"Though I had always wanted to be an opium addict, I can't claim that as the reason I went to China. The opium ambition dates back to that obscure period of childhood when I wanted to be a lot of other things, too—the greatest expert on ghosts, the world's best ice skater, the champion lion tamer...."

So begins a fascinating chapter in the life of Emily Hahn—and in her intimate and amusing story spanning almost half a century of round-the-world adventure. If most of these early dreams were indeed forgotten, Miss Hahn did enjoy a short but heady affair with the pipe; she also stole her sister's best beau, crashed the all-male precincts of the University of Wisconsin geology club, and traveled alone to the heart of Africa, at a time when such things were not done by proper young ladies from proper St. Louis families.

With an eye for the curious and a heart for the exotic, she finds the offbeat and the unexpected at every turn: on board a steamer bound for Tokyo, in Chinese towns and villages, in Dar-es-Salaam, in Santa Fe, in Greenwich Village, and also in the venerable reading room of the British Museum. Wherever Emily Hahn is, *there* is a happening, vividly evoked in anecdotes, vignettes, and conversation.

Like that unlikely Christmas in Africa, for example, when the "ways of men" finally king, expecting dates and dancing, and ended up in a new world of war and fire bombs.

Emily Hahn's vivid impressions and reactions are notable not only for their frankness and for the light they shed on her fascinating life, but for their colorfully detailed close-ups of people and places. And beyond her diverse company of native guides and colonial officers, of village dentists and eccentric anthropologists, her personal odyssey is a unique record, written with gusto, humor, and affection. From it emerges the portrait of a delightful woman with a deep gift for living.

Books by EMILY HAHN

Hongkong Holiday
Raffles of Singapore
Miss Jill
England to Me
Purple Passage
Love Conquers Nothing
Chiang Kai-shek
Diamond
The Tiger House Party
China Only Yesterday
China to Me
Africa to Me: Person to Person
With Naked Foot
Romantic Rebels
Animal Gardens
Times and Places

EMILY HAHN

TIMES AND PLACES

THOMAS Y. CROWELL COMPANY
New York • Established 1834

1818

All of the material in this book
appeared originally in *The New Yorker*.

MANUFACTURED IN THE UNITED STATES OF AMERICA

L.C. Card 70-132312 ✓

ISBN 0-690-82499-8

1   2   3   4   5   6   7   8   9   10

TO CHARLES

CONTENTS

TIMES AND PLACES

THE ESCAPE

Not long after my family moved from St. Louis to Chicago, I ran away from home. It is only honest to admit that the affair didn't amount to much; indeed, nobody among my relatives remembers it, except my sister Rose, today a psychiatric social worker, who claims she does. She says I ran away because I was disturbed, and she adds that we were all disturbed at the time, and that the move to Chicago was bad for us. She speaks, of course, as a social worker, but when she talks like that I'm visited by the ghost of an old resentment. "There they go again," I say to myself, "crowding in on the act." But the annoyance really is only a ghost. It is nothing like the frustration and rage I felt back in 1920 at the slightest hint that any one of the rest of the family was as miserable as I was. Mother once tried to tell me that she was unhappy, too, but I only walked off, shaking my head. The misery was mine and mine alone. I was fifteen, and entitled to undisputed possession. Had I not been forced to leave St. Louis against my will? Wasn't I always being pushed around? No one but me had my sensitivity; no one but me knew how to suffer; the others were clods. It was clear that I had to run away.

"There must have been something wrong with you," my husband said recently, when I told him the story. "Girls don't usually run away from home."

"All normal girls do," I said loftily.

But, having thought it over, I will concede that I may be mistaken about that. My family weren't really clods, and they weren't abnormal, yet out of five girls and one boy, of whom I was the next to youngest, I'm the only one who ran away.

Very likely it happened not so much because we moved to Chicago as because I had a hangover from books. I was a deep reader, plunging into a story and remaining immersed even after I'd finished it. Some of it was apt to cling for a long time, like water to a bathing suit. The "Jungle Books" clung, for example. Mowgli was a natural wanderer. I was surprised when he went back to his home cave once, after he'd grown up, to confer with Mother and Father Wolf. I assumed that he had forgotten them. I had. I was also a natural wanderer, or wanted to be. Mowgli was the real thing—the best example—but there were others. David Copperfield, for instance; *he* ran away, and a lot of Dickens' other children were admirably mobile, too. I was certain that Little Nell, though she thought she was sorry to slip away from home with her grandfather, must have felt some hidden enthusiasm for the road. Nor did I have to depend on Dickens for vicarious running away. I drifted downriver with Huck Finn, and got lost with Tom Sawyer, and sailed here and there, all over the world, with any number of other people, scorning the stale air of indoors.

At the same time, I much preferred to be indoors in fact;

2

there I could read in comfort of the wild hawk to the windswept sky, the deer to the wholesome word. My mother was always sending me out to play, partly because the open air was healthful and partly because she thought reading, done to excess, ruined the eyes. We all had good eyes, and she was a keen reader herself, but she dreaded some future day when we might use up our allotted sight, so she instituted a rationing system: her children up to the age of twelve might read for pleasure only half an hour a day; when they reached their teens, they were allowed an hour. The rest of our leisure time had to be spent in the open air. This was the era of the sleeping porch, or, if you couldn't have that, of the window gaping wide all the winter night, which may have been a legacy of Theodore Roosevelt—himself a great one for wandering in the open air—or a reaction to central heating, which we rather overdid. At any rate, I found playing outdoors boring until I learned to hide books under the back porch or in a peach tree's cleft. After that, it was simply a matter of finding some spot out of sight where I could read in peace.

Later on, in Chicago, it suited me to mope as if I'd lost a paradise when we moved away from St. Louis, and I began to dream of running off—if not to that one, then to some other. And St. Louis was, in fact, a pleasant place. There must have been other towns along the Mississippi with a similar charm— places where cement had not yet tamped down everything and nature still showed through—but I thought mine unique. I firmly believed that the little girl from New York who came out every summer to visit her grandparents next door was as miserable, when the time came to return to the brownstone fronts of the East, as Persephone going back to the underworld. In New York, we children told each other, there were no back yards. That unfortunate Eastern child had to live in a flat, with no place to dig in the dirt. Actually, what should have bothered us was that St. Louis was a hell of a place for a summer resort. It rests in a topographical hollow, and the air is usually quiet, growing humid to an extreme degree in summer, except for the times

3

when everything blows up all at once in a cyclone. Our cyclones and tornadoes were inconvenient, and even dangerous, but we were proud of them.

Fountain Avenue was where we lived, across the street from Fountain Park—an oval-shaped tract of land about three blocks long, with trees and paths and benches and trimmed grass. My parents often said contentedly that it was a splendid place for children, but I preferred our back yard—a much wilder place. I didn't know much about jungles, but I pictured them as something like the back yard. There were hibiscus bushes in it, and peach trees. Somebody else had a persimmon tree, not far off; I know it couldn't have been ours, because the fruit bounced on someone's coach-house roof when it fell, and we didn't have a coach house. A ripe persimmon that has hit a roof on its way down is a badly squashed persimmon, but those tasted wonderful, in spite of twigs and bits of dead leaf that had to be pulled off or spat out. Bitten at the proper angle, a persimmon seed puckers the mouth, and when it splits open, a little white spoon lies inside it in silhouette.

Our yard was divided from its neighbors by a high board fence, always in need of paint. It had an occasional knothole and looked like the cartoon fences through whose holes little ragamuffins steal glimpses of baseball games. The upright planks were reinforced near the top by a ledge, on which daring children walked, balancing. In time, the fence was replaced by a low wire one—everybody who was anybody was getting wire fences—and privacy was gone in our block. You could see both ways as far as the eye could travel, and I was sorry. Progress marred our alley, too. To begin with, when I pulled myself up to stand on the rim of our ashpit and peered over a wall into the alley, what I saw was almost rural. The alley was cobbled, bounded on one side by a vacant lot and a couple of wooden outhouses and a stable. In the stable lived a horse, who kept his head resting on the lower half of his divided door and always regarded me amiably. The whole place smelled of horse, cold ashes, garbage, and open ground. But one day men appeared and dug in the vacant lot, and practically the next day a tall red brick apartment building stood on it. About the same time, the stable, shed, and horse disappeared, to be replaced by concrete and brick and glass, with a lot of earthenware pots in evidence. It must have been the back of a flower shop. In the same abrupt manner—my memory moves as jerkily as an early silent movie—the rough alleyway became smoothly paved and good for roller-skating. St. Louis changed, but it was nice.

Late in May, it would begin to heat up. Then we were permitted to go barefoot, outside of school hours—a privilege I did not appreciate, for the sidewalks burned my feet and the asphalt in the streets melted to a mushy consistency, streaking my legs with tar. Wherever potholes in a street were being mended, there was a little heap of soft tar nearby, and I remember—though I hate to think of it—that we filched little pieces of the tar and chewed it. The parched grass of Fountain Park was easier than asphalt on the feet, but if one simply *had* to stay outside, the back yard was best. There we could turn on the garden hose and wallow. When the classroom thermometer at our school rose about ninety, we were sent home.

Then came vacation, and after a few weeks everybody, including us, went away. My father would go with us to Michigan, settle us in, stay a couple of weeks, and return to work. My mother always filled the family scene to a greater extent than he did; she could hardly help shouldering him out, for he was away a good deal of the time, "on the road," sellings things for a company of which he was half owner. But my father was not self-effacing. He enjoyed entertaining people, telling stories, and singing. Nevertheless, it is Mother I remember, and it was Mother I preferred. When Daddy wasn't on the road, we children went down to the streetcar stop to meet him. As he stepped off the car, we made a great demonstration, jumping and yelling and rushing to embrace him, scuffling like puppies, but I'm afraid I carried on in this manner only because the others were doing it. I was afraid of him, really. It was one of the foremost facts of our life that he was nervous and couldn't take too much noise. Nervous people, I knew, were as unpredictable as nervous dogs. Also, he affronted my vanity in the matter of what would now-

5

adays be called sibling rivalry, by adoring my older sister Dorothy and paying less attention to the rest of us. It was only when I was older and braver that I learned to like him, and he in turn learned to recognize me. But if I didn't love my father, I certainly never realized it. I thought I loved him, and we were always in holiday mood when we set off all together for Michigan.

I wonder why Michigan. Presumably my parents thought it cooler than St. Louis, and it must have been, because anywhere was, but we didn't visit the northern woods; we went to a farm right in the heat belt. We didn't drive, of course. Cars were not quite unknown, but I can't remember anybody who actually went from one town to another by auto. We travelled on a train, taking with us a big trunk and many suitcases, getting aboard in the late afternoon and sleeping in flimsily constructed rooms of green cloth. The moldy smell of that cloth is still evocable in my nostrils. Arriving in Chicago next day, we rode across town in a Parmelee horse-drawn bus to another station. The bus was upholstered in something shabby and slippery, and the streets were bumpy. I kept sliding off the bench, but my mind was not on keeping my place, because I was looking out with horror at the streets. No skyscrapers today, not even the nightmare canyons of Wall Street, can match the towering height of Chicago's buildings as I saw them in my childhood. Not only were they tall, they faced each other across narrow streets into which the sun could not reach, and they were black all over with grime. At this point, angry Chicagoans may declare passionately that it simply isn't true, and that the Parmelee bus never followed such a route, so I hasten to assure them that I know it—now. I have tried, myself, to find those hellish buildings and the nightmare sooty pavements we rode along, but I couldn't. I can only conclude that I didn't really see them at all but read a description of such a place—some demon world—in a book, and mixed it up with reality. And yet it is vivid in my memory—the dreadful buildings, and ramshackle wooden sheds, and the brick façades of miserable tenements. It seemed natural, therefore, when my sisters spoke disparagingly of Chicago. "How dreadful it must be to have to live in Chicago!" they would say, and look with

6

pity from the bus windows at the miserable people in the streets. Though I did not live there yet, and did not dream that I ever would, it was a place I was already glad to escape from.

Now, with one of those sudden cinema jerks, I remember myself at fifteen, in high school and already halfway out of the existence I had known best. Real life was no longer a mere transition from one story world to another. I looked at and saw flesh-and-blood people of whom I'd never before been aware. I looked at, and fell in love with, an assistant teacher at the art school I attended on Saturday mornings. I was waking, but it wasn't a tingling awakening; it was a sort of drifting. There was something in me that worried me, because I had never read or heard about it—a slowness to react, a drowsiness of the spirit. When other people were hurt, they cried immediately. When I was hurt, I cried a good deal later, and half the time only because I thought it the thing to do. I thought that I might be incapable of feeling, especially when I looked around at my relatives and saw how different they were. My sister Dorothy and Mother were volatile and excitable, and clearly revelled in scenes. My father couldn't read anything emotional aloud without choking up with laughter or tears; wiping his eyes, he would say, "I'm sorry, I know it's a weakness." Yes, I thought, he was weak, but perhaps that was the way to be.

I was jealous of my privacy, but I was inconsistent about it. I wanted desperately to be noticed and equally desperately to be let alone. This wasn't a new state, to be sure. Some years before, there had been the affair of the Teddy bear. Probably I wouldn't have been so wacky about him if we'd been permitted to keep live pets, but my parents thought dogs and cats were not good for children—Mother was convinced that cats carry typhoid germs—and they were sure children were bad for dogs and cats. Mad about animals, I lavished emotion on other people's pets, until I saw the bear in a shopwindow. I was no tot in search of a cuddly companion—I must have been eleven—and the bear was a miniature Steiff model, about five inches long, but I went crazy with love and longing. I saved up my allowance. I earned money running errands and cutting grass. Finally I got the bear, and I carried it everywhere for years. In those pre-Freud days, nobody worried about such things, though I drew pictures of its face on my arithmetic papers and songbooks, and made clothes for it, and built it a house. Even now, it's a struggle to call the bear "it," and not "him." One day I took it to school. Such small bears were a novelty, and the other children in my class made a fuss about it and vied for the privilege of keeping it in their desks for allotted spaces of time. Inevitably, the teacher noticed the disturbance. She investigated, discovered the bear, and confiscated it—an act that triggered off one of the most humiliating experiences I can remember. I burst into tears—in the sixth grade, mind you, and over a Teddy bear. But that was not the worst of it. To demonstrate that I didn't really care and was unwounded, I also laughed. The effect was appalling. Laughter mixed with the weeping came out in a series of whoops that wouldn't stop. The other children stared, and so did the teacher, while I gasped and whooped and sobbed until my breath failed. In the ensuing pause, the teacher said quietly that she would give me my bear after school. I got the bear back as the teacher had promised, and nobody ever dared to tease me about the incident or even mention it again, but I still shrivel when I think of it.

So, at fifteen, I admired and envied my sister Dot, who was very much the other way and would never shrink from scenes. When she felt like it, she threw things. Even when she threw them at me, I admired her swift passion, as well as her aim. I was sadly aware that my own rebellions and quarrels were cold in comparison—thoughtful and sluggish. My attacks were planned and few. But these self-doubts were finally submerged. Dot was away at college, and her splendid tantrums no longer enlivened the day. The eldest of us, my brother Mannel, married at the close of the First World War—he had been in the Air Service—and Rose was training in psychiatry in Boston. Dauphine and I, the younger ones, now found the house spacious and calm.

8

I had been in high school more than a year when the shock came. We were going to move to Chicago, because my father and his partner thought their business would expand there. It was almost too outrageous to believe. Live in Chicago—that gritty, high-built town? My parents must have gone crazy, I thought, or were in the grip of some higher power than themselves, mysterious and malign. It was incredible that they should want to go. Taught by them, we thought St. Louis was the best city—with the possible exception of New Orleans, where Daddy had relatives, and Denver, where they'd gone on their honeymoon—in the States; that Fountain Avenue was the most charming part of St. Louis; that our friends in St. Louis were uniquely wonderful; and that St. Louis schools were the best to be found anywhere in the world. That my parents should voluntarily give up all this privilege was inconceivable, unless—as I suddenly thought, for the first time, *might* be possible—they were not, after all, the kindest, wisest people ever born.

With this horrid doubt gnawing my mind, I followed sulkily in Mother's path, through the upsets and nuisance of selling the house, packing, perching for a while in a hotel in St. Louis and then in another in Chicago. The North Side, where we were to spend many years, has a reputation for elegance, but for a long time my eyes saw only what I already knew I would see—awful Chicago. Even when my senses convinced me that the street where we lived was not as dark, not as hemmed in as I had expected, I *felt* dark and hemmed in. At that, it wasn't a pretty place. My father found an apartment on Lawrence Avenue and signed a lease without consulting my mother, and she was not pleased, though it wasn't really as squalid as she said it was. Later, we were to move several times, and each removal would find us in a pleasanter place, but I couldn't look into the future, and I thought we would be stuck forever, without escape, in that narrow red brick building with its curious strung-out arrangement of rooms hitched to each other like boxcars.

Dauphine and I enrolled in the nearest high school, the Nicholas Senn. It was Dauph's first term in high school, and she was pleased to be where she felt she belonged—among older people.

She was always gregarious and immediately made a lot of friends. In short, she committed infidelity and came to like Chicago, was glad we had come, wanted no escape, and made no bones about it. I dropped her flat. Slowly and reluctantly, I, too, made friends, but only a couple of them, and I hated Senn. It was too big. It wasn't Soldan High School, in St. Louis. Still, little by little, even I had to put out feelers, no matter how grudgingly. Lessons and weekly tests, lunch at the corner store with my new friends Betsy and Caroline, working on the school magazine— these activities dented me, but even they left the dark well inside me undisturbed. Every afternoon, I went back to Lawrence Avenue and put on my misery again, like a pair of comfortable old slippers. Perhaps that simile is not a good one, because slippered people stay at home, and soon I was itching to get out of the apartment again. I was considered old enough now to have a certain amount of freedom, so I spent most of my allowance on bus rides along the lake, all the way down to the Field Museum and back. Even wrapped in my cloak of grief, I was aware of—for I remember it—the pattern of the city. First, the ride took me past relatively humble houses, a good many still retaining wooden porches of oddly rustic appearance. Then, as the bus approached the center of town, the surroundings swelled with splendor. The large residences of the rich were of varied styles, but they all imitated something in Europe: there were Bavarian castles, Queen Anne mansions, and Scottish fortresses side by side, having in common only their distance from the street and their surprisingly small gardens. Without a park to surround it, a mansion looked peculiar to me, but the millionaires apparently did not agree. They seemed to want to huddle together. I was indifferent.

Beyond this belt, the private houses grew less overwhelming, because fine new apartment houses and luxury hotels had taken over. This part of the Gold Coast left me as indifferent as the other. Here my eyes were fixed on the opposite side of the road, where, most of the time, I could look out over Lake Michigan, and sometimes down at the beach. Even I could not claim that there was something like it, but better, in St. Louis. Even I could not imagine anything better to do at dusk than bowl along by Lake Michigan in the front seat of the top of a double-decker bus. The wind from that great sea was never quite like ordinary air. It had a delicious foreign smell. But the most enchanting thing about the lake was that you couldn't see to the other side.

"How happy are they that till the land, did they but know it," wrote the Dorset poet William Barnes. How happy was I on that bus, did I but know it! Brooding over my sorrows (and, when I thought of them, the lesser troubles of Byron and Shelley and Keats), borne forward like the figurehead on a ship's prow through waves of gusty wind, I was busily preparing myself for new regrets, oncoming losses. When I got home afterward, Lawrence Avenue would be that much less bearable, with its close air, and with the dining-room table, under a circular hanging lamp, cleared and ready for homework.

I have forgotten exactly why I ran away on the day I did. No doubt Mother said something that brought all my sorrows to a head—but what? It could have been anything. During that time, she and I sparred a good deal, and even when we weren't bickering she often indicated impatience by sighing. She had a very eloquent sigh, and I hated it. I preferred it when she slammed doors, but she didn't often do that to me, reserving the gesture for the older children and my father. Perhaps she didn't say anything that day; perhaps she only sighed once too often. At any rate, *something* was the last straw, and I decided to run away.

True to my nature, I laid plans slowly and thoughtfully. It was Friday, before school. I emptied my money box of its few savings and put them into my pocket. At school, in history class, I approached Betsy Cummings. "Didn't you ask me if I could come home with you for the night sometime?" I said. "I could tonight, if you like."

Betsy said she was delighted, and if she was also surprised she didn't show it. That afternoon, I walked home with her in the direction away from Lawrence Avenue. Betsy lived on a street that led downhill to the lake front, in one of the apartment houses near the edge of Rogers Park. The houses there were new, which gave them a cachet. Betsy impressed me by having her own key. She unlocked her apartment door and led me into a living room furnished with a shiny new sofa and chairs, and curtains made of crisp flowered stuff. It looked very pretty to me; it wasn't home.

"Mama doesn't come home until about six," Betsy said. "She works. She manages something downtown. Let's put your things in my room—but where are your things?"

I'd thought that out. I said, "I had my bag all packed, and then I walked out of the house and left it."

Betsy said she was always doing things like that herself, and it didn't matter; she could lend me a nightgown, and I could brush my teeth with a finger. We went into the kitchen and made fudge. While it cooked and we dropped bits of it into cold water to see if it was ready, she explained her family life. Her father did not seem to be a part of the daily routine, and I didn't quite understand whether he was dead or just missing. He and her mother may have been divorced; if that was the case, Betsy would naturally have ignored the subject, because most people didn't talk about divorce. I didn't ask awkward questions, because I appreciated that it was hard enough on Betsy as it was, with her mother working. Working mothers were pretty *outré* in our circle.

Mrs. Cummings came home at six—a tall, deep-bosomed woman with carefully marcelled hair and the motherly manner characteristic of many career women. She was so wholesome I found it hard to like her. She went straight to the kitchen and put on a starched, ruffled apron, and told us to do our homework while she cooked supper. "It's no use your saving you have the whole weekend," she said merrily. "I know all about that. I'm not going to spend my Sunday afternoon driving Betsy to her books."

After supper, something rather surprising happened. Mrs. Cummings actually suggested to Betsy that she call up Howard, a fellow-student at Senn, and ask him over for cake and ice cream and to play the Victrola. It didn't startle me when Betsy welcomed the idea, because we all knew she was sweet on Howard. It was Mrs. Cummings' suggesting it that seemed so queer. My mother would never have done a thing like that. For one thing, she thought I was too young to fool around with boys, and, for another, she had a horror of appearing to chase young men for her daughters. She had always impressed on us carefully that we must never telephone boys; we must wait and let them telephone us. I asked myself if Mrs. Cummings could be quite *nice*. All through the evening, during which Howard politely danced with Betsy and me alternately, to the music of records like "Margie," and Mrs. Cummings beamed on the young people and brought in refreshments, I thought about her amazing behavior. Truly it was a variegated world I was stepping into, and Chicago mores were shockingly different from those of St. Louis. What ever must Howard be thinking? How shameful for poor Betsy!

After Howard had gone, and before we went to bed, there was some desultory talk about plans for the next day. Betsy and Mrs. Cummings expected me to stay for lunch at least, but I would not consent. I couldn't tell them why—that I intended to take a bus downtown, get a job and a room, and settle in for the next phase of freedom, which included plans to join a circus in the South. Instead, I told them politely that my mother wouldn't permit it, because she needed me at home.

"Surely she wouldn't make you work on Saturday," said Mrs. Cummings. "I thought you girls might like to go to a movie in the afternoon."

"I'm awfully sorry, but you see how it is," I replied.

Early next morning, before Mrs. Cummings woke up, Betsy and I tiptoed out of the apartment and went down to the beach to go swimming. Salmon sunrise clouds still streaked the sky as we swam out into the lake. Everything was unfamiliar to me, and suddenly a miracle took place. Not only the lake, with its waves creaming up the sand, but Chicago itself became beautiful. Even

13

after we had come out of the water and were jogging back up the street to the apartment, Chicago was beautiful—fresh, vivid, and exciting.

I replied absently to Betsy's chatter as we dressed, keeping my eyes on the changing sky I could see through the window. It was a new sky; I felt as if I'd never seen it before. Breakfast was also new—the fried eggs tasted wonderful. Had I ever tried to *taste* fried eggs before that morning? Possibly not. My heart pounded with excitement, and then the telephone rang.

"We'd love to have her for the day," Mrs. Cummings was saying, and I realized it was my mother she was talking to. Mrs. Cummings' voice was calm and pleasant and showed no surprise; apparently Mother wasn't giving anything away. I listened. "You're quite sure?" said Mrs. Cummings. "I see. Yes, of course. Some other time, then. She's right here." She turned and called me, saying that my mother wanted to talk to me, and I went over and picked up the receiver and said, "Hello?"

Mother's voice, flat and heavy, did not waste time saying hello. "Well," she said, "I hope you're satisfied. You've had your wish. I've been worried sick all night. It was Dauphine who just thought of Betsy Cummings."

For the benefit of the Cummingses, I said pleasantly, "Yes?"

"Come home now," my mother commanded.

I said, "All right."

But this time I wasn't talking for the benefit of the Cummingses; there was no reason not to go home. Mother was right about that. I had escaped. I'd had my wish.

BE NOT THE FIRST

My little daughter, Carola, aged three and a half, was raising a considerable stink. "I wanna wear it!" she yelled, and jumped up and down, kicking at the floor in a rage. "I wanna wear my new dressing gown! I want to, Mommy!"

"Listen, darling," I said, "you can't wear your new dressing gown to school. You've got a lot of good, hard work to do at school. You've got to climb all over that nice progressive equipment, and a dressing gown would only be in your way. And there's finger painting. You've got to have perfect freedom for your creative instincts, and I don't have to tell *you* what that

15

means, Carola. You know all about you and finger paint. Personally, I don't see eye to eye with the school on that, but never mind. Suffice it to say that you wouldn't want to wear your new dressing gown when you do finger painting. In short, Carola, you don't want to wear your nice new expensive dressing gown to school."

Carola jumped up and down with fresh abandon. "I do!" she said. "I *want* to!"

"Listen, darling," I said. "Let's start over again from a new angle. Maybe what you want to do isn't the point. Maybe *Mommy* doesn't want you to wear your new . . ."

All of a sudden it came over me, just like that, and I remembered my school in 1920. Of course, I was a good deal older than three and a half then. I was fifteen going on sixteen. I was what they still call young for my age—not boy-minded, and well padded with puppy fat. One's figure at fifteen didn't matter very much in St. Louis, but in Chicago it was a serious matter. But then, even thirteen, in Chicago, seemed to call for a degree of poise and experience that my kid sister, Dauphine, could not achieve overnight, and we two talked about this bitterly whenever the rest of the family would listen to us, which was not often.

The family's emigration had been hardest on us. We had to *live* there, whereas our older sisters, the lucky ones, would be away from home at various universities. At first we had both hated Chicago for various reasons—for example, the school situation. Back in St. Louis, nobody had any notions about education; you went to the neighborhood public school and that was that. In Washington School, the teachers had practically been old family retainers, because all six of us children had attended their classes from kindergarten on. Now and then, a teacher would get us a little mixed up and would call me Helen, for example (Helen was the fourth), or Dorothy (the third), but that was only natural. Even my father did that occasionally; none of us ever dreamed of resenting it. The important point was that you went to public school. Everybody did. I suppose there were private schools in St. Louis; there must have been. But we thought of private schools only as places for children who had something the matter with them—feeble-mindedness or divorced parents.

Therefore we were shocked, after our arrival in Chicago, by my eldest sister Rose's report on educational methods there. She had been asking around among her classmates at Smith. "The city schools are terrible, Isabel says," she announced. "Those children haven't got the right background, and incidentally the teaching isn't any good either. Isabel says we just simply can't send the kids anywhere but Francis Parker."

We all gasped. Mother said, "Francis Parker? Isn't that a *private* school?"

Rose turned pink and squared her shoulders. "This is a much bigger city than we've been used to, Mother," she began. "We'll have to readjust our ideas. We've got to remember that people of our class . . ."

Really, Rose should have known better. It wasn't as if she didn't know all about Mother's democratic principles and wasn't locked in grim battle with her most of the time on one point or another. Rose was a girl of her times, but Mother was ahead of hers. Mother was not a career woman only because career women had not yet been developed. She showed most of the earmarks of the species in its earliest phase—she wrote a paper once a month for her club, and every four years she objected, without fail, to my father's Presidential choice, arguing with him each evening at the dinner table for a full month before the election. She also took an intelligent and humane interest in such matters as fur trapping in Canada. As long as we girls lived at home, none of us was permitted to use fur or feathers on our clothing. However, aside from the Presidential elections, she didn't pay any attention to politics. That would have been going too far, even for a free-thinking female like Mother.

She had other convictions, strong ones. We girls were all going to have college educations or she would know the reason why. My brother's education was taken for granted. Mother was far more interested in seeing to it that her daughters were emancipated females, and this caused trouble between her and Rose. Rose didn't much care about being emancipated. Like Dauphine, she was more her father's girl, but Dauphine was easygoing and Rose wasn't.

Dad constantly frustrated Mother, not only by being unsympathetic but by not offering opposition. He didn't give her restless spirit the exercise it craved. He was a quiet man who loved to read. Mother, though she was a perfect lady and glad of it, just had to be arguing with somebody. She worked out some of her energy on our aunts. They usually considered Mother a harmless madcap, but sometimes they thought her downright dangerous—Rights for Animals, for Women, for Enslaved Peoples, Religious Tolerance. . . . The aunts were sorry for Dad and Rose, but I wasn't.

I thought Mother was just about perfect. It wasn't only that I agreed with her and burned to go out and save a few trapped fur-bearing animals myself; it was also that she had such excellent moral reasons for diving into battle, and had a hell of a good time doing it. Mother always did exactly what she wanted to do, but she always richly justified herself in advance. For example, there was her job before she married, which I loved to hear about. Mother had gone out and got herself a business training and worked in an office, long before most girls dared have such excitement in their lives. She had refused to stay home and cook; she had two sisters who could cook, she argued. And why had the headstrong girl done this, nearly breaking her poor old parents' hearts and dragging down their heads with the shame of it? Because women have the same right to earn a living as men have, that's why, and it was Mother's moral duty to demonstrate this. She hated housework, anyway. Deciding to marry Dad and to keep house must have been a struggle, but she was in love. That wasn't why she married him, of course. Mother married Dad because he was an orphan.

Mother approved highly of the democratic principles set forth in the Constitution. Now here was her own daughter talking about this class and that class, just as if she hadn't been brought up a good American. It was a shock to Mother, but it gave her a long-desired chance for a little legitimate excitement. She exploded, and they had one of their good old-fashioned arguments. At the end of it Rose retired to her bedroom and wept, while Mother, flushed with the pure emotion of the crusader, put on her hat and went out to enroll Dauphine and me in the nearest high school.

The only flaw in the setup was that Rose seemed to be quite correct in her opinion; the nearest high school was a pretty bad school.

Dauphine and I didn't suffer more than most other children from inadequate teachers and a poorly planned schedule, because there was something wrong in those days with the American high-school system in general, and we would probably have been just as bored and badly informed in any other institution. The real difficulty for us was social. We couldn't get the hang of this new crowd of schoolmates, and they didn't care so much for us, either. Some of the males looked like thugs. In time, I am sure, they became genuine professional thugs on a highly successful scale. They were the social leaders of the school. Their little group was exclusive and only the highest-ranking, most enviable people were admitted. They were the élite and we recognized their position at once.

It was the period just after the success of *The Sheik,* when *This Side of Paradise* was a best-selling novel and people were dancing to the strains of "Dardanella." Our high-school men—one couldn't call them boys—shaved every day, and sported the lacquered hair and bell-bottomed trousers of the current John Held drawings. I suppose we called them parlor snakes. I'm not sure. Dauphine and I, wholesome little girls from St. Louis, thought them absolutely beautiful and just about as unattainable as gods. And they were indeed unattainable. We would have been more profitably employed in dreaming of and yearning after football stars and swimming-team champions. The high school had its quota of those, too, but they didn't have the glamour of the bad boys or their girls. Those girls! I wonder where they are now. I can make a shrewd guess. I don't know what their mothers were like, but I'm sure they didn't look any older or more sinful than their little daughters. The accepted costume for class attendance was a skimpy black satin dress, black silk stockings rolled to the knee, opera pumps, and a tight cloche hat, worn over a frizzy hairdo. The girls also went in for what we still knew as "paint," thick-spread on their tough little faces.

I can't say honestly that Dauphine and I were shocked by them, because we were not. We were merely thrilled to death. We would go down to the corner candy store from school at twelve o'clock and buy our lunch there just because that was where the glamour boys and girls went. We listened eagerly to their talk as we munched hamburgers and dill pickles, wondering what the cryptic phrases meant. "Helen's some vamp, huh?" "You'd be surprised." "Oh, boy! No future, but what a past!" "Come awn, come awn, don't hang on to that canteen all day. I gotta rench my mouth."

Mother couldn't understand why we never brought any little friends home. "The house in St. Louis was always full of young people," she said wistfully. "What do these children do after school? I suppose they go and sit in the movies."

"Maybe," I said doubtfully. It was my private opinion that they were out cracking safes somewhere or rolling around on the floor of some opium den.

"Well, I don't approve of that," said Mother. "I'm surprised that you children aren't more sociable, though. We always wanted to know your friends. We want them to feel welcome to come in any time."

Dauphine finally put in a request, without much hope, for a black satin dress; she didn't get anywhere. So she and I went our unobtrusive ways in Chicago, skating in the park when the weather permitted and sighing after strange gods. Nobody at home realized how very strange they were.

When Mother saw an advertisement for knicker suits in the paper, she probably didn't realize what a delicious upset she was in for. Ostensibly, knickers for her two young daughters were just a good, practical idea. They seemed to settle the long-standing problem of how to dress us so that we could attend school and then go straight out to play rough games without ruining our clothes. Actually, it was a matter of deep calling to deep. Mother, in her young, office-going days, had created a mild scandal in St. Louis by wearing bloomers for bicycling, and she was hurt and puzzled that Dauphine and I scorned bloomers. The knickers, however, met with our approval. They looked just like the clothes little boys wore before they graduated to long trousers, and, as successors to the comfortable rompers we had worn in childhood, they seemed pretty good. In 1920, remember, slacks had not yet been invented, and nobody wore pajamas in public except as Oriental fancy dress.

We were completely innocent about it, all three of us. Mother went downtown and bought the knicker suits, and one morning Dauphine and I put them on and started out for school.

On our way to the streetcar line, it began to be apparent that the public was going to consider the costume startling. A man driving a delivery truck reined in his horse and asked us if we had not forgotten something. It took us a little while to catch on. Then we flounced off indignantly, blushing. A group of street urchins followed us, making loud remarks. By the time the streetcar came, we were suffering badly from jitters.

"Do you think maybe there's a law against it?" whispered Dauphine.

"Of course not, or Mother wouldn't have let us wear them," I said. "Why, they couldn't have sold them in the store. These crazy people!"

The other passengers in the streetcar took a lively interest in our appearance. We stared ahead of ourselves with grim and rigid dignity. "Don't you let them scare you," I counselled Dauphine. "I guess we've got a right to wear knickers if we want to."

Fortunately, a group of girls from school boarded the car a few stops along the line, and they broke the tension. They were squealingly enthusiastic about the innovation, making blithe, clearly insincere plans to convert their mothers to the idea. Though they weren't representatives of the bright young set, the support of anybody, however obscure and dull, meant a good deal just then. We clung to them with pathetic eagerness all the rest of the way.

By the end of that first morning, my sister and I had learned a lot. We had tasted the sweets as well as the bitterness of notoriety. There was now no doubt that the high school was aware of us. We knew what to expect from people approaching us in the narrow corridors. We became all too well acquainted with the first startled jump, the second glance, the amused stare, the craned head, the animated discussion between bystanders, as each of us made her lonely way from class to class. It might have been less painful if we had been able to go together.

Most of my teachers, timid by nature, took the easy way out and ignored my knickered legs. Only one of them, an elderly spinster soured by too many years of teaching history, spoke about the costume when I entered her room. "What, Emily, is that extraordinary outfit?" she demanded. "What do you call it?"

In a husky voice I told her what it was called and where it had been bought. I really thought at first that she must want a pair.

"Looks completely ridiculous," she said in hearty tones. "All you need is a red parasol for the finishing touch. Reminds me of one of those Africans the missionaries talk about. Tell your mother I said so."

"My mother likes knickers," I said. "She would like to wear them herself. She said she was sorry she's too old."

"Well, that settles it, of course," said the history teacher.

"Yes, Ma'am," I muttered, and buried my flaming face in a book. Neither Dauphine nor I had bargained on the teachers. We had never thought that teachers would have opinions about clothes.

There was a choice of two paths. We could give in and try to live down the knickers, or we could brazen it out by insisting on our rights and wearing the things again. On that first day two newspaper photographers lay in wait for us as we came off the school grounds. We should have gone over to the basketball field, for now was the moment to justify and vindicate those knickers by playing games with all the freedom and grace we were expected to feel. We didn't, though. We made for home like scared rabbits.

"Are we going to tell Mother?" Dauphine asked on the streetcar.

"Tell her what?" I asked haughtily. "That a few fools looked twice at us? I guess she'd expect that, anyway. *She* wouldn't pay any attention to that."

"Oh," said Dauphine, and at her forlorn tone I looked sharply at her. "Then you're going to wear 'em tomorrow?" she asked.

"Aren't you?" I turned on her and she shrank back.

"I wanted to wear my pink dress," she faltered. "I never meant to stop skirts altogether. We've got a lot of dresses to wear out. . . . Well, all right. If you do, I guess I will, too," she said.

The next day there was a piece in one of the evening papers, along with our photographs. The Board of Education had refused to make any statement about knickers, and some enterprising reporter had tried to discover whether there was any ordinance on the subject of proper clothing for public-school students. He couldn't find any. There was only a vague city ruling about immodest attire.

"Immodest?" cried Mother, her face lighting up with the familiar glow of battle. "Do they dare to call these suits immodest? Why, the girls are covered from head to foot with good, thick wool! When I see some of those skimpy little things, with their rolled stockings and their low necks, I'm very proud of our girls. Isn't that so?"

"Of course it's so," I said heartily. Dauphine did not reply, nor did my father, but then he wasn't listening.

Dauphine and I continued to wear our knickers to school. The excitement among the students soon died down, and the teachers managed to relax and pay attention to their jobs. A few girls in knicker suits were seen in the streets, and the newspapers worked up more and more interest in them. My Aunt Lillie made a trip from the suburbs to speak her mind to Mother about it, "I may be old-fashioned," she said, "but if the good Lord had meant girls to wear pants, they'd be born with 'em on."

Mr. Clarke, our principal, called an assembly one day, and, as usual, there was free speculation about its object. Mr. Clarke knew the authoritative value of the dark hint, and in the discharge of his duties he was always mysterious. I may be maligning him in saying his actions were the result of deliberate policy. They may have been the result of not quite knowing what to do next. In the *affaire des* knickers, for example, he was definitely up against it, because Mother had him on toast and we all knew it. Mr. Clarke had stuck his neck out; he had written her a letter signifying his disapproval of our costumes, and Mother was joyfully able to point out that his disapproval was purely private and personal. Besides, the newspapers had already made it clear that the Board of Education, upon due examination of its rights in the matter, had admitted that it couldn't expel Dauphine and me from class or dictate what we were to wear as long as we didn't come to school in a state suggesting nudity. Mr. Clarke didn't reply to the letter.

An assembly was a sort of emergency function in the auditorium, to which the entire school personnel (with the possible exception of the janitor) was peremptorily invited. In spite of the principal's cumbersome secrecy, I had a pretty good hunch that he intended to be pompous about knickers. It would be his only way to talk back to Mother.

Against Dauphine's protests, I dragged her down to the front row that afternoon and sat her next to me, directly below the rostrum. I was quite right in my hunch.

Mr. Clarke stood alone on the platform, a solid, stubby man with impressive thick white hair. After the rustling and whispering and the squeaking of folding seats had subsided, he still stood there in silence, solemn and awe-inspiring. He always started out that way, no matter what the occasion. He would lower his white head and stare at us fiercely, lips compressed and nostrils dilated, until our nerves were definitely strained. Then he would open his mouth and speak.

This day he was slow about opening his mouth, and from

where I sat, bright-eyed and expectant in my knickers, I could detect a certain lack of assurance. Obviously, Mr. Clarke didn't quite know what he was going to say. At last he raised his head, placed his feet a little further apart, and declaimed, while avoiding our eyes.

"The immortal Shakespeare always has something pertinent to say," he began. "I cannot do better than to quote his deathless lines

> Be not the first by whom the new are tried,
> Nor yet the last to lay the old aside.

I am grieved to tell you that our school's fair reputation has suffered. Owing to an ill-advised experiment made by two of our young women, who think themselves, no doubt, very modern . . ."

Mr. Clarke loved to speak in a deep, stern voice that could swell to a roar. On this occasion he let himself go, but he didn't really say anything in an entire half-hour except that knickers were immodest and that any girl wearing them rendered herself ludicrous and unwomanly. He did not, I marked with interest, forbid them. He didn't say anything that Dad would have to resent legally. He merely advised females against wearing pants, on the general grounds of morality, world civilization, and taste. Then he came to a stop, blew his nose, and started off the stage, with an avuncular wave of the hand to signify that we could adjourn. An English teacher ran up the steps and whispered to him frantically. Mr. Clarke clapped his hands to call us back, and walked to the center of the platform.

"I have just been informed—that is, reminded," he said, "that it was not Shakespeare, as a matter of fact, who penned those immortal lines. It was Pope—Alexander Pope, Miss Jensen?" Miss Jensen, hovering offstage, nodded. "Yes," said Mr. Clarke, "it was Alexander Pope who wrote those words, as it happens. However, they are so wonderful that they *might* have been written by Shakespeare. And with that thought I will leave you."

"Well?" asked Dauphine as we walked out, last in the line of students. The others were looking back to see how we had taken it. My mouth was stiff from smiling carelessly.

"Well," I said, "what?"

25

"You wearing them tomorrow?" asked Dauphine.

"Sure," I said. "Aren't you?"

"Of course," she said savagely. "He doesn't give us any choice. Oh, dear, and I'm so tired of this color."

"Mine are wearing out," I said. There was a traitorous note in my voice, a note of hope.

"You don't want to wear your new dressing gown to school, Carola," I said, "and I'll tell you why."

"Why?" asked Carola.

"Because," I said, "the other children will laugh at you. Nobody wears dressing gowns to school. They'll *laugh* at you. Think of that! You wouldn't want the other children to laugh at you, would you, Carola?"

Silently my daughter put down the dressing gown she had been clutching to her breast, allowed me to put a dress on her, and trotted off to nursery school meek as a lamb.

RAYMOND

I was shocked, recently, when a neighbor said laughingly of her thirteen-year-old daughter, "This morning she got flowers from her boy friend to celebrate their anniversary. They had their first date just a year ago. Isn't it mad?"

Mad? When I was thirteen, my mother would probably have called the police at any suggestion of a boy friend, but at that age no boy looked at me and I looked at no boy. Even when such exchanges did begin, several years later, and Mother didn't mind, I was reluctant to bring the boys home; I tried to keep anybody I liked away from the family as long as I could. I wanted to keep him to myself, and, as I knew all too well, once a new friend was admitted to our jolly family group he entered the public domain and was no longer exclusive property. My parents, my four sisters, and even my brother, had a way of pouncing on people and in the most friendly way possible tearing them to pieces and swallowing the bits. If I seem to exaggerate, allowances should be made; that is how I viewed the operation at the time. After such an experience, a boy never seemed the same to me again. I don't mean he disliked the process. Not at all—he enjoyed it. But *I* didn't.

As soon as a stranger was led into the parlor—which is what we called our sitting room—the place got terribly crowded, because everybody piled in, curious and full of hospitality. En masse, the family took over, and it was just like a party. The parlor really wasn't very comfortable—most of the furniture was upholstered in shiny green short-haired fur—but the piano was there, and, quick as a wink, if someone who could play it happened to be at home everybody was singing, whether I wanted my friend to be sung at or not. It was a pretty fair guess, too, that somebody who could play the piano *would* be at home, because our musical accomplishments had been carefully distributed. What instrument a child wanted to play, if he or she wanted to play one at all, had nothing to do with it. My parents had alternated the piano with something else, down the list according to age, so Rose played the piano, Dorothy the violin, Helen the piano, I the violin, and Dauphine, the baby, the piano. My brother Mannel, the eldest, played everything, even the clarinet, and Mother played the piano. Daddy sang. Hell, we all sang. What chance had a strange young man in the midst of a crew like that?

Even without music, they could be overpowering. Daddy was courtly, but as soon as he warmed up he grew anecdotal, and Mother retailed embarrassing stories of my childhood. She did it in a good-humored way, but there was just a hint, a glitter, of hidden steel. Even so, my parents weren't too bad, taken alone. Parents are parents. It was the crushing mass of sisters that got me down. Most of all it was Dot—warmhearted, quick, clever Dot, full of life and bent on grabbing everybody who showed up.

And once she had grabbed people, she kept them. Long after we others had lost interest in Tom, Dick, or Mary, Dot still corresponded with them, keeping up, mentioning them now and then casually as if *she* had seen them first. I think she really believed she had.

Admittedly, Dot was seldom a sore trial to me in that particular respect, because we were a long way apart in age. I had only two grudges against her, dating back to childhood. For one thing, she snitched my soldier in World War I—*my* soldier, for whom I knitted peculiar khaki-colored washcloths and made fudge. Not every little girl had a soldier—I got this one through my brother—and I was very proud of my acquisition and boasted a lot about him in school. He sent me a diamond-shaped insigne patch to wear on my sleeve, and once I got a postcard from abroad decorated with a drawing of a German officer in a spiked helmet, standing over a dead woman in torn clothes. Was she Marianne? One of his booted feet rested on the corpse, and in his raised hand was a skull, out of which he was drinking blood. The legend was "The Triumph of Kultur." I took the postcard to school and showed it around, but pretty soon Dot wrote to my soldier, and after that his letters were addressed to her, with an occasional message to me in a postscript.

There was also the affair of my Airedale pup. Even today, the phrase "my pup" has special meaning, for it was a tremendous step forward to have a dog in the house, and a greater one to have a dog of my own. In a big family, almost everything is a community possession. I had nothing but sympathy for a cousin of mine whose notorious habit was to put all her treasures into a box, close the box, and sit on it all day. At any rate, the family knew that Dixie, the Airedale, was mine, and for a long time no one disputed my claim to him. And, of the whole ravening lot of them, Dot was the one I would least have expected trouble from. She feared and hated dogs. But late one evening Dixie, in the middle of a romp, gave a shrill scream, ran into a dark corner, and went on screaming. We tried to reach our vet on the telephone, but at first we couldn't find him. We moved Dixie to an upstairs sleeping porch, where he continued to yelp. I hung over him, spouting tears, imploring him to stop. Then I heard my mother say to Mannel, "Shouldn't he be put out of his misery?," and my screams drowned out those of the dog. At last, the vet was located and a palliative applied to Dixie, who, said the vet, was suffering from inflammation of the intestines. The dog settled down, as did the house altogether. But when, at bed-time, I went back to the sleeping porch to spend the night near Dixie, Dot met me at the door and barred the way. She drove me off with noisy abuse, declaring that I was not to bother the dog, and she was too much my senior for argument. She spent the night there, usurping my position, and I never forgot it.

I understood. Though Dot hated dogs, she had to be in on an affair as dramatic as that one, and wherever she was she had to manage things. I understood—but understanding does not neces-sarily bring forgiveness. Neither of these grudges had anything to do with boy trouble, however. All that came later, by which time the identity of my chief opponent had shifted.

In our St. Louis house, *Webster's Dictionary* lay open on a lectern. Some of the pages had come loose, and on the infre-quent occasions when the dictionary was closed they stuck out. Its binding was as scuffed as my school shoes. Webster must have been used a lot, though I don't recall anybody's using it very much until I learned how. Before I learned to look words up, I realized that the book was excellent for pressing flowers. The pages already sheltered a number of cruelly flattened roses and violets faded to a dirty yellowish pallor, and skeletons of leaves, and even old dance programs. In my flower-pressing phase, I once or twice looked speculatively at a set of fairly large, heavy books ranged behind glass in the parlor. Piled up, three or four of the volumes would press a violet adequately, perhaps even a rose, but somehow I thought we were not sup-posed to meddle with them. I may have been mistaken about that. The series was a sort of "Child's Treasury," and, much later, on an idle afternoon, I unlocked the bookcase and ex-amined one of the books. I liked it, and quickly read through the lot. Then, emboldened, I started out on an upper shelf of books not so pristine in appearance, bound in battered tan calf —the complete translated works of Victor Hugo. Ultimately, it was Hugo, not the "Treasury," that sent me to Webster, for M. Hugo's vocabulary was way above my head, especially whenever I reached the most fascinating point of the plot. Off I went to the dictionary, every time. For some reason, most of the unknown words I looked up started with "l"—"licentious," "libidinous," "lascivious" (mostly out of *Le Roi s'Amuse,* as I remember)—but there were other terms, and I was badly disappointed with some of them, such as "venal." Nevertheless, I learned a lot from the dictionary. Not everything, though. I never had occasion to look up "ambivalence"—naturally enough, because it wasn't a word in use at the time and I wouldn't have found it even if I tried. Yet it would have been a good, useful term to apply to a split point of view of my mother's that puzzled me.

Her attitude toward dating was indeed ambivalent—double and incompatible. Dating—or, as we called it then, "going out with"—was either good or bad, right or wrong, but my mother showed signs of both approving and disapproving. Sometimes she behaved as if she hated the idea, at which times girls who went out with lots of boys were condemned as boy-crazy. At other times, she spoke admiringly of popular girls. My father followed her lead, no matter where it took him, and you never knew where you were. One day, I heard Mother discussing my sister Helen with Daddy. Because the discussion was about Helen, who was next-older to me and thus within my orbit of interest, and also because they spoke in low tones, I pricked up my ears.

"She's going to be a beautiful girl. Beautiful!" Mother said, and my father assented, with pride. It was not news to me that curly-haired Helen was beautiful, but I found it worthy of note that our elders should consider this a good thing, since, when talking to us, they never took the position that pretty children were any better than plain ones. Distinctions were drawn along quite different lines: it was good to get high marks, to tell the truth, and to show courage, and bad to mistreat your little sister, to make a noise when Daddy was home, to pat strange dogs, and to tell lies. Beauty was never mentioned, and now I believed that my mother spoke softly because she didn't want Dauphine and me to hear her, since we were not beautiful. Naturally, Mother wouldn't want to hurt our feelings.

My feelings may not have been hurt, but I was certainly jealous. Until then, I'd felt superior to Helen, in spite of her seniority, because her beauty was so painful to maintain. Every time the "upstairs girl" (the one who did housework and looked after the children, as opposed to the "downstairs girl," who cooked) combed Helen's ever-tangled hair, there were screams and tears. Style decreed that she wear it in glossy sausages of equal plumpness and length, dangling to the collar. Propriety demanded that these sausages be reglossed every morning, but the upstairs girl, as well as Helen, shrank from the ordeal. I'd always thought, smugly, Poor Helen, but now I realized that it was true what they said, or at least implied, in the fairy tales: it was good to be beautiful.

After that day, I studied pictures of princesses in the fancy fairy-tale books that Dorothy had begun to collect—special full-page illustrations in color, protected by tissue-paper pages, by Maxfield Parrish, Arthur Rackham, Edmund Dulac. Their princesses often bore a distinct resemblance to Helen, with their large blue eyes and thick dark lashes and pretty smiles. No princess in any of the pictures looked like me; none of them had straight bobbed hair and a round face.

I didn't repine over my shortcomings or refuse to believe they existed; I conceded them. If the world wanted graceful, blue-eyed princesses with curls, it would have to make out with Helen. I had *Webster*. But though I aimed at self-sufficiency, I couldn't attain it. In spite of myself, I occasionally tried for my turn at the center of the stage. A small child finds it comparatively easy to get there. He has only to open his mouth and yell, or use some innocent, lovable pretext like that of Dot, when she was four, who plucked at a visitor's sleeve and said, "This is me. This is Dorothy." But it is not so simple as you grow older. Besides, I was fifth in line and had to compete with others who had already learned to dispute the field, so I didn't try hard or often.

People were always telling us how lucky we were to be a big

family. The world we grew up in was secure; our brother and sisters were always our champions. Though we might have our little spats, who didn't? In the end, the family was the important thing, cemented by love and loyalty. I have never doubted the fundamental truth of this concept, but I'm not so sure the spats were all that trivial. Dot did her best to live up to the temperament everybody automatically attributed to her because of her red hair. She was passionate and bad-tempered—partly, I was sure, because it was expected of her. But I didn't often make allowances for Dorothy. I belonged to Rose. Dauph was Dot's. To Dauphine and me, it seemed that our older sisters had never been in our humble class; they'd always been adults. Most of the time, we obeyed their commands, though we expressed feeble defiance first. And it worked both ways, for Rose felt a special responsibility toward me, as Dot did toward Dauph. I would fetch and carry for Rose, though not for Dot, and when the two of them faced each other in the arena, it was Rose I rooted for. It didn't occur to me then that I might ever be a full-fledged gladiator myself, but the time was coming.

I grew older, and began going with Helen to Saturday-morning classes at the art school at Washington University. The school was housed in an edifice of great, if accidental, distinction. It had been created as a pavilion for the World's Fair of 1904, with an Italian sunken garden and porticoes on all four sides. By the time we got there, it was as romantically decrepit as any real Italian ruin. Leaky roof, peeling paint, mounds of dead leaves and bushes run wild were fit surroundings for drawing in charcoal from casts of antique sculpture. I drew Apollo, Hercules, and Hera, then moved on into the sculpture class, where I modelled dogs, horses, praying hands. I loved it all.

St. Louis's bohemians used the school as a center, and put on a pageant there every year—their own Chelsea Arts Ball, or Beaux-Arts. The last year I was there, for some reason that escapes me, we younger students wore costumes of vaguely Egyptian appearance and danced all together to music from *Aïda*. I was thrilled, especially when somebody took a photograph of me at the dress rehearsal looking dreamy and noble in profile against an empty sky. I could not be so fat after all, I thought, if they wanted to photograph me, and after the performance I hung around waiting hopefully for compliments. Mannel said, "You looked like a butter tub next to Helen."

This may have been the point at which I made my resolution to step into the ring. Yet, at that time, there was no rancor in my feelings for Helen. We got on well; our interests were compatible. Helen liked to paint and I preferred sculpture, which kept things comfortable; we went to museums together. She wasn't a passionate reader, but she didn't mind listening, so I would read aloud. She played the piano and I the violin, or we sang together or made up songs—Helen the music, I the words. If I couldn't keep up with her in the gym and she cared little for my interest in natural history, the balance still tipped to the side of friendly relations, and I appreciated above all the fact that, as the elder, she never pulled rank on me, as I was always doing to Dauphine.

But Helen had a side that I couldn't understand—she didn't want to remain a child. She was always rushing her fences; it had been that way, I reflected, since she rose up in rebellion against the early supper of cereal and milk we three youngest used to have in the kitchen and insisted on eating later, with the others, in the dining room. This desire for the dull world of grownups mystified me then and continued to mystify me when I was twelve or thirteen and Helen, at fifteen, was still straining at the leash.

There was a sort of climax, one evening, over a party dress that Helen had inherited from Rose. All our clothes were passed down from sister to sister. We never minded that; on the contrary, we sometimes waited impatiently for our turn at some favorite garment, and I had always loved the dress Helen was wearing that evening. A white net, it had skipped Dot on its descent, because of its salmon-pink bolero; according to the immutable laws of dress, a redhead could not wear pink. Redheads had to wear blue, green, yellow, or tan; brunettes were best in red, blondes in blue; gray-haired women must wear black or

34

gray or purple; and nobody less than thirty could dress in black except for mourning. When the white net with the bolero had been made—like all our things, it was made at home, by a dress-maker—there was some anxious argument about the trimming of tiny crystal beads, designed by Rose. Mother was afraid the beads would look cheap, but she gave in at last. There had been no trouble over the neckline, because it was high and demure. (Mother worried about necklines that gave any hint of secondary sex characteristics. "Can you see the divide?" she would ask suspiciously.)

I thought the bolero and the beads were beautiful, and at the party that night—I've forgotten what it was, perhaps a university party for all ages—I kept looking at Helen. But one thing puzzled me: I didn't see why she kept retiring to the powder room. She took me with her every time, to talk with, and she didn't do anything but mope.

"I don't want to go back out there," she said when I got bored and tried to coax her.

I said, "What's the matter, Helen? Oh, come, let's get some lemonade. Let's sit near the band. Come on, Helen."

She flared out, "I don't want to, I tell you! I hate the way I look. I just hate it. I wish I hadn't come."

I thought she had gone mad, and said so. Hate that lovely white net and pink taffeta? What on earth could be said against it? Helen replied bitterly that everything in the world was wrong with it; it had sleeves, it had a high neck, it was revolt-ingly childish. "This is an evening party, and I ought to be wearing an evening dress," she said.

A tall young woman came into the room, wearing a low-necked sleeveless garment of pale-yellow chiffon with ruffles on the bodice. You could see the divide.

"There—like that," Helen whispered. "That's what I ought to have on."

She was obviously out of her head.

But in the last analysis I was on Helen's side; it was a question of solidarity. She might be wrongheaded about beaded taffeta, but we were still companions and belonged to the same club. Whether or not she liked it, we were all together in the boat—Helen, Dauph, and I. To do Helen justice, she seldom complained about my company, though in her own mind she had long since crossed over to the other side. If she thought about it at all, she probably reflected that it wouldn't be long before I joined her over there and then I would stop holding her back.

Summer camp probably gave me the necessary push. As we grew up, our parents shipped us off, two by two, to a place on the northern peninsula of Michigan, where we spent six weeks of the endless summer living under canvas at the edge of a swamp, and learned such useful arts as shooting with bows and arrows, decorating birch bark with porcupine quills, and driving mosquitoes out of the tent with a smudge pot. We must have looked rather odd. We didn't want to wear skirts, but, as I have said, slacks and shorts for women had not yet been introduced. Bloomers were out of the question; bloomers were passé—nobody had used them for quite two years. Instead, we all wore shirts and boys' pants, and had the same difficulty that boys do in keeping our shirttails tucked in. Since nobody outside could see us, this hardly mattered, but the discomfort I experienced may be one reason I was so willing, when the time came, to adopt the style of girls' knickerbockers.

I didn't like camp very much, but I didn't detest it as much as I claimed to. There was far too much exercise for my taste and very little time for reading, but late every evening, when the smudge pots had been lit and then removed, some of us gathered in a big tent and listened to one of the older girls reading aloud from *A Girl of the Limberlost*. We were crazy about it. We all wailed when it was finished, and no wonder—Elnora's love affair was pretty hot stuff. Though I didn't always grasp the significance of certain remarks made by other girls when the reader came to some particularly tense part—for instance, where Elnora carelessly hugged her young man and he turned absolutely white with passion—I pretended to, and laughed as heartily as anybody. I soon learned at camp that quite a few of the girls were odd in the same way Helen was.

In fact, they were even more peculiar. They talked incessantly of boys. Going out with boys was an old story to some of these hard-bitten maidens, and furthermore, to hear them tell it, they had been indulging in sinful practices—driving around in roadsters and petting—for years. I went to Helen and asked her opinion, and she shrugged it off. "Oh, that's a fast crowd," she said, so I went back and listened some more. I learned a lot that summer at camp, but I hadn't learned how to handle Helen by the time we got home.

By now, of course, Helen was a veteran; she'd been going out with boys for a couple of years. She was also a problem. Helen took men away from other girls. It was not the sort of piracy Dorothy committed. Dot swiped people—men, women, and children—but Helen concentrated on men. She disregarded the barriers of age and poached wherever she liked. How did she get away with it? We other sisters theorized about that—alone at first, but then, as the menace grew, together.

It was not easy to figure out the answer, because Helen's methods were not showy. She didn't come into a room and take a man by storm, as it were. Instead, she seemed to seep into his consciousness. Certainly she was beautiful—especially once she got away from home to the safety of Smith College and cut off those curls that had long been the bane of her existence—but beauty couldn't account for everything. Helen took men away from other girls who were just as pretty. Dauphine thought it was the manner in which she played the piano, looking up in an alluring way as she sang. Dot thought it was something more heinous; Dot said Helen pawed boys. (Pawing was anathema. It was fast. A girl who patted a man's arm while talking to him, or snuggled while dancing, was pawing him.) I didn't go as far as Dot. What Helen did, I said, was to show her feelings—a proceeding I considered shameful—and this meant that men were immediately aware that she liked them. A man was naturally flattered and delighted to be thus bombarded by Helen with delicate signs of affection, or at least approval. A man would naturally fall flat at her feet, I said. I added, "I don't think she does it on purpose. It just happens."

The others scouted my theory—that is, Dorothy and Dauphine did. Rose wasn't in on these talks very often, because she was away. I wasn't sure what Mother thought about the situation. I suppose it was still a case of ambivalence with her. Half the time, she deplored Helen's popularity, and the other half she was proud of her.

After we moved to Chicago, many things changed. Rose married. Dot was engaged. Dauphine started at once to go out with boys, because such behavior, precocious as it might be in St. Louis, was the accepted thing in Chicago. Daddy grumbled and Mother made a sour face, but nobody put a stop to it. I had already started going out, if only just. Dauph and I followed separate social paths and did not bother each other, but we didn't enjoy peace and quiet for more than a few months at a time. There was always the day of reckoning when, with a whoop and a holler, Helen came home from college on vacation.

The devastation she wrought was appalling. Talented as she was at bowling over adults, our very young men didn't stand a chance. It was hell, but I would never admit that it was hell for *me*. I would say indignantly, "Dauph's so young, it isn't fair. A kid like that can't possibly hold her own against an older woman like Helen."

Dauphine took the poaching with droll resignation, though I couldn't. Accepting the inevitable, she once even made Mother admit there was dirty work at the crossroads. Dauph had brought home—foolhardily—a particularly good specimen, a man of more maturity and charm than we youngsters usually rated. After dinner, Helen sat down at that damn piano and began singing *bergerettes* at him. She was awfully good with French songs, now and then looking up and smiling with her eyes, inviting him to join in her enthusiasm for them. The man was stunned. He stood there like a statue, until Helen moved over on the piano bench and asked him to sit down. His knees gave way and he sat.

Mother reported later to Rose, "Dauphine was the funniest thing I ever saw. She tiptoed up to him behind his back, kissed her fingertips, and touched the top of his head in farewell, then tiptoed out of the room." She laughed, but I didn't see anything to laugh at.

Not long after that, Helen decided not to finish the four years at Smith, and she came home to attend daily classes at the Chicago Art Institute, later taking a job. What had been merely a seasonal menace now loomed over Dauphine and me all the time. Everything got worse and worse. Young men around our house lost whatever identity they had ever possessed and were known simply as "Helen's, formerly Mickey's" (I was Mickey) or "Helen's, formerly Dauph's." It was all becoming intolerable, I reflected; it would have to stop.

According to family legend, I planned what I did in cold blood, but that is not true. If plans formed, they did it down in my subconscious. The way I remember it, the idea came over me in a rush on the day Helen brought home a man of her own, for a change. No, that's not fair—she often found men outside. This one was French, named Raymond de Something, and he spoke with a charming, if complicated, accent that was both French and British, because he'd been to school in England. Helen addressed him as "Ray-monde" instead of Americanizing and calling him Ray, as most other girls would have done. Obviously, she was delighted with him; not only was he good-looking and very well mannered but he was foreign, and that was always a good thing around our house. We were all fascinated by the world abroad, where none of us had ever been, and Helen, moreover, was exceptionally quick at languages. She and Raymond kept talking French at the table that first evening, and after dinner they read Verlaine and Mallarmé to each other before getting around to the inevitable *bergerettes*. After Raymond had gone, we all pronounced him charming.

"Yes, isn't he!" said Helen, gratified. I did not miss the sparkling eyes and pink cheeks—though, of course, her eyes would have sparkled and her cheeks would have flushed even if Raymond had been all wet. Helen never thought men were all wet; she liked every one of them, but I could see that she liked

Raymond more than most. She told us where she had got him, but I don't remember that. Details about Raymond's outside life did not interest me, even later.

The ceremonial visit to the family had been polished off, and the next time or two that Raymond saw Helen it was downtown, where he would call for her after work and take her to a restaurant or a show. When he brought her home, it was easy to see that he was in that state of dizzy infatuation we all recognized so well. Helen told me in confidence that Raymond was sure she would love France, especially if she stayed awhile with his people. But she was vague about that. Life held so many possibilities for Helen that she was in no hurry to marry anybody, even a good-looking Frenchman. "Still, he's awfully cute. Isn't he cute?" she said, and I said yes.

It was springtime. Helen's other friends grumbled and complained that she neglected them, but Helen spent most of her spare time with Raymond. After two weeks, he came for lunch on Sunday, and by that time I felt ready to begin. He arrived in a serious, questing mood. Apparently, he felt it was time to get better acquainted with his wonderful girl's family, and he set out to do it. He listened to my father and mother, laughing when Daddy made jokes and becoming grave when Mother was serious. He was introduced to Rose and her husband and made an excellent impression on them. He chatted in the kindest fashion with Helen's two little sisters, Dauph and me, asking about our lessons and games. I noticed that he would avoid looking at Helen for minutes on end, then sneak a quick little glance, like a man taking a sip of refreshment. I was sure she returned the glances, but I didn't look to see, because I looked at nobody and nothing but Raymond. I stared at him, and stared and stared.

If Helen did it—conveying to a man that he had all her attention—I could do it, too. I didn't only stare; I listened. No matter what he said, I hung on his words. I thought of this first attempt as practice—I never supposed it would work right away—but nobody could have undergone that fixed stare without feeling it, and soon Raymond began to fidget and cast hunted glances in my direction.

So far so good. I am still not quite sure why Raymond didn't simply decide that Helen had a lunatic sister and let it go at that, but young men from the Continent are apt to think the best of themselves, and after he'd gone home that night he wondered if he hadn't perhaps made a deep impression on an innocent child who had then fallen in love with him. I know this; he told me so later. It seemed to him the only explanation, but he came back next day to make sure. After all, what did he know about young American girls? Helen was at her office, but he had an excuse to come by—he had left a book in the sitting room. Raymond retrieved his book, had a little talk with me, and confirmed his suspicion. I was still staring at him, still listening raptly when he spoke. So when I showed him out he whispered quickly the suggestion that I meet him next day at Goethe's statue in the park. I didn't have to counterfeit delight when I agreed to this; it was all I could do not to clap my hands for joy. The system worked!

We met at Goethe, we paced the nearby paths, Raymond talked, and I listened. At least, I assume I listened, though I can't recall anything he said. At the end of the afternoon, when he left me on my doorstep, neither of us proposed that he come in. Instead, Raymond put his hand to his forehead, saying, "Darling, my mind is made up. I've been so confused I didn't know what to do, but now I've decided." He thrust out his chin and stared dramatically over my head. "I cannot be a rotter," he said. "Wait. Do nothing. I shall—" He dashed off into the dusk without finishing the sentence, and I ran in and upstairs.

Any family but mine would have noticed my elation that night, but I was safe with them. Dauphine was talking, Helen was talking, Daddy was talking—oh, I was quite safe. But by the middle of next morning things had started. Helen telephoned from her office. Mother answered the ring, listened for some minutes, and then came hurrying to say the call was for me. She followed me back to the telephone, talking as we went: "It's

Helen. I can't make head or tail of what she's saying—something about you and that Frenchman, Raymond. But surely not! What have you been up to? What—"

By putting the receiver to one ear and my finger in the other, I was able to hear Helen's voice, but at first she was so excited as to be almost incoherent. Her voice shook with hysterical giggles. Calming down, she said, "Raymond's just been here, and I still can't believe it's happened. He was in a terrible state. You little devil. He burst in and started talking before he got through the door. He said, 'Helen, the most dreadful thing, but I'm not a rotter, I'm not a rotter, I must tell you now that it's Mickey I love. It's not you. There's been a terrible mistake, but I don't want to be a rotter.' What in the world?"

She paused for a reply, so I said, "Yes, I know about it."

"Know about it? I should think you do," said Helen. "I called up to tell you it's all right with me."

Again she paused for a reply. I managed to say, "Oh?"

"Yes, I told Raymond it's perfectly all right, he mustn't give it another thought," she said. "And I really don't mind a bit. I really don't, Mickey." She stopped to giggle. "You little *bitch*!" she added, and hung up.

I was left with the astonishing impression that among the emotions struggling through her voice admiration had been uppermost. I turned away from the telephone to face Mother, who had been thinking fast. She said, "So. It's true, then. And you did it on purpose, didn't you?"

I stammered slightly, because, for the first time, I was afraid. "I g-guess so."

"Oh, well," said Mother calmly, "it was time somebody did."

I don't remember what finally happened to Raymond.

THAT YOUNG MAN

I remember my father toward the end chiefly as a gantlet to be run whenever I had to pass through the living room. He never let me or my mother or my younger sister go through without making some excuse to stop us. All day he lay stretched out on a sofa, reading, while the radio made a noise in his ears. You couldn't exactly say Dad listened to the radio, though there were certain programs which he did concentrate on; he just depended on the noise that came from it to keep him from getting lonely. Even when he dozed off, he needed it. We soon learned not to switch the radio off while he slept. If we did, he always woke up immediately and turned it on again.

Getting past the sofa unobserved was almost impossible. Evidently Dad lay there thinking of nothing but how to waylay us and what to ask for, just as a child lies in bed wondering if he dare ask for yet another drink of water. Before he was stricken, his days had been crowded and he had been busier than he liked to be, but the last three years of his life were terrible for him. Each day yawned ahead of him, an empty canyon. He had always been a friendly, gregarious man, too busy even to separate his six children into six distinct entities in his mind, though he was sure he was very fond of the family. Now he lay helpless and childlike, begging the three of us who were left—my brother and three older sisters were married now and had homes of their own—to stop and talk to him, to bring him a crumb, however tiny, of life from outside, or to lend him our ears for just a while, only a little while. A child, after the third or fourth drink of water, can go to sleep, but Dad could not. He dared not. He was fighting off the last sleep. For an old man, he put up a good battle, and stayed out of that endless slumber for three long years. Watching him, I would become frightened. I was in my twenties, but even I was no fonder of life than he was. If seventy-five can fight for life like that, I said to myself, when does one begin to feel reconciled to death? Never? Nobody dares tell you that when you're young and strong.

So I always tried to get past the sofa without disturbing my father. He had a way of lying there, his head on a pillow hung over the sofa's arm, his eyes closed, as if he were sound asleep. I always hoped he really was sleeping. I would tiptoe very gently, avoiding the board that I knew squeaked under the blue velvet rug, and sometimes I would get so far that I was sure I had made it. Then:

"Dolly!" my father would say, opening his eyes. He called all his daughters Dolly. "I wonder if you would mind just handing me that *Nation* on the table. . . . That's it. Thank you, Dolly. Just a minute," he'd add, if I took a tentative step toward the

44

door and freedom. "There's something here that I think will interest you." And, feverishly eager, without waiting to select a passage which might actually have caught my interest, he would begin to read aloud something, anything, while I stood on one foot and then on the other, waiting for a chance to break away.

Dauphine and I tried to avoid being caught, and we tried to get away as soon as we could once we had been caught. It was cruel, of course, but we couldn't help ourselves. Dad was too much a part of everyday life for us to be anything but natural with him. It wasn't so bad when we had been away from him for a while; it was even pleasant to come home from a trip downtown and tell him all about it—pleasant and heartwarming, for an hour or so. But after that hour or so there were things to do, —telephones to answer, letters to write, books to read, life to live—and Dad never, never, never had enough attention. You couldn't just sit with him quietly and read to yourself; he didn't want that. He wanted to make his mark on you, lacking a larger audience. He wanted the great, yawning chasm to be filled up. He wanted to be himself again, to find reality in the eyes of the people around him as he had found it before he was imprisoned.

I shouldn't allow myself to remember Dad as an old man, because I knew him a lot longer as a man who moved around, went out for the day, took long trips. I knew him when Mother wasn't always being kind to him, when she still felt free to act natural. I can remember very vividly the quarrels between Dad and Mother, and though I know that the books say such things sear one's childhood and leave indelible marks on the soul, I can't believe it. Perhaps in those days children just didn't have any psychology. My parents certainly did all the wrong things, according to modern rules, but we didn't react as children are now supposed to. Why, they even called us in to arbitrate for them. I remember Dad's appealing to my sense of justice while I was still small enough to be taking an afternoon nap in my cot: "Now, just listen to this, Dolly. I want you to see for yourself how unreasonable your mother is."

45

Certain things my father did, certain remarks he made, invariably annoyed Mother. She reacted in exactly the same way every time; it was like pushing a button, and her husband was constantly, irresistibly tempted to push it. If we were at the dinner table, especially if there were guests, Dad would do something to make Mother glower at him. Then he would look guiltily at her, sitting in proud, offended dignity at the other end of the ten-foot table, and he would say, "Quit kicking me under the table!"

We children lived in what amounted to a matriarchy. We knew that Mother was the judge and the jury. People who didn't know us very well thought this was Mother's doing, and they pitied my father, poor, good-natured man, whose wife seemed to have grabbed all the authority around the house. They didn't understand that Dad wanted it that way. His business took him away from home a great deal, sometimes for several months at a stretch, and if he had been presented between trips with the job of sitting in judgment on some child's dispute, he would have fled in horror from the scene. Theoretically, he loved his children, but in the flesh they scared him to death and wore him out. He thought that most of the natural manifestations of childhood were just plain, original sin. Children worried him when they made a noise or jumped about; they worried him when they enjoyed games; they worried him when they made themselves noticeable in any way at all. So when we began to grow out of the noisy, running-around stage, it looked as if almost everyone would be better off.

Only Mother bewailed the ways of nature and thought sorrowfully of her vanished babies. And soon she had no leisure in which to do any bewailing, because a new trouble had developed, and the name of it was Sex. Though that word was not permitted to be spoken in our house above a whisper, the awful fact of it pervaded the entire group. First, Mother tried to cope with it by ignoring it. She seemed to think that if she pretended vigorously enough that no such force existed, Sex would cease to annoy or threaten us. She didn't talk it over with Dad, because she never talked about Sex, even to Dad, but he evidently decided, quite on his own, that it was time for him to start taking care of the children.

Dad had a lot of notions, it seemed, about Sex. He must have realized all in a rush that he was the father of five growing girls and that something would have to be done about protecting them. Dad was a Southerner, not a half-hearted one like Mother, whose native town was St. Louis, but a real Southerner, from Memphis. And a real Southerner—well, he has notions about womanhood. Somewhere, buried in Dad's soul, there had slumbered through the years of our childhood the conviction that when we started to grow up it would be up to him to take over the reins from Mother. Mother, of course, wouldn't be able to handle such matters, Dad figured, because she was one of them herself—one of the mysterious, ignorant, adorable, horrible, sinful, purer-than-snow creatures called women. Day after day had passed over his head until years of married life had been rolled up, during which Dad lived comfortably and cheerfully with Mother, perfectly content to think of her as a partner. a pleasant, sensible companion. Then, all of a sudden, along came Sex, and he had to face the fact that Mother and five of his six children were females.

The prospect might have daunted a less sturdy character, but Dad wasn't daunted. He knew just how he would have to train us. Since we were his daughters (and Mother's, of course), we would be ladies, not the other sort of woman. Ladies were ladies more by virtue of the things they didn't do than by the things they did. The other sort of woman had a different, more positive set of values. To begin with, ladies didn't use powder on their faces—not in Dad's world, they didn't. Ladies didn't adjust their hats in public, he decreed, or stand before mirrors to see whether they looked all right, because ladies were not supposed to care whether they looked all right or not. Ladies most decidedly did not smoke, that being one sure way, Dad said, of telling the sheep from the goats. Ladies never discussed clothing from the point of view of sheer adornment. There were other things ladies didn't do, but they were so dreadful Dad didn't like even to think of them in connection with his daughters. He put that whole matter out of his mind, he thought, but actually he didn't. It stayed right there—a little below the surface, perhaps, just barely out of sight, but there it was, waiting.

Dad became, to me and my sisters, a nuisance. Much to our mystification, after years of being no bother at all, of not even taking us seriously save for a very occasional slap or scolding, he began to concentrate on our conduct. It was most annoying.

The family usually met in strength only in the evening, at dinnertime. It was at table that we chattered about all the little affairs of the day. Because we were so preponderantly female, the conversation had a way of slipping over into things which interested women, especially clothes. Well, Dad took to listening. He would prick up his ears when we spoke of dress, alert against the slightest sign of vanity. He permitted us to discuss clothing in its primary function, as a protection against the elements, but that was all. As long as Mother said something harmless, such as "It's time to get you a warm coat, Helen. Your blue won't do for really cold weather," or Dauphine spoke up for a new pair of rubbers, nothing happened down at Dad's end of the table. But the talk never stopped there. Sooner or later, one of us, usually one of the older ones, would begin describing the divine red party dress she was planning for spring, or someone would set up a howl for a new hat, and there the fat would be, sizzling right in the middle of the fire.

Dad would clear his throat loudly. Mother sometimes would hear the danger signal and change the subject, but usually she would be so absorbed in it herself that she would pay no attention. After a moment of outraged silence, Dad would push back his chair, making a loud scraping noise as he did it, stand up, pick up his teacup and saucer—he was very fond of tea—and walk majestically from the room. He would finish his cup alone in the living room, having registered a protest and done his duty toward protecting the morals of five little potential prostitutes.

Mother betrayed us by going over to Dad's side in several small matters. Evening dress, for instance. Dad thought décolleté evening dress was the Devil's cleverest invention, and Mother supported him in this opinion. As long as we children lived at home, we wore sleeves to parties and covered our bosoms up to the neck. Often, when the family dressmaker triumphantly exhibited one of us dressed in the latest example of her skill, Mother shook her head in disapproval and condemnation.

"No," she'd say. "You need more *here*," indicating her chest.

When Rose or Dot or Helen dressed for a party, even though her sleeves were long and her neck properly concealed behind a lot of tulle, Mother would arrange it so that the madcap party girl didn't appear at dinner. She would eat in the kitchen, and when she went out she would be careful to swathe herself in a long cloak, just in case Dad should catch a glimpse of her in the hall, on the way to the front door. Even if he had no cause to complain about décolleté, he worried just the same when any of us managed, in spite of all Mother's efforts, to look pretty.

One after another, my sisters and I grew up, met young men, and began going out in the evenings. The first few occasions were very hard on Dad, but, luckily for me, by the time I entered the lists, he was beginning to feel less desperate about life and its dangers. He was aging, spending more and more time at home, and, by attrition, his bump of shocked sensitivity was getting smaller. When Rose, my oldest sister, had her early beaux, Dad made a brave attempt to keep track of things. He always got himself introduced to Tom or Harry or Dick and tried to spend a few minutes during each of the young man's visits in courteous conversation, taking the boy's number, as it were. But time went on and the boy friends piled up—more and more and more of them. Helen's list alone was staggering. She could scarcely keep track of them herself. Dad ultimately gave up the struggle and took to referring to all of them, no matter whose, by the generic term "that young man."

He never thought of asking where these young men took his daughters once the parental door closed behind them. I suppose he assumed, without question, that they were always going to some properly spied-on party. But sometimes the young people didn't go out at all. Sometimes they just sat in the parlor and visited. It worried Dad that Mother thought it unnecessary to be present on these occasions, and one evening, when she was out, he resolved to do a proper job of chaperoning. When Helen's date arrived—it was at the time of Helen's dizziest popularity—Dad was all prepared. He came into the parlor, bringing with him an enormous heap of magazines, back numbers, for months, of the *Saturday Evening Post,* and under Helen's startled gaze settled down in an armchair, lifted the top magazine, and began to read. The effect of this invasion was tremendous. In our circles this sort of thing just wasn't done. The young man was uneasy, and Helen was in an agony of shame. They couldn't speak about it openly or take issue with Dad, but neither could they talk to each other. The young man went home very early.

Next morning, of course, Mother heard all about it from her outraged daughter, and she went to town on Dad, but he wouldn't give an inch. "When I was a young man," he said, "a young lady's parents always sat with us when I called. Why not? Why should they object? What does Helen want to do that her old father shouldn't see?" This was a question so difficult to answer that nobody answered it, and Dad retired master of the situation. We all felt worried. Something would have to be done, but what?

I was the next sufferer. I was, at seventeen, in a difficult mood anyway, just old enough to have beaux yet painfully self-conscious about them. It was a Saturday evening. Once again, Mother was out—there must have been a club meeting or something. I know I was wary, expecting trouble, and I was right. When Jimmy, my young man, came to call and Dad brought out the old pile of *Saturday Evening Post*s, I controlled myself. Remembering Helen's experience, I bit back the hot words of protest that rose to my tongue. Jimmy didn't seem to be daunted by the silent, reading figure over in the corner under the piano lamp, so I decided that I wouldn't be either. Jimmy and I sat side by side on the sofa and had a reasonably good time. There were salted peanuts, there was candy, and everything was all right for a while. I was almost able to forget Dad.

Suddenly, however, he spoke up. "Dolly," he said, "it's ten-thirty."

Jimmy jumped nervously to his feet, but I grabbed him by the coattail.

"What about it?" I asked my father, honestly bewildered.

"It's bedtime," said Dad.

"No, it isn't," I replied confidently. "You've forgotten. It's Saturday night."

I was referring to the set rules of the house. Bedtime was ten-thirty on most nights, it was true, but Saturday night was different. Saturday, since the beginning of time as I had known it, had always been special. On Saturday night we stayed up until midnight, because Sunday was the day for sleeping late. It never occurred to me that Dad wouldn't be aware of this ancient ruling, but either he wasn't, or he simply didn't approve and so ignored it.

"I don't care what night it is," he said testily. "At ten-thirty, it's time for sensible people to be in bed."

"Well, I—" began Jimmy, miserably.

The blood rushed to my head. "Jimmy, you sit down!" I snapped. "If you go now, I'll never speak to you again! I guess I know my rights."

Jimmy wet his lips, opened his mouth, and sat down again, limply.

"Very well," said Dad coldly. He picked up another *Saturday Evening Post*.

For several minutes, Jimmy and I sat silent and miserable. I was licked. I was also humiliated, furious, and more than ready to leave home.

"Oh, all right," I said at last. "You can go, Jimmy. I'm *terribly* sorry."

The front door closed behind one lost boy friend. Not trusting myself to argue with the tyrant, I went to my room and slammed the door. It was the first time in my experience that a hard-and-fast family rule had been questioned, and I was badly shocked.

"Daddy just didn't know any better," my mother said soothingly next morning. "Poor Daddy, he's away from home so much . . ."

Scornfully I shook my head, rejecting the olive branch. She

51

couldn't give me that. I knew dictatorship when I saw it. Fortunately, for Dad, and for me, I went away to college a few months later.

After college, I had two years in New York and three in Europe and the Congo. When I came home after those five years, the change I found in Dad was dismaying—he could move about only with the aid of crutches. For the first time, perhaps, I realized something of what was in store for him. After a little while, though, things settled into a normal state. True, the table wasn't as long as it had been. Four of us had married and gone away; Mother, if she had wanted to, would have been able to kick Dad right in the shins at dinner. But home life seemed quite familiar, quite as if I'd never been away.

The phone rang one evening while we were dining, and it was for me. A man I had known as an undergraduate was living in town, in a downtown hotel. He wanted me to go dancing with him. Making arrangements to meet him, I felt my parents' anxious gaze on the back of my head as I stood talking into the phone.

"Yes, Cap. . . . Sure. Oh, I think it will be easiest to pick you up down there, don't you? It saves time. . . . Sure. I'll stop by and call up from the lobby, and then you come down. O.K.?" I hung up the receiver and turned back to my dinner, but stopped short at the expression on Mother's face.

"You're *calling* for him?" she demanded, shrilly incredulous. "You're going into a public place, a hotel, and *ask for a man*? At the *desk*?"

My jaw dropped. For years I had been living on my own—sometimes without excitement but more often on the verge of disaster, financial and otherwise. I looked at Mother; Mother looked at me. She also began to cry.

"What will they *think* of you?" she asked tragically. "Whatever will those people *take* you for?"

"Why, I . . ." My voice faltered and stopped. There just wasn't anything that could be said. Mother was getting old. It was simpler to capitulate. "I'll call him up, Mother," I said. "He can come out here and call for me, I guess."

"Well, I should think so!"

A minute later, I broke the silence in carefully natural tones, just to start the ball rolling. "I'll wear that short black thing I bought coming through San Francisco," I said. "Isn't that what they use in the evening here?"

"That would be all right," said Dauphine, growing animated. "What kind of a hat would you wear with it if you wore a hat? We don't use them much around here, but when we do, we go in for small ones."

"I had a darling one in New York," I said. "It was a ballibuntl straw—Oh, Dad!"

Down through the years came the scraping noise of Dad's chair on the floor as he pushed himself back. Mother's face fell; she shook her head dolefully. Dauphine bent her head over her plate. Slowly, impressively, my father stood up, ready to register disapproval by leaving the room. But there was something wrong, something new since I had last seen that gesture. It took me a second or so to recognize the trouble. With his crutches, Dad had no hand to spare for his teacup. He stood there on his crutches, looking helplessly at the table.

"Wait a minute, Dad," I said. I picked up the teacup. Solemnly we marched out of the dining room and into the living room, and there Dad settled down to drink his tea in dignified solitude. Nothing, after all, had changed very much at home.

The years added themselves to my life and escaped from Dad's. Day in, day out, he lay there on his sofa and grasped at our flying garments as we hurried past. I wanted again to get away. I hated watching him. I used to reflect that things would be easier if he would only change, but apparently he didn't. He seemed to be the same old Dad, only Dad a few years before would never have been tiresome or have bored anyone. Even now, he had flashes. Moving fretfully on the sofa, on days when his legs hurt more than usual, he would say all of a sudden, "Oh, damn! Sometimes I'm sorry I ever *got* sick."

53

He did develop, he did show a different point of view, if you observed closely from year to year. In the first months of the really bad time, when the doctor was sure that he would soon be dead, he wrote a good deal in his journal. Sometimes he quoted a bit of poetry at the head of a page. The journal had been begun thirty years earlier, and most of the quotations in the beginning came from Tennyson. Toward the end, the entries were just as copious as ever, but there were differences in the tone. Even the quotes were different. They were from Walt Whitman.

The biggest change of all, though, came over him imperceptibly.

Before Helen married, among her many boy friends was one, John, who was particularly constant in his attentions. He took Helen out, and came to dinner at our house, and sent her books and letters when he went away, for more than two years. Then, after she married another boy, John began to pay attention to me. He took me out to concerts and plays and meals; he sent me books; he came to dinner with the family. And all the time, like most of the young men who came to see us, he spent some minutes, while he waited for Helen or me, conversing with our father. Dad was always the same, courteous and chatty and just a tiny bit vague. I never for one moment thought that he knew John from any of the other beaux. He always referred to him by the cognomen which had become his special labor-saving device—"that young man."

Well, the days went by, and I got my wish at last. I went away again, out of the house, out of town, away from that sorrowful living room with the sofa in it. That meant we were all gone now, all of Dad's children but Dauphine, the baby. Whereupon, John began paying attention to Dauphine.

On the first evening he called to take her out, a little box of flowers in his hand and his nice new cravat just so, John paused, as always, for a few moments of polite conversation with my father. Dauphine kept him waiting a minute or so while she pinned his flowers on her cloak, in her bedroom. She came down then, and John shook hands with Dad and said goodbye to

Mother, and Dauphine kissed both the old folks, and she and John went out, and the front door closed.

Dad lay there as he always did—dozing, perhaps—with his eyes closed. Mother would have been sure he was sleeping except that she suddenly saw his lips move. Then he spoke up, quite loud. "It's all right with me," he said, "but tell John he can't have the old lady."

B.Sc.

My career as a mining engineer has this much in common with many success stories—it was founded on an accident. Otherwise, there is no comparison, because mine is not a success story. As an engineer, I have been a flop, but there were a few glorious weeks, back in 1926, when it might have been otherwise. Flushed with the glory and the triumph of my B.Sc., excited by the publicity which I received as the First Woman Graduate in Mining Engineering from the University of Wisconsin, and generally on top of the world, I completely forgot the reason for my acquiring that extraordinary diploma and actually took a job with a mining company. Yet the facts are simple and stark. I never meant to be a mining engineer at all. The whole thing was a complete misapprehension.

At the age of seventeen, I was an earnest, plump young woman, much annoyed by my parents' insistence on my going to college, because I felt that I was destined for Art. Once installed at the University of Wisconsin, though, I had to study something. At first I enrolled myself in the College of Letters and Science, where by temperament I belonged; it offered that potpourri of language, literature, history, and science that made, I thought, for Culture. It was the required science course which led me astray. A half-year term of freshman geology stirred me up to try chemistry. I had heard that among the chemistry professors at Wisconsin there was a really good teacher, Kahlenberg, but when I tried to get into his class, I ran into a trifling technical difficulty. Kahlenberg's course, the dean explained, though it exactly paralleled that of the Letters and Science brand of chemistry, was usually taken only by engineering students.

"Well, that's all right," I said. "I'm sure I can persuade Professor Kahlenberg to give me special permission to go to his lectures. Since they cover the same ground, what's the difference? May I do it that way?" Now, the dean may have fought with his wife that morning, or maybe he was worried about his bank account, or perhaps it was necessary that he say no once in a while, just to prove he was a dean. I'm sure that he never intended thus carelessly to mold my future life with one hasty word, but that is what he did. "No," said the dean rudely, and turned back to his desk.

His manners hurt my feelings, but that alone wouldn't have done the mischief. Like many young people in my day, I was bristling with principles, eager to find abuses in the world and burning to do away with them. In five seconds I had condemned the dean's decision as an abuse. He was wrong in saying no—wrong on technical grounds, because Professor Kahlenberg's consent would have been enough for any dean in a reasonable mood, and wrong in principle, because a student should be allowed to select his own teachers. Anyway, those were my sentiments.

I was mad. Boy, was I mad! I couldn't have remained in the same college with that dean for one single day more. Before the registrar's office closed that afternoon, I had transferred myself to the College of Engineering, enrolled for the chemistry course I wanted, and sent off a confused letter of explanation to my parents. There, if only anybody in the Engineering College had had a grain of sense, the great revolt would have ended. I would have listened to Kahlenberg's chemistry lectures, shaken hands with him, and transferred myself right back to Culture and a chastened dean at the end of term. The engineers, however, were not wise.

They were stunned when they discovered me, a seventeen-year-old female freshman, enrolled in the Engineering College. The university had a long-standing tradition, as well as a charter, for being a coeducational institution. Women studied medicine at Wisconsin, and the "pure science" courses were full of girls; the Agricultural College, too, had them. Nobody argued about that. But nobody had yet heard of a coed engineer. The engineers' immunity through the years had bred in their ranks a happy confidence that it could never happen there, and I was a horrid surprise. They lost their heads and went into a panic and, in the ensuing weeks, actually appealed to the state legislature to heave me out. After due consideration, the legislature regretfully refused. It couldn't heave me out, it explained, much as it would like to as a group of red-blooded he-men, because the university was a coeducational, tax-supported institution, and if a woman wanted to study any course it offered, and if she fulfilled the requirements and behaved herself, you couldn't turn her down.

Even then, if the engineers had only known, all was not lost. They couldn't keep their mouths shut, though. They were the engineers—hearty, simple folk. All of them, faculty members and students, tried to live up to the college pattern—the awkward guy, the diamond in the rough. To a man, they wore stiff corduroy trousers, smoked pipes or chewed tobacco, and looked down haughtily on the other colleges, which they condemned as highbrow. It was not in them to be diplomatic, and I maintain that they brought upon themselves what followed.

The custom in college is to allocate each student to a professor, who acts as his adviser. In the College of Letters and Science, my adviser had been a fragile lady who taught French literature, but my new adviser in the Engineering College was a mining engineer. I had elected mining engineering as my particular course. Professor Shorey was no pedant, nor was he tactful. My first advisory hour with him was given over to a violent argument.

"But why?" he demanded. "Why should a woman want to be an engineer? I never heard of such nonsense!"

"Why did *you* want to be an engineer?" I retorted. I was still talking in a more or less academic spirit, of course. I meant to leave engineering in peace, and before long. Sooner or later I intended to break down and explain the circumstances to Professor Shorey and reassure him, but in the meantime his attitude interested me. I wanted to hear more about it.

"It's not all the same thing," he said. "In the first place, you'll never get a job, even if you should take your degree, which is very doubtful. If I were running a mine, I'd never hire a woman in any technical capacity. You wouldn't have the practical experience, and you'd be a nuisance around the office."

"Why wouldn't I have the experience, Mr. Shorey?"

"How would you get it? Who's going to let *you* go down a mine? Why, the miners would go on strike. They'd call it bad luck and expect a cave-in. It's too foolish to discuss. It's all a waste of time, anyhow—your time and mine—because you won't get your degree."

I moved closer to the desk, all alert. "Why won't I get my degree?" I said.

Shorey sighed. "The female mind," he explained carefully and kindly, "is incapable of grasping mechanics or higher mathematics or any of the fundamentals of mining taught in this course."

That remark, *tout simple,* is why I am a Bachelor of Science in Mining Engineering. From that moment until graduation, I completely forgot that I had not always, from my earliest youth, intended to become a mining engineer. Every day offered fresh reason for forgetting. I was awfully busy for the next three years, up to my neck in mechanics and drafting and calculus. It was enough to make any girl forget a little thing like Art.

One afternoon soon after my argument with Shorey, I attended my first class in surveying. We met indoors to get our instructions. I sat on a separate bench a little way off from the men, and none of them looked at me. The instructor, too, avoided my eye in a sulky manner. He explained, with chalk on a blackboard, the simple rules for running a line with a hand level. Then he announced, "We will now go to the instrument room and take out our equipment. You people choose your partners for the term—surveyors always work in pairs. Go ahead and divide yourselves up."

He leaned back in his chair behind the desk. There were fourteen men in the class, and in two minutes there were seven couples. While the other students got up and scrambled to make their arrangements, I just sat still, wondering where I went from there.

"Well," said the instructor, "let's go and get our instruments."

We straggled after him and waited as he unlocked the storeroom. The levels we were to use, the type called "dumpy" levels, are heavy, metallic objects on tripods. Seven men stepped up and took one apiece, and then, as the instructor hesitated, I walked over defiantly and picked up an eighth. The instructor rubbed his chin and looked at me furtively. I looked at my feet.

"Damn, I was sure we had an even number in the class," he said. "I guess Bemis has dropped out."

Fourteen men and I stood there tongue-tied, impatient to bring all this to an end. Then I noticed a tall, lanky boy, who had not been in the lecture room, leaning against the door looking on, a good-natured sneer on his freckled face. He now gathered his bones together and shambled over.

60

"Aw," he said gruffly, "I'll take her. What the hell!"

"Oh, there you are, Bemis. O.K.," said the instructor, loud in his relief.

Bemis picked up my level and tripod and, with his free hand, waved me toward the long rod which one man of a surveying pair always carries. "Come along," he said. "I know these things. I've already run a few, working in the summer." He turned and started to walk out, and after a second, during which I stared at him registering eternal devotion, I scampered after him. Behind me there was a loud general exhalation of relief and wonder.

Reginald Bemis—for Reginald was his name—found out all too soon that his responsibility was not temporary. Whatever whimsical impulse of kindliness had pushed him into his offer vanished when he realized that he was stuck with me for the term, but once he learned this bitter fact, he decided at least to bring me up the way I should go. He had worked in open-pit mines before coming to the university, and it was typical of his scornful attitude, that of a veteran miner, that he hadn't deigned to come to the explanatory lecture. He was one of those gangling, undernourished boys who work their way through college; he waited on table at a hash house when he wasn't in class, and got good marks and had a future. As a surveyor, he knew his business as well as our instructor did. By the time we graduated from the dumpy level to the transit, Reginald and I had the best record of any pair of engineers for our reports and drawings. None of this excellence, obviously, was due to my talents.

Not that I didn't do my share of the heavy work. I did. We took turns carrying the cumbersome instruments. Sometimes our trail led us to a very public spot, and when passersby suddenly noticed that I was a female—that took a moment or two, for I wore khaki coveralls most of the time—Reginald became very touchy. The minute a stranger paused to take another look at me holding up the rod or squinting laboriously into the transit, Reginald would make such ferocious noises and wiggle his fingers at his nose so insultingly that the passersby would soon move on. His attitude was brutal but right, and I tried to show him that I appreciated it.

One evening, near the end of the surveying course, as we plodded along through snowdrifts toward the instrument room to turn in our equipment, I said to Reginald, "Excuse me for saying so, but you've been awfully nice. I don't know what I would have done that day if you hadn't said you would take me along for a partner."

"You was all there was left," said Reginald gruffly.

"Yes, but you didn't have to go on with me after that day. It must have been very hard sometimes."

"You ain't kiddin'," said Reginald, with deep feeling. "You know what they was calling me all year? Her Choice—that was it. Once I hadda fight a guy."

"It's a shame," I said. "But anyway, I've learned how to survey."

"Oh, you ain't so dumb," he admitted. "Only trouble with you is, sometimes you don't think straight. It's like you was dreamin'. Like today, when we couldn't find that bench mark. You just stood there with your mouth open while I went around kicking snow up, trying to find it. Lazy, that's your trouble."

"I'll try to do better," I said.

"Anyway," remarked Reginald cheerfully as we entered the door, "the worst is over. I got only one more week with you."

"You've been *awfully* nice," I repeated.

I knew one of the geology professors socially, as it happened, and though I never crossed his orbit in an official way, I did drop in on him once in a while to unburden my soul. He gave me a piece of advice early in the game. "These boys are just afraid you'll interfere with their daily routine," he said. "As soon as they realize you don't, it will be all right. They've got some idea, for instance, that they'll have to be careful of their talk when you're around."

"You mean," I asked, brightening, "that there are words I don't know?"

The professor ignored this and said warningly, "Don't pay

any attention, no matter what they say. Don't expect special privileges just because you're a woman. Try to let them forget you're a woman. Pretty soon everything will be all right."

As a result, I trained myself to keep very quiet and to maintain a poker face wherever I was in the college. The mining-engineering course was a stiff one, and we were all too busy to indulge in any feud, anyway. Now and then, however, some complication cropped up. I was excused permanently from one lab course because there was no ladies' room in that building. I was also formally excused from the gymnasium classes the other coeds had to take, on the ground that I got enough exercise just learning to be an engineer. The khaki coverall garment I wore for surveying and ore dressing had to do for more orthodox classes as well, and I could see that my French teacher didn't like it, but she never complained.

It was at this time that I acquired the name Mickey as a permanent label. It was a nursery nickname of mine which had been more or less forgotten by everyone but Mother. The engineers heard it and adopted it as a more acceptable, masculine-sounding name than my real one, which was hopelessly ladylike. Of course, there were brief flareups and resentments now and again. Some of the boys were unfair, I felt. At the beginning of a math course, one of them yelled at me, "You'll never be able to get through this! You're a girl!" Yet at the end of term, when he asked me what grade I had and I replied exultingly that I was in the first five on the list, he said, "Huh, that's just because you're a girl you got that mark." It was irritating, but after all I *had* stuck my neck out. I continued to keep mousy quiet, and our mechanics instructor finally said to a friend, "You know, I've been dreading the day that girl would have to come to my lectures. But now that she's here, she's—why," he said in astonishment, "she's quite a lady."

As I look back on it now, I am amazed that I passed any of those examinations. Half the time and energy I should have given to my work was used up in the effort to prove that I could hold my own without being in the way. I was painfully self-conscious. My professor friend's words had sunk in so deep that

I couldn't get them out of my head or my behavior. I took it as an insult when some absent-minded engineering student so far forgot himself as to hold open a door for me or stood up and offered me a chair. In time, though, most of these little frictions wore away. The one serious problem was the matter of field trips.

Field trips are study journeys into the country. Students, both of mining engineering and geology, go out with instructors and wander about looking at rock formations, geographical features, mines, or whatever they are interested in at the time. Of course, I went out on the small trips that were over in one day, but from the longer trips, including one expedition to mines in the West, which took up a whole summer and taught the boys how to work in the tunnels, I was barred. It was simply impossible to surmount that obstacle. The Wisconsin state legislature couldn't help me this time, because the State of Montana would have kept me out of its mines. How, then, was I to qualify for my degree?

I figured something out at last as a substitute for the mining experience. I went up that summer and stayed with relatives who had a farm in Michigan. Every morning I went out with a hand level and a Brunton compass and ran lines back and forth at half-mile intervals, straight across the township, until I had made a respectable contour map of the region to take back to the college. The authorities studied the map, smoked a few pipes over it, and unanimously voted to give it the status of the summer's field work the boys had put in. Perhaps this really definite triumph went to my head a little. Perhaps the summer of walking alone under the Michigan sun had sweated out of me my hard-won humility. Anyway, that autumn, the beginning of my final years, I was in a mood to fight my great, all-out battle with the Geology Club.

Again, it wasn't my fault. I didn't start it; the men did. They should have known that the sign they put up on the bulletin board in Science Hall would be enough to knock me off balance. A stranger would not have understood. All the sign said, in formal lettering, was that the Geology Club was holding an extra-special meeting that night for two purposes—first, to introduce the semi-yearly crop of newcomers to the group, and, second, to hear the highly respected visitor, Professor Such-and-So, world-renowned expert on volcanoes or coral reefs or something, deliver the first of his series of lectures. But someone had added a significant line in red pencil: "Women not invited."

I recognized this as an insult aimed directly at me. No other woman would have been crazy enough to want to go to a Geology Club meeting. The sign was the worse for being unnecessary. I knew perfectly well I wasn't invited; I had not been invited, repeatedly, for three years. They had thrashed the matter out many times. I always pretended not to know, but it was an old grievance, because all members of the mining-engineering courses had heretofore automatically been invited to become members of the Geology Club. Once I showed up, though, the Geology Club members maintained that they were not a formal institution of the college but a social organization, and, as such, didn't have to abide by the cruel law of coeducation, which forced open their lecture halls to the female sex. True, I did belong to the Mining Engineers' Club—we held our meetings in the ore-dressing laboratory and cooked hamburgers in the blast furnace—but that club, said the geologists, was different, somehow—more entangled in the web of the educational setup. The geologists claimed that their taking mining engineers into their club was a voluntary courtesy, and they said that they preferred not to extend it to me. Inviting me would, they said darkly, establish a precedent.

For three years I had silently accepted this argument, because I was, thank God, a lady, and besides there didn't seem to be any way around it. This red-pencilled message, though, affected me strongly. I was as angry as I had been that long-ago day in the dean's office, back in those prehistoric times when, for some reason, I wasn't yet studying engineering.

It wasn't fair. I hadn't been bothering their old Geology Club. Yet there the men were, jeering and making faces at me in this bulletin-board announcement. Rub it in, would they? I'd show them!

My eyes narrowed as I read the sign through for the fourth

time. Somebody had slipped up. Professor Such-and-So had been invited by the college faculty to give that series of lectures, and, as one of the college students, I was, of course, entitled to hear the entire series. Entitled? Why, I was probably *required* to hear them. Not that I had ever felt any particular emotional yearning for information about volcanoes or coral reefs or whatever it was. That was not the point. The point was a matter of principle. The point was that the Geology Club, in thus selfishly arrogating one of the visiting professors' lectures to their own session, sacrificed their standing as an amateur social organization. They had made themselves, at least for the time being, one of the college classes, and that class I was entitled by law to attend. I was a perfect lady, all right, but just the same I decided to visit the Geology Club that night.

The most painfully uncertain people are the ones who seem poised and self-assured. I walked into the club meeting as bold as brass, but the slightest push would have upset me, and my old pal, the friendly professor, quite unwittingly almost administered it. As I made my way past the rows of dismayed, silent, flummoxed men, he shouted in a whisper, "Bravo!" It took a gigantic effort to finish the walk, to sit down demurely in an empty chair, to pretend that nothing at all extraordinary was happening. This was my first overt rebellion. Just when I had almost captured the good will of the college, too, and was so near to graduation and release. Just when they were about to confer on me the ultimate honor, the priceless boon of indifference.

The visiting lecturer saved my face, though he couldn't have known that, by climbing to the platform and breaking the tension. The ensuing hour must have gratified him, for the whole roomful of young people sat in a dead hush while he told us about volcanoes—or was it coral? If some of the graduate students hadn't been polite enough to ask a few perfunctory questions at the close of his talk, he would have noticed a strain in the atmosphere, but the amenities were properly observed, and

66

after a vote of thanks he said good night and left us alone to wash our dirty linen.

The club president, a kindly soul named Clyde, took the floor and went through a few formalities—minutes of the last meeting and a brief résumé of the club's aims, for the benefit of the new members. Then he said, "It's our custom, just to make things less formal, to ask the men who are new to the club to introduce themselves. I'll call on them in order of seating. Mr. Blake?"

"Class of twenty-eight," mumbled a scarlet Mr. Blake. "No other clubs. Transferred this year from Michigan College of Mines. Majoring in petrology."

Everyone grew quieter and quieter as the introductions proceeded. I wasn't just quiet; I was rigid. Were they going to pretend that I wasn't there? If Clyde skipped me, I would have to make a demonstration of some sort. I would *have* to. I held my breath until I nearly strangled. Clyde's eyes fell on me and he cleared his throat.

"Since our friend Miss Hahn has taken the bull by the horns," he said, "I will call on her to introduce herself to our new friends."

Everybody let out his breath a little; the crisis was postponed. I stumbled to my feet and duly made my recital. The meeting proceeded without interruption. Clyde finished up the official business of the meeting by announcing that it was the evening for collection of dues. If the members would kindly pay their dues—a dollar a head—to the treasurer, he said, we would be able to proceed with refreshments—the customary coffee and vanilla wafers.

We stood in line, with our dollars in our hands, and that was when the trouble started. When I reached the collection table, the treasurer shook his head. "Can't take it," he said.

"Why not?"

"Well, uh . . . ." The unhappy boy swallowed hard, and then in desperation raised his voice. "Clyde! Come over here, will you?"

67

It had all been arranged in advance, evidently. Clyde came over and took my arm with a sort of reluctant affection, and said, "Come on out in the hall, Mickey. I want to talk to you."

I pushed his hand away. "Talk to me here," I said.

"Come on, Mickey. Do me this favor, won't you?"

We marched out between serried ranks of embarrassed young geologists.

"It's this way," said Clyde miserably. "A bunch of us tried to—I mean, this thing came up again, the way it always does, last week, and though I personally, and some of your other friends, tried to persuade the fellows, the thing is—"

"All right," I said abruptly. "Here's my dollar, anyway. Take it for wear and tear on the bench. Nobody wants to—" To my horror, it suddenly became urgently necessary to be alone. My unhappy nature had played me false. Whenever I am keyed up to violent anger, tears begin to flow. I ran down the hall, completely routed. This was disaster. I had committed the one unforgivable sin: I had been feminine. I wanted to kick myself for shame. I wanted to die.

What happened after that is public knowledge. Clyde walked slowly back into the clubroom and shook his head in misery when the boys asked him what had happened. "Was she awfully sore?" they asked. "Did she make a scene? Did she say—"

"Oh, gosh," said the president, "don't talk about it. She—she cried."

"Cried?" Appalled, they stared at each other. Cried! They lowered their eyes, unable to meet each other's gaze.

Somebody proposed a vote. There and then they voted.

A half hour later I was sitting in the study room at Science Hall, huddled in my chair, despair clutched round me like a blanket. There Clyde found me and brought the news. Practically unanimously, I had been elected a member of the Geology Club. One lone man who still stood out against me, admitting that his attitude spoiled the record, was yet unable to give up his convictions, and so he had left the room while the vote was taken. Public opinion had demanded that he do this.

"And in conclusion," Clyde said to me, "permit me to say that I'm sure all the fellows are *awfully* sorry it all happened."

Though stunned, I managed to say a few gracious words of acceptance, so that Clyde would leave me the sooner. I needed solitude; I had a lot of reorienting to do. I sat a long time at my desk, looking backward at a three-year program of mistaken strategy. It was the friendly professor, I realized, who had started me off on the wrong foot. Well, it was all right now. I knew better now. Just in time, too.

I blew my nose and started to search my briefcase, diving far down, trying to find a long-forgotten pocket mirror.

THE SURROUNDING HILLS

I must have been a pest as an undergraduate, restless and complaining most of the time, but there were fewer coeds than men students at the University of Wisconsin, so I had dates anyway. One of them used to scold me about my restlessness. He would say, "Why do you talk all the time about getting away? Isn't Madison good enough for you?"

"Madison's all right, I guess, but no one place is good enough," I would answer. "I want to get around. I want to see things."

"You've already been around more than most other girls," he

would say, and though the remark always irritated me, the fact was incontrovertible.

For that year, 1924, and considering my Middle West origin and surroundings, I was an experienced traveller. I had spent my childhood in St. Louis, and I had been to Chicago, where my family lived now, and to Michigan as well as to Wisconsin. On one occasion, I had penetrated Indiana for a winter-sports festival. And yet, for all this rich background, I was unsatisfied. "If other girls are happy with the Mississippi Valley, that's their affair," I once told my critical friend. "I want to go farther afield. Even you hiked all the way to California last year."

It was a foregone conclusion that he would retort that it was different for a man, yet when he did say it I was ruffled, and remained so until I got home and told Jane, my sympathetic roommate, about it. She agreed that men were the absolute limit. Then we took another of our innumerable soothing looks at the atlas, and talked once again about our projected tour of the district of Lake Kivu, in the Belgian Congo.

As I look back, I see more clearly than I did then. I see, for example, that Jane's energy might perfectly well have been directed elsewhere than toward travel if I hadn't swept her into my own designs. In the end, it didn't make any difference to her. People do what they are inclined to do, no matter where they are, but for a while I did affect her, though I didn't realize it at the time. Indeed, I would have been amazed at the idea, for she was a strong character; I considered her the leading spirit of our partnership, and was quite content. She was the type of girl I had always admired—enterprising and athletic. I have never been athletic. Her exotic background fascinated me; she had come all the way from that unknown land Ohio. Her father, a man of liberal ideas, had heard that Wisconsin was politically enlightened—it was well known that the university authorities had rejected Rockefeller's tainted money when it was offered to them—and had made up his mind to entrust his only child to the Dairy State. As if all this were not romantic enough, Jane had actually been to New York. I used to beg her to describe the fabulous city, but she wasn't much of a hand at that sort of thing; she was better at action than at words. She could drive, she skated well, and she had several medals for swimming and diving. When I had first spoken of my ambition to see the world, she had quickly joined the project. It had been my idea that our first practical step should be getting degrees as geologists—this, of course, before I took a really giant step, and possibly not such a practical one, into the College of Engineering. "If we were geologists, we could go just about anywhere," I explained. "Some geology graduates have gone to South America, and I've heard of Americans prospecting in Russia and the Near East, and anywhere you can name. So we'd better major in geology."

"Why not?" said Jane, in her amiable way, and we signed up.

I was not always the one with the ideas, however. It was Jane who thought of Lake Kivu, during a lecture on geography. Afterward, she pointed it out to me on the map, saying, "If we could get ourselves sent here, it would be marvellous. Just look—all that water. We could swim every day."

The lake did look inviting, even on something as impersonal as a map, but I was cautious and practical, and spoke of crocodiles.

"That's exactly why I chose Kivu instead of some other lake," Jane said. "Look at the text. It says the water's too cold there, by three degrees, for crocodiles. What's more, Kivu has a white man's climate, and possibly the surrounding hills contain deposits of gold and silver. What more do you want?"

"Nothing," I admitted. "It sounds perfect. We'll go to Kivu."

It had been a relief, all along, to have that much settled and out of the way. On the other hand, though we knew exactly where we were going, the years of training stretched out wearily ahead of us. All around us, in the spring of 1924, we saw lucky young men planning the summer adventures open to their sex. Some boys had jobs as chauffeurs, some were going to work their way to Europe on cattle boats, and a few declared their intention of hitchhiking across the country. It was exasperating. I made suggestions. "No, we certainly can't ride the rails, or hitchhike, either," Jane said impatiently. "Be your age. What would your father and mother do if you tried that? I tell you what we *might* do, though. If we had a car, we could drive out to my uncle in Albuquerque. That's in New Mexico."

I had not thought of anything like that, though the motorcar was already an important part of life in America. A few students owned cars of one kind or another, Stutz Bearcats being the most admired, but they were considered short-haul vehicles for the most part. Roads generally were unpaved and risky, motels had not yet been invented, and most people who made long trips overland went by train. So I realized that Jane had suggested an adventure of respectable proportions. The West! It was not the Belgian Congo, but I had entertained romantic thoughts of it ever since my father had brought me, as a souvenir of Colorado Springs, a paperweight that contained under glass a little mineral collection (iron pyrites, or fool's gold; native copper; calcite). Besides, there might be the sea, for Jane went on to propose that we continue west, after visiting her uncle, to the coast of California. The Pacific would not be too much of a revelation to her; she had looked on the Atlantic. But for landlocked me it was the biggest attraction of all.

The Model T Ford that we decided on was not considered expensive by sophisticates, but I believe Jane's parents bore the brunt of its cost, pointing out to my parents by letter that she was their only child, whereas I was one of six. For the rest of what the trip was to cost, I had some money put away, and my father and mother, figuring that I wasn't going to be an expense otherwise that summer, gave me some more. The Model T arrived, splendidly black and shiny, sitting high on spindly wheels, and we rode in it all around Madison and the gentle, glaciated hills of the countryside, past grazing cows and farmhouses, while Jane taught me to drive. Driving a Model T was simple. You pushed a pedal halfway in to disengage the clutch, and used the same pedal hard for braking.

Later, we took the car to a garage for a major operation designed to let us dispense with most of the cumbersome camping gear used by other tourists. We had the back support of the front seat hinged, with a hook at each side to keep it upright while we drove. At night, we could fill the well between the front and back seats with luggage, lower the hinged back on top of it, and make up a bed. If we kept our feet still, so as not to kick the steering wheel or the other controls, the car was long enough. Privacy was to be afforded by the car's rain curtains, of cloth and isinglass, and we bought a mosquito net that fitted nicely over the entire equipage.

Spring brought, as usual in Madison, the promise of happy days by the lake and moonlit evenings in canoes, but I was deaf to the promise. I didn't smell the flowers and the new-mown grass. Already, in my mind, I was out of Madison, driving toward the sunset. I can't remember whether or not I went to the prom. If I had any dates at all, they didn't make much impression, and, naturally, I paid even less attention to Jane's social activities. As a consequence, I was surprised by what took place on the morning we set out. We were moving everything out of our room and into the car. Belongings we didn't need to take were to be left in Chicago, at my house, so to begin with we would be overloaded, and the packing was a big job. I welcomed the help, therefore, of two of our friends—Terry, who was Jane's property, and an occasional date of mine called Will. The four of us worked for a while, and then it dawned on me that Terry was very much all over the place, bustling and anxious. Will's help was not nearly as intensive. There was something so proprietary in Terry's behavior that I wondered why Jane didn't slap him down, but she didn't. Even when he criticized our arrangement of the loading, she accepted it in astonishingly meek fashion. When he said, "That big bag is better in the middle," and moved it accordingly, she merely thanked him. The next thing I knew, the two of them had their heads together over our driving map and Terry was laying down the law. We must never tackle questionable roads except in broad daylight, he said firmly, and Jane nodded, as if in gratitude.

I said, "Come on, Jane. We've got to go."

Will whispered fiercely, "Leave them alone, can't you?"

So! I bit back my next words and waited. Terry was telling

Jane, evidently not for the first time, that he would certainly write to her at St. Louis to start with, and then he would get a letter to her in a town at what he estimated would be two days' drive west of there. He had a list, it seemed, of post offices all the way along the road, and Jane brought out a companion list of her own to show him.

Now, however, even Jane realized that it was time to leave. She and Terry kissed each other, and Will immediately, in loyal imitation, kissed me. I accepted the gesture, though we both knew it was hogwash. With Jane at the wheel, we left the boys and, waving, drove down the street. It was as well that I wasn't driving. Dark thoughts, fears for the future, distracted my attention from the solemn moment. I reflected that I might have to revise my hopes of Jane as a companion for later tours. She did not seem to be made of stern enough stuff ever to get to Lake Kivu. Then I cheered up. After all, any girl had a right to correspond with people, and we would be gone for weeks.

Jane and I had agreed that the next few days were bound to be a trial, because of relatives, and they were. Not only was my family in Chicago, but Jane's parents were there as well. They had come on from Ohio to see us off. We listened to a lot of reiterated counsel as we laid in stores and repacked—about taking care of ourselves, sending frequent telegrams to assure our families of our safety, and never giving lifts to strangers. I hope we were patient and polite, but I can't swear to it.

Even when Chicago was behind us and a new road lay ahead, we knew we hadn't truly embarked. I had another large clutch of relatives to see in St. Louis. As that city was only a two days' journey away, we didn't try out our sleeping arrangements on the way, in tame old Illinois. We slept in a cheap hotel. But in St. Louis we did use the car bed, parked in an aunt's side yard. Cousins and other connections lined up to peer at us lying inside the mosquito net and to thank God *they* didn't have to do it. And the next morning, when we got up at sunrise, I was almost sick with joy and excitement, tiptoeing with Jane into the house to cook breakfast. It would be the last time for weeks that we would be boiling coffee and frying eggs in a civilized kitchen. From then on, the whole way west, it was to be virtuous, healthy discomfort—at least until we landed in Jane's uncle's kitchen in Albuquerque.

As the Ford left St. Louis behind, we both laughed very hard for no reason and remarked what a wonderful day it was. Raining, but wonderful. "Oh, boy!" we said, several times. I was driving. The impression I still have of the countryside I saw that morning must be exaggerated. I have never gone back to look at the region around that highway leading west, and it would be different now anyway, but even then it couldn't have been as beautiful as I thought. Nevertheless, I still think with love of rich, wet color—the green of summer trees and the dark, glistening red clay of the road winding between them, distant blue hills across valleys that were as simply verdant as if a child's crayon had drawn them. There were cracks of lightning in the lowering sky, too far off to be frightening. Obviously, I have forgotten all about the long dull stretches, and though the little towns must have been just like those of Wisconsin and Illinois, my mind has retained no memory of boredom or disappointment. All was new and new-washed.

Occasionally the rain stopped and we had sunlight, but the road remained slippery, and occasionally we skidded. "We aren't making very good time," Jane said, but her tone was light-hearted, and she suddenly thumped my knee with her fist, saying, "We've done it! Do you realize that? We're on our way!"

I agreed. "On our way, on our own, on the road. From now on, nobody knows us and we don't know anybody."

"You said it. I get so tired of being someone's daughter or somebody else's niece, don't you? Wait, you're skidding. Slow down. Slowly, now. Not too sudden. Woo!"

I braked as cautiously as possible. The road had taken us around the corner of a hill and almost into a big mudhole, but I managed to steer the car onto a sketchily indicated track that led around the worst of it. Someone else had not been so lucky; another car stood in the middle of the muck, sunk to its hubcaps. Sloshing in the water nearby, looking forlorn, was the driver, carrying his shoes in one hand.

Jane called, "Do you want a tow?" and the man looked at us hopefully and started to reply. Then something happened; he swallowed the words and stared at us. "Well, hello there," he said at last. "I know you, don't I?"

This sounded like an old gambit, and Jane ignored it, repeating testily, "Do you want a tow?"

"Not you," the man said to her. "You at the wheel. Aren't you one of the Hahn girls?"

"Oh, God, yes," I said in disgust. "Who are you?"

"Don't you remember? I was engaged to your sister Dot last summer," said the man in the mudhole.

For quite a while after we had carried word of the plight of my sister's ex-fiancé to the nearest garage, Jane and I didn't have much to say to each other. Little or nothing was said about getting away from people. But by evening our faith was largely restored, and driving through Missouri was once more like being the first travellers on the moon.

The sun began to set. It was time to look for a tourist camp, and soon we saw, at the outskirts of a town, an arrow, crudely lettered on a bit of old plank, pointing to one. At that time, people still behaved as if motoring was a passing fad; some were willing to set up services for it in hit-or-miss fashion, but they weren't sticking out their necks. The tourist camp was a field, surrounded by a low fence, with one other car already in occupation. We paused at the gate, locked by a huge padlock, and honked until a boy in a wide-brimmed straw hat came out of a nearby house, collected a quarter from us, and let us drive in. With a bored wave, he indicated a pair of outhouse sheds, and told us that water could be got out of the pump back of the house, if we had a bucket.

Of course we had a bucket, we told him haughtily; we had everything. Actually, however, we were not so sure when we saw the litter of things unpacked from the other car. A large family and a dog were busy with all the gear. Suitcases, crates, and odd bits of furniture had been unloaded, and now the family was making camp. "They must have left their house empty," Jane said. Already a tepee had been set up, and now the father and some children were stretching more canvas over a frame attached to the car, like a small porte-cochere, while the wife cooked something over a rusty portable stove.

Greetings were exchanged. "How are the roads your way?" asked Jane, first crack out of the box. This opening, obligatory in any conversation between tourists, had been unknown to me until that moment, and my admiration for Jane increased. How much she knew of the world! The inevitable question soon followed from our neighbors ("You girls alone?"), along with comments on how worried our parents must be. Soon we were deep in chat—that time-consuming, easygoing, meaningless talk with which Americans both fill any void and hold each other off. Our neighbors had not, after all, emptied their house to fill their car, because they had no house. They were migrant workers, who followed the harvest, zigzagging across country to catch the ripening crops, slowly making their way north and south by way of east and west.

All the while we talked, we were working, each at his own camp. Jane and I wanted to make up our bed before dark and afterward stroll into town for supper, but we were delayed by the other party's friendly wonder at our arrangements. It was like having relatives around us all over again. Still, we got fed and we went to bed remarkably early, for after dark there was nothing else to do.

All along, it was that way. We would go to sleep with the sun and, as a result, we got up with the sun as well. The first two hours of driving took us through a deserted landscape where everyone else, including restaurant workers, still lay in bed. Though snappish with hunger, we never quarrelled. Jane was stubbornly good-tempered even when I drove badly, as I often did. In fact, I can't remember anything about that trip that wasn't good, except for the times we picked up our mail.

I was always reluctant to go to the post office, but the more I hung back—suggesting that we fill up first with gas, perhaps, or eat our lunch—the more eagerly Jane insisted on getting her letters immediately, as soon as we entered a town. It wasn't only because of Terry that I hesitated. Letters in general were an intrusion, I felt, on this otherwise wonderful existence, reminding me that I had not always been free, that I would someday have to go back to my past. All letters were like elastic bonds, pulling us back to reality, but of course Terry's were the worst. Terry's threatened everything in the future.

I must be wrong to recall the tour as long. Even in 1924 it was not a matter of months to drive to Albuquerque from St. Louis. Nevertheless, that is the impression I have kept. I seem to remember night after night in tourist camps, and one night especially when we tried to do without a camp, because it was late and we couldn't find one. We pulled up at the side of the road near a small town and went to sleep, but we were soon aroused by the sheriff. He insisted that we follow him into the town and make our simple arrangements once more outside his house, where we would be safe. He said he couldn't imagine what our parents were thinking of anyway, letting us gallivant around alone at our age. We resented him deeply—especially when, in the early morning, we found the town's entire population thronged around the Model T, gawking at us. Still, I could not be wholly displeased, for the sheriff wore blue jeans and a Stetson, and it was borne in on me that we were really approaching the West, where my paperweight had come from—the West, with its mountains and its cowboys.

Jane was not as excited by the prospect as I was. She had seen mountains in the East, and she knew enough about the difficulties of driving cars along hilly roads to be somewhat apprehensive. Hitherto, the Model T had behaved beautifully, she admitted, but we would shortly have to cross a high range between Colorado and New Mexico, where the air would be thinner than the car was accustomed to breathing. The engine would get overheated. We must change the mixture, look to our brakes, and have a general overhaul before we tried the pass. All this was duly carried out in a town in the foothills, where Jane and a garage mechanic went into serious conference while I stared, rapt and foolish and useless, at the heaped-up landscape ahead. Eventually, Jane broke into my trance and sent me shopping for canvas buckets. "Extra water to take along," she explained.

That evening, we ate in a diner with the garage worker, who had by this time become a close friend. He was a youth of thoughtful mien, with a habit of going off into fits of abstraction. After an especially protracted one, he apologized. "I can't get this car off my mind," he said. "Not yours, but one a fellow brought in last night. I can't quite figure what's the trouble. Been working at it on and off ever since it came in. I've checked everything, but—" He broke off and shook his head in a worried way, adding, after a moment, that it might be something about the carburetor. He was like a physician fretting over a difficult diagnosis, especially when he announced his intention of staying up all night with the patient. After eating, we went to the movies, but in the middle of the Colleen Moore feature he said, "I've just figured out about that car. You girls excuse me, will you? I want to go back and try something on her. Meet you at the drugstore after the show, O.K.?" Then he hurried out—a happy man, who has stayed in my mind all these years as the true Spirit of the U.S.A.

Once he was gone, I began worrying belatedly about the next day's ordeal. I recalled various anecdotes told by camp acquaintances about the terrors of the pass, and Jane was no comfort. She said, "You'll have to be careful, you know, with the brakes. You still step down on them awfully hard, and you don't get two chances on a mountain road. I'd better do all the worst bits, I think."

"That's a good idea," I said sincerely, but before I got to sleep that night I had unpleasant visions of driving around bends and down impossibly steep slopes without time to relinquish control to Jane. In fantasy, I saw the Model T toppling forward head over wheels, then rolling sidewise off the road into a kind of Grand Canyon.

It hardly needs saying that after all the fuss we negotiated the actual pass without incident. The radiator tended to boil going uphill, but that did not constitute a crisis. We pulled up and waited until the bubbling subsided, refreshed the radiator with cool water, and proceeded until the next warning gurgle. Even today, when I smell the odor of rust in steam, I feel elated, as if I have just surmounted some tremendous obstacle.

The change of landscape that greeted us as we moved into New Mexico was magically sudden. It was like straying off one colored postcard and onto another. Here, with no gentle transition, was the true West, with mountain ranges trailing their long blue-and-purple skirts, right-angled mesas standing sharply against the great sky, and under our wheels arid, yellow ground that bristled here and there with grudging grayish shrubs. Tumbleweed moved with us, the tangled combings of a giant caught in the wind. I felt lightheaded, and no doubt was, for Albuquerque, which we were approaching, is five thousand feet high. Jane, too, seemed to be affected. Again she pounded my knee, laughing with triumph as we swooped around a hairpin turn, saying, "Well, we did it!" After a pause, she added, "I bet we'll have stacks of mail waiting," but for once I didn't let this worry me. Any mail waiting for us now had come such a long way that it was bound to have cooled off.

I didn't mind fixing breakfast in a New Mexico kitchen; it was different. Everything in New Mexico was different. Elation went with me every day, all day long, no matter what was going on—meeting friends of Jane's uncle and aunt, parties at the country club, a sightseeing trip to Santa Fe. Everything was brushed with the clear, sparkling gold of altitude; nothing was dull. So I was not surprised when Jane announced that she wanted to live in New Mexico. "After we've been to Lake Kivu, of course," she added. I was not surprised, but I was gratified to think she had at last forgotten Terry.

We had said we were going on to California, so we did. I was still keen to go, but I suspected that Jane now looked on it in the light of a chore. But before long the road lulled us into the old mood, and something of the former urgency came back. We even managed to work ourselves into another lather, this time at the prospect of getting the Model T across the desert. We were careful to fill the water buckets, and we drove most of the hottest part by night.

California itself seemed at first an anticlimax, with nothing along the road but one dull orange grove after another. We had given our hearts to a country without so much green stuff in it, and nothing pleased us until the last, when we reached the coast. I don't remember where we came out of the hills, but I know it was just before noon, and a fine bright morning. We'd gone past a few houses, some foothills, and a curve in the road, and there lay the sea below us, just the blue-green I had imagined, with white-edged breakers roaring along the beach and all eternity beyond. For a long time we looked, until Jane stirred impatiently and I said, "Well, there it is. We'll have to cross a lot of water like that before we reach Lake Kivu."

She nodded. "Might as well start back to Albuquerque now. We've seen the Pacific," she said, and turned the car around. So much for California.

My parents complained that I was never the same after that summer in the Model T, and no doubt they were right. I was restless and discontented at home, and, as they said, anything served as an excuse to get away somewhere, even if it was only a weekend in Libertyville or Milwaukee. But now that I think it over, I don't think it was fair to blame the Model T. It wasn't the car that did it. Look at Jane. Her life wasn't affected by the trip in any serious way, though no doubt it altered a few details for her. After we finished college, we did go back West, but this time Jane got married. Admittedly, she married an Albuquerque man instead of Terry, but what's the difference, really? If that's the way you're going to be, that's it. Why, by the time I actually got there—to Lake Kivu—Jane had had two children.

The other day, when I was in Albuquerque, I saw her again. After all those years, she hadn't changed much, because, as I say, people don't. We talked for hours—about her late husband, our children, and, of course, the Model T. Jane said, "I've often

82

wondered why on earth our parents let us do it. They must have been nuts. I'd never let *my* daughter go off like that, would you?"

Before I answered, I took a deep breath of the cold, high air. "Yes," I said.

THE INNER
WORKINGS OF THE ATOM

I thought that the letter that came to me in the spring of 1926, offering me a job in a St. Louis mining company, was the most exciting, delightful thing that had ever happened. I saw nothing incongruous in the offer and nothing unaesthetic in the idea of a girl's working with lead and zinc. I had hardly dared hope to get a job. My professors and classmates, trying to get rid of me, had warned me that I was insane to go after a degree; they said I would never in the world get a chance to work. Though they didn't quite succeed in getting me out, they did scare me silly. Yet here was this incredible letter, a full week before graduation, when few of my male classmates were getting offers. In 1926, things were not so hot for mining engineers. There had been a lot of gloomy discussions of the unpromising future. It was agreed that nobody ever paid an engineer a decent wage, that the boys who made good were those on the business end of mining, and that nobody with his eye on money ought to go in for science at all. "Just look at the facts," I remember a boy named Shorty saying as he puffed at his pipe. (Nearly all the mining engineers, except me, smoked pipes.) "Look at what they pay a top-rank surveyor in the Panhandle. Two hundred a month! That's the best he'll ever do. Just the same, I wouldn't want a job on the business side."

The rest of us echoed the sentiment. I, for one, meant it fiercely. On the subject of science, I was very touchy. It was my religion, and since I had realized it late, I took it hard. I had always hung around museums gawking at the dinosaurs and the mineral specimens, and I'd had infant dreams of living in the wildwood, friend to the shy fox and the possum. But the true call didn't come until I learned, in college, in a lecture on crystallography, about the inner workings of the atom. Those were the days before we had discovered too much about the atom, and I was able to grasp the current theory. The thought of atomic particles revolving in orbits, of atoms composing molecules, of molecules arranged in latticelike patterns within crystals and the crystal forms depending on these molecules' dictation, excited me much as philosophical conclusions excited other students. It was like an explosion. Suddenly I understood that crystallography was logical, and from this fact concluded that nature itself was logical. I had never before trusted in the independent existence of logic. I knew one could reason out the solution of a mathematical problem, but I had always suspected that mathematical problems and their solutions were inventions of mankind—a made-up game. The atom was independent of man, and *still* it obeyed the rules of logic. Besides, it reproduced the makeup of a solar system. Each atom was like a solar system, with each molecule's nature depending on its atom, and we ourselves were made up of molecules. The possibilities were endless, and I wondered why people wasted so much time on the dogmas of formal religion when this was such a satisfying truth. I thought of my atheist father and his hobby of tracing inconsistencies in the Bible. It seemed childish to bother about that sort of thing with science waiting in the offing—science, which settled everything.

On my next visit home, to Chicago, I tried to explain all this to him. He was reading Mencken. "Look at calcite, Daddy," I said. "It's a mineral—calcium carbonate—and it shows what I mean about the universal design. The calcite crystal is rhomboidal, and the molecular planes . . ." I drew it for him. "Think of the crystal as a stack of cards. Here's a cross-section, with the loose layers running horizontally. Now, look. If you bear down along the obtuse-angled side with a knife blade, the thing suddenly gives way and shifts position. It's still solid, but it's changed shape." Seeing his face, I judged he was skeptical, and I added urgently, "I've done it myself in the lab. Isn't it beautiful? It proves the whole thing, don't you see? The universe is summed up."

My father picked up his Mencken again. "I'm afraid that's too deep for me, Dolly, but it's nice to see you so interested in your studies," he said.

Obviously, my father was too old to see the light, but my life from then on was dedicated. Now getting the mining-company job seemed a happy augury. Looking back, I can't understand why I was so sure that working in a lead-and-zinc company would afford so much bliss. I must have envisaged the place as a super-laboratory where I would be able to work at research for the rest of my life. It was intoxicating to feel that I would go home this time with my status improved, and I must have strutted around quite a lot when I got there, between bouts of packing for St. Louis. As I recall, my parents didn't talk much about my opening career. I was their fifth child to go out into the world, and they had seen it all before.

Of course, the mining company was a horrid shock. There was no laboratory. Instead of a place at a table full of retorts and Bunsen burners, I was put at an ordinary green metal desk that stood in an ordinary office. Next to me, at a similar desk, sat Miss Lowry, the girl I had been hired to replace. Within call were stenographers and an office boy. Our boss, Mr. Dixon, reigned from an inner room. It looked like an insurance office, a real-estate office. What was I doing in such surroundings? Indignation mounted as I listened to Miss Lowry's explanations of the routine and fiddled with a lot of objects on the desk—pencils, memo pads, paper clips, stuff like that.

Miss Lowry was undeniably a nice girl, but I could hardly take her seriously—a geology graduate who intended to be married to an industrialist, leaving science flat. I simply could not comprehend her mental processes. Furthermore, it was plain that Miss Lowry liked the office, was fond of Mr. Dixon, and felt some regret at leaving them. For the sake of the firm, she kept a sharp if friendly eye on my aptitude, and when the time came to report to Mr. Dixon on it she gave me a recommendation. "Intelligent and eager to learn" was what Miss Lowry said. This, too, is a mystery to me, even today. I couldn't have been intelligent, and certainly I was not eager to learn, especially after I discovered that Mr. Dixon and the company had all but given up on lead and zinc and were now concentrating on oil.

Like most of my colleagues at Wisconsin, I had an intense prejudice against oil geology. It could have been fascinating, I now realize, if we had looked at it fairly, without snobbishness. The occurrence of oil, its origins, its association with certain rocks—yes, it could have captured the imagination. But oil had always bored me, and I knew it had a grasping way with geologists, tempting them from other paths because it was so important in business.

If Mr. Dixon knew I was harboring subversive sentiments—and I don't suppose I tried very hard to hide them—he didn't care as long as my work didn't suffer. He was a dramatic, dynamic type, who liked to keep things at high tension, and he handled his office staff with the technique of a football coach. We had periodic pep meetings at which he exhorted us all—stenographers, office boy, me, and whatever company geologists happened to be in town—to think constructively, be loyal, and remember that

87

we were in business to make money. Afterward, I always went back to my desk in a painful state of guilt, because, I told myself, I was serving false gods. This was high-flown language for what I was actually doing—organizing and filing correspondence, keeping maps of the company's holdings up to date, and plotting from the information that came in records of well drilling and production—but after a pep meeting with Mr. Dixon one did tend to think in high terms.

After a few weeks of this routine, even prospecting for oil seemed to me an enviable activity, and I was sorry I had ever called it ignoble. Our geologists would clump into the office straight from the field, in sweaty khaki shirts and breeches, to talk to Mr. Dixon about their journeys, compare notes, and file reports. I listened to them ardently, and talked, when I got the chance, of my own desire to get away from desk work. It seemed to me that I would be perfectly happy plodding mile after mile under the Southwest sun and pitching camp in the Dust Bowl. They laughed. So did Mr. Dixon, when I begged him to let me do it. Things were even worse after he hired a surveyor from my college. I had to sit glowering at my desk, watching him swagger off to the field. "Well, we told you and told you," he said. "Didn't we?"

The long, hot days of the St. Louis summer marched past. I caught the same streetcar every morning, went out at the same hour for my lunch, had the same date every Saturday night with a strictly non-geological man. I began reading novels. At the local museum, I went out of my way to avoid the natural-history displays. I was a scorned suitor. If science didn't want me, I didn't want it. But I kept a savings account, into which every week I put as much money as I could. Someday I would escape from this pool of oil and forest of paper clips and get back to the world in which I could think again the old, deep thoughts of calcite.

"By the way," said Mr. Dixon one morning, "I've hired another one of you girls—another geologist."

Annabel was her name. Here was another anomaly, like Miss

Lowry: she showed no dismay at all at the discovery that no-body intended to use her knowledge of fossils. On the contrary, her eyes brightened when she heard that she was to spend a lot of time filing. She said she loved filing, and forthwith flew at the correspondence in a manner that Mr. Dixon obviously admired. At least something about her evoked his admiration—possibly her appearance. Annabel was very pretty in a blond, blue-eyed way.

At lunch one day, she asked me, "Where do you live? Have you got an apartment?"

"No, a furnished room," I said.

"That must be awful," said Annabel. "A girl wants a place of her own. Let's get an apartment together, so we can cook for ourselves and be comfortable."

I shook my head, though not really with decision. I said, "Don't you hate housework? I'd rather use my time for things that interest me—things that when you've done them you have something to show for it."

"Like what?" asked Annabel, and this stumped me. I recol-lected that I was no longer a scientist but a mere breadwinner.

"It's much better to have an apartment," she went on. "I like cooking, so you wouldn't have to bother too much with that. You can do the cleaning and dishwashing. You'll like being in an apartment, once you get used to it. Any woman would."

"Oh, all right," I said.

So we found an apartment, and bought things from a second-hand furniture dealer, and set ourselves up. Annabel was really happy about it. She gloated over the furniture.

"You'd never guess it was second-hand," she said. "Don't you really begin to feel just a bit domestic now?"

To keep from being nagged, I said I did, and I tried to show reasonable interest in the details of life in the apartment, but a lot of them irked me. It wasn't easy, in 1926, to keep house and go to work as well. There were no drip-dry clothes, no nylon, no refrigeration except what the iceman supplied with his tongs. Because we were out all day, we were constantly toting things upstairs at night or early in the morning—we lived up several flights—from the grocery, the butcher's, the laundry, and the dairy. Annabel didn't mind, but that was natural; we never agreed on anything. I can't conceive of two girls with less in common. On the other hand, we never quarrelled, either. Indeed, as time went on I confided many things to Annabel. Over a gin daisy in the evening, I would expatiate on the frustrations I suffered at the office. I was particularly bitter about Mr. Dixon. I called him an exploiter of science and a sweater of female labor—I had recently discovered that I was being paid less than any of the male geologists. Annabel would listen to all this with no comment, her wide blue eyes full of calm.

It was the period of prohibition, and the gin that went into the daisies was made by Annabel and me out of alcohol and essence of juniper. Like most other people of our acquaintance, we got the juniper from the corner drugstore and used fairly hit-or-miss methods to get the alcohol. Annabel didn't drink much—not as much as I did. But I wasn't a real drinker, either. I hadn't had much practice. Until my last year at college, all the liquor I'd had was the warm, evil-tasting stuff we used to suck from hip flasks at football games and dances, with more giggling and innuendo about it than intoxication. And since I hadn't gone to many games or dances, my experience was strictly limited until my senior year, when I decided to investigate the subject once and for all, as a scientist. I got a small bottle of grain alcohol from a friendly attendant at the lab in Science Hall. He swore it had never been used. With this and half a dozen bottles of Coca-Cola, I drove out into the country one night and got to work. Pouring a third of the Coke out of a bottle, I filled it to the brim with alcohol, shook it vigorously, and drank it down. Then I sat waiting for sensations. Nothing seemed to be happening, so I mixed another bottle and tried again. The sensations must have hit me fairly quickly that time. I got to thinking about life. My thoughts made me laugh, and then I cried, and then I was sick, and then I passed out. It was a long time after that before I could get anywhere near liquor.

In St. Louis, however, I at last conquered that prejudice. You could get used to the taste if you kept trying, I decided, and I did try, successfully, especially after my social calendar changed. I began going around with two new young men named John and Jeff, who worked on a local newspaper. I was always going out with one or the other or, more frequently, both. We would spend hours mixing our essence of juniper with alcohol and then drinking it mixed with lemon juice or Coke. We talked, too. Neither of the boys knew a thing about science, but I often told them about calcite and the rest of it, and once they had agreed with me on the villainy of oil geology I could be persuaded to switch the subject. They preferred to discuss F. Scott Fitzgerald, baseball, and poetry. They tried to get me interested in politics, too, but they failed. I wouldn't even read their newspaper. Newspapers had nothing to do with what interested me, I told them.

I liked the boys, but Annabel didn't seem to. It was too bad; double-dating would have been more convenient for all concerned, but it was no use arguing with Annabel. She was invariably polite to John and Jeff, but when they invited her to come along with us she always had another date. I gave up, finally, and advised the boys to do likewise. We decided that she preferred men of a more regular fashion of life—men with season tickets to the opera, men who played bridge and went to church on Sunday.

Winter came. With John and Jeff, I went to the movies and ice-skated. Then March melted the snow and April brought a foretaste of summer. I grew restless, especially after I got a letter from Jane, who was now working as a tourist guide for the Fred Harvey company in Santa Fe. "I don't suppose you'd consider coming out here and working with me," she wrote. "You're doing so well in mining that you're probably happy where you are." If I hadn't been so old, I might have sniffled a little.

I went home to Chicago for a vacation. I must have hoped the trip would jounce me out of my gloom, but the sight of the city made it worse than ever. It was awful to think of everybody in that big place getting up at the same time every morning, taking the same bus or streetcar to work, doing the same things every day at the office. Where in the world were people who did things simply because they wanted to—because they were interested? Did no one ever strike out along new paths? All these people were no better off than I was. "But what *is* it you want?" my mother asked. "A few years ago, you were bound and determined to do engineering. There was no stopping you. Now you're tired of it. . . ."

I went back to St. Louis meekly, and back to the office. Soon May was more than half over. I felt as if I had been collating oil records my entire life. One morning when Annabel and I were sitting at our desks, Mr. Dixon came out and asked for a set of Oklahoma leases. Annabel got them with her customary speed and efficiency, but Mr. Dixon lingered, chatting pleasantly. He divided his glances between us whenever he paid us such a visit, but it was to Annabel alone that he said, "By the way, I've had interesting news in the morning mail that has some bearing on our discussion last night."

It was Annabel who gave herself away. I was only half listening, and the phrase "last night" would have passed in my mind for a reference to late yesterday afternoon if she hadn't looked sidewise at me. Her eyes, usually so expressionless, were hunted and guilty. Suddenly something clicked in my brain. I bent over a chart on my desk.

"Emily," said Annabel, when Mr. Dixon had gone.

I looked up and found her regarding me with a fair approximation of her old, calm gaze. She said, "I suppose you must be wondering about that remark."

"Oh, not at all," I said.

"But you must think it strange. I admit I *have* been seeing Mr. Dixon outside once or twice. Not very often, believe me. The only reason I haven't mentioned it before is that he said I shouldn't. You know how people talk in an office. They wouldn't understand, and it seemed safer not to let even you know."

"But it was Mr. Dixon himself who mentioned it just now."

"Yes. I suppose he forgot," said Annabel.

"Anyway," I said, "it's none of my business who you go out with."

I was lying. I thought it was very much my business when I recalled the things I'd said to Annabel about Mr. Dixon. I kept remembering more things, each one worse than the last. She must have told him some of them, I thought. It would have been only natural. And, of course, he'd given her two raises since she'd joined the firm. She was earning more than I was. Oh, of course Annabel had been telling him everything she'd ever heard in the office.

Anyway, what did I care? I didn't. I repeated this to myself, over and over. Angrily, I said to myself, "You listen to office gossip, and suddenly you're in the midst of horrid intrigues. This is what comes of letting life break in."

On the evening of May 20, 1927, I went to dinner with John and Jeff at a beer garden. Beer gardens were still called that, though we had to fill up on gin before going to one, for we could only buy a near-beer concoction called Bevo when we arrived. The men talked excitedly about the day's big news story, on which they were working, while I mopped my face, swatted mosquitoes, and sipped. Our table was in a corner near a lot of potted plants. Around us, at other tables, sat other sweaty people. The garden was really a paved yard with fading shrubbery, but it was better than being indoors. We were all lit by strange, unearthly colors—blue, green, and pink—that drifted across us in blotches from electric lights in festoons overhead. On a platform, a band played tunes from *The Chocolate Soldier* and *The Count of Luxembourg,* operettas familiar to St. Louis because they were performed regularly at the St. Louis Municipal Opera Theatre in Forest Park.

>With love, Nadina Popoff,
>   'Tis right there!
>No! With scorn, Nadina Popoff,
>   'Tis right—there!

I hummed with the band. Looking up, I found my friends still talking as hard as ever. I said petulantly, "What is all this, anyway? Who is Lindbergh?"

They exclaimed in horror. "Don't you know anything at all? Lindbergh's the greatest man of the century," said Jeff. "At this moment, he's up there flying across the Atlantic to France. Solo!"

"You mean this is the first time it's been done?" I asked.

Yes, they said, it damn well was.

I said, "Oh, well, once you've got a plane in the air I guess it doesn't make any difference how far you go."

The men exchanged glances—clearly I was hopeless—but then they tried to explain. The dangers Lindbergh was facing, I learned, were many. He had a very small plane, like a chicken coop, but he might run short of fuel anyway. He might go off course. He might blow up. "Most of all, think of the loneliness," said Jeff emotionally. "Good Lord, just look up at the sky."

I did. Between the festoons of lights, it was sullen and black. Heat waves darkened the stars.

"He's up there in the dark for hours on end. That's courage!" said Jeff.

"Well. Well, yes. I see what you mean." I stared again at the black above us, and a slow thrill started between my ears and moved downward. "Yes," I said.

John was looking at his notes. He said to me, "This might interest you particularly. It seems that Lindbergh was at your university, and in your college—the College of Engineering, wasn't it?—just two years ahead of you."

"Honestly?" I asked.

"Yes, but he didn't finish. Otherwise you might have met him. It says here that he dropped out because he got sore at the system used in teaching physics. Students have to write up all their experiments, don't they?"

"Yes, of course. What of it?"

"I don't know if this is true, you understand," John continued, "but the story goes that Lindbergh said it was just plain foolish for all the students to write up the same experiment every term. Writing it up took more time than the experiment. He said it was an awful waste of time and labor."

I thought this over. I found I was excited by the suggestion; I had never thought of the point before, but it was true, it was true. "Why, yes," I said. "It *is* a waste. What happened then?"

"Oh, he refused to write the experiments. He did the work, but he wouldn't turn in reports."

"Now, *that's* wonderful, if you like," I said. "That's *wonderful*."

The boys looked at me so oddly that I didn't go on to say what I'd intended—that Lindbergh's rebellion seemed far more important to me than did his flight across the Atlantic. At any rate, however belatedly, he was now my hero. I was silent for the rest of the evening, and still silent when I crawled into bed, for fear Annabel might wake up. It was embarrassing nowadays having to make conversation with Annabel.

I had a bad dream. I was standing somewhere, in a limbolike country without landscape, waiting for a procession to pass by. When it came, it was made up of young geologists marching smartly, four abreast, in field clothes, with cups and compasses hanging from their belts. Though I recognized them as my old friends, they walked straight past as if they didn't see me, until, as the last four came swinging by, one head turned, and one face—later I couldn't recall whose—looked at me. It was a look of grave contempt that pierced me painfully. Shame, grief, and a feeling of intense loss filled me. A cloud of dust welled up in the wake of the geologists and blotted them out, and when I woke I was still heavy with pain. Was I the betrayed or the betrayer?

It was Sunday. Annabel still slept, breathing softly. As I sat up, the morning sun glared on the sheet, burning away the mists in my brain. Suddenly I remembered what day it was, and what news the morning could bring—news with, I felt, a special message for me. During the night, I had somehow made a decision: If Lindbergh had landed in France, it followed with logical progression—the same clear logic that I knew existed in crystallography—that I was as free as he was, and therefore that I could quit my job. Of course, if he hadn't made it I would have to stay. Fair was fair.

In a tearing hurry, I dressed, no longer caring whether or not I woke Annabel, and rushed downstairs and along the street to the corner drugstore. For the first time in my life, I was going to buy a newspaper. The papers were stacked on the counter, and I grabbed the top one, shaking. My heart bounded. Sure enough, Lindbergh had settled it. I could quit.

TILL THE WELL RUNS DRY

"To think that you're going to be a Harvey Girl!" wrote my father, in 1927. He had things a bit wrong, but I was so relieved by his good nature that I didn't argue the point. I had expected stern disapproval. Without first consulting my parents, I had thrown up that good steady job in St. Louis to go to New Mexico and be a Fred Harvey courier, which was merely a fancy term for tourist guide. I wasn't even to be a regular guide, I had confessed—just one of the extra staff for the busy season in Santa Fe and environs—and for all this I could give no better reason than that I loved New Mexico. My mother had written; her letter had been perplexed, dismayed, and, finally, bitter. What was the sense, she asked, of having had a good education if I was going to throw it away? She pointed out that there was no future in guiding, and I could not bring myself to tell her, truthfully, that the last thing in the world I wanted was a future. You didn't say things like that around our house. Of all the lyrics I sang as a child, picking out tunes on the piano with one finger as I read a big green book called "Heart Songs," I remember best the following chorus:

> "Waste not, want not" is the maxim I would teach;
> Let your watchword be dispatch,
> and practice what you preach.
> Do not let your chances like sunbeams pass you by,
> For you never miss the water till the well runs dry.

There was another song, even more disturbing, presumably uttered by birds, which we sang at school:

> Oh, field and wood were passing fair.
> Today, alas, the world is bare.
> The summer's gone from hill and plain,
> And after gladness follows pain.

I can't recall the rest, but the idea is clear. Well, that was my family's philosophy. If I'd said to my mother that I didn't want a future, she would, of course, have asked what I did want, and that would have been awkward, because I didn't know. I merely wanted to live, without aiming for anything— though I was aware that this was a shameful attitude. After all, I was no fretful adolescent but a mature woman of twenty-two. Still, there it was—the very idea of taking care of the future sent me into a bad temper. At least, Daddy's letter showed that he could be reasonable, and still laugh about Harvey Girls.

The Harvey Girl as an institution had always been one of our family jokes. Years before, when my father had travelled every year in the West, Harvey Girls stood for much the same thing businessmen's secretaries often do today—they were hazards to stay-at-home wives. They were the waitresses for the Fred

Harvey restaurants, set up at wayside stations for the benefit of railway passengers on long trips. Fred Harvey, who founded the company in those days of no dining cars, made a fortune out of his monopoly, and his Harvey Girls were famous for looks as well as dexterity. Mother had half believed that my father was carrying on a flirtation with one of the young ladies, though even if he was it couldn't have amounted to much— a gallant remark or two thrown at her, as she rushed past, across the heavy railway china.

"You've heard Fred Harvey's famous last words, haven't you?" my father's letter continued. " 'Slice the ham thinner, boys.' "

He knew perfectly well I wasn't really going to be a waitress; it was just that the old name stirred memories in him. No, I was going to learn all about the mountains and pueblos of the Santa Fe country so that I might convey to tourists the same sensation of delight and adventure that it had given me when I visited it. I had thought the Indian Detour (a bargain excursion through the Pueblo territory, dreamed up by the Fred Harvey company) a splendid idea. Of course, the original Fred Harvey, the man with the ham, was by this time—1927— long since dead, and his restaurants, now that dining cars were everywhere, had been forgotten. But his name had been taken over by new people, and the desire to aid travellers live on in these successors. They didn't need to worry any longer about feeding tourists, but even in '27, in spite of electric fans, observation platforms, and the tremendous speed that trains were achieving, a trip across country from coast to coast was a severe ordeal. Travellers would appreciate a break, the company felt. Besides, coast-to-coast tourists never got a chance to see Santa Fe itself, because the main railway line didn't go that high into the mountains. Instead, it ran to Las Vegas—the New Mexico Las Vegas, not Nevada's—on a lower level.

The Harvey company figured out a way to solve all these difficulties at once. Motorcars met the travellers who were taking the Detour, at Albuquerque if they came from the west, at Las Vegas if they came from the east. They were whisked into the hills, to Santa Fe, by way of points of interest peculiar to the Southwest. Ever since Teddy Roosevelt had gone ranching, the American public had realized that the West was romantic, and in local color of that sort New Mexico outdid the other states. Tourists were taken to Indian villages, ranches, museums, and all the rest, and slept in La Fonda, the spanking new Harvey company hotel in Santa Fe, before going on their way refreshed. The Indian Detour didn't cost a lot, and, with its Thunderbird emblem, it was rapidly becoming popular. Now the company was planning new, elaborate private tours farther afield, and that meant more couriers.

When I arrived in Las Vegas, Jane met me, picking me up courier-fashion. Jane had been with the Detour a year. It was on her recommendation that I'd been accepted for the job—though I didn't exactly have it as yet; I was to start out as a summer extra hand.

I hardly knew Jane when I saw her on the platform. She was wearing a strange rig that didn't suit her at all. Indeed, I can't imagine anyone it would have suited. I was taken aback when I found that it was the courier uniform, which I, too, would have to wear. It comprised a khaki skirt, a bright velveteen overblouse of clumsy cut, a heavy silver girdle, or concho belt, and, most dreadful of all, a stiff Stetson hat. I still speculate with awe on the brain that designed that outfit. But I didn't really care what I looked like. Apart from the uniform, I found the life of a courier enchanting once I had started it. I had a bed in the house Jane shared with a never accurately determined number of other girls—nothing more than a barracks, but in Santa Fe even a barracks had charm. Our ranks shifted and changed, because girls were always going out on the Detour or being summoned suddenly to chaperon a longer trip. The house could take in any number of camp cots. Like most other Santa Fe buildings, it was of adobe, with whitewashed walls. The girls had a rough-and-ready system of paying expenses out of a pool, and though I was paid on a piecework basis, earning six dollars a day only when I worked, I made out all right. I never gave money much thought, even when somebody in the house stole the sixty dollars I had brought out to Santa Fe with me. More than once, Mother wrote to ask what on earth I would do if I should suddenly need an appendix operation or something like that, but she didn't scare me. Why should I have a faulty appendix, for goodness' sake? Only other people had operations.

We novices attended lectures and acquired a quick smattering of Amerindian ethnology, Southwestern history, and a few rudiments of archeology and ceramics. Then, after a training trip each had to make with an old hand, we were ready for work. I remember waiting for my first group of dudes, as we quickly learned to call tourists, on the platform of Las Vegas station. Las Vegas had none of Santa Fe's charm, and very little of its own, but at sunrise even the unlovely conglomerate of frame houses and the dusty road running between sand-colored scrub took on a golden, rosy glory. The mountains in the distance were suddenly crisply outlined by the glow. I felt a rush of gladness that I was there, wasting my life instead of pegging away in a St. Louis office and saving up for an appendectomy.

When the day was over for the tourists and they had been taken at La Fonda and given their proper room numbers—when they had seen Indians and bought pottery at Indian villages, and looked at the desk in the Governor's Palace where Lew Wallace completed *Ben-Hur,* and visited the cave city at Puyé—the courier's work was done. I caught on quickly. There was a rhythm to the job—three days with one party from Las Vegas to Albuquerque and another three days doing it backward. I didn't always get six days in a week, but when I did I enjoyed it. I enjoyed everything. There are people on whom altitude works like a stimulant, and I am one of them. I would come into the house from a day's guiding thick with dust and my voice reduced to a croak. Off with the uniform, into the rusty bathtub, into clean clothes, and out again with keen appetite to a party or a moonlight horseback ride and picnic. I simply never got tired, even when the party went on all night, as Santa Fe high jinks were apt to do. It was all right with me whether or not I got a good night's sleep. When I did, I slept like a dormouse, and when

I didn't I greeted the morning as alert as ever, ready for anything. It is all the more remarkable that I felt so well, in view of the stuff we drank at those parties. The Middle West had been a bathtub-gin district, and I was used to that. In Santa Fe, we had two staples—tequila and corn liquor. Corn had to be smothered in Coca-Cola or chased down with beer, whereas tequila was drunk then, as it is now, with a dab of salt in advance and a bite into a lemon afterward. The point of all this is that I drank them both, often during the same evening, and though I can hardly claim not to have shown any effects, I would wake up in the morning well and happy. Actually, it was a waste of either drink to give it to me. I would have been just as exhilarated without it.

Santa Fe was not merely my state of mind. It was really an interesting place—possibly the only town of its kind anywhere. You couldn't dismiss it as a resort for pleasure seekers, because it was also the state capital, as well as a refuge favored by doctors for tuberculosis cases. Santa Fe was a mecca for American Indian experts, being a living museum of Mexican and Indian culture. Most of all, it was an artists' colony. These differences didn't leap at once to the eye—I doubt if my Detour dudes saw them—but Santa Fe was a rich, rare city to live in. Strolling around the plaza at lunchtime on an idle day, I would pause every few steps to chatter with friends—an English girl training to be a vet, a hopeful t.b. case, a sculptor, a curio dealer, an archeologist, a millionaire in search of something to do. They all dressed the same, too, in Levi's, boots, and bandannas. It was the holiday uniform—the Santa Fe uniform. Nobody could have told the difference in people's social strata. They didn't fit neatly into categories there; Santa Fe had a way of mixing them up. A local banker turned to painting and became a professional; one of the Mexican workmen had an operation for tuberculosis that attracted a lot of attention and cured him; summer visitors fell in love with the town, bought land, built houses, and became permanent residents. Everyone fitted in, I reflected comfortably—and then discovered, to my dismay, that *I* didn't fit in at all. None of the couriers did, for lots of the people who lived in Santa Fe didn't like or want the Detour.

I should have realized this from the beginning, but I was so dazzled I couldn't see. The discovery came at a studio party where I was the only courier present. Incidentally, it was often like that—my being the only Detour employee at a party—because most of the girls preferred playing bridge or dating. At this party was a painter named Sylvia Howard, and suddenly I heard her voice above all the others, talking indignantly about a proposed improvement of the road leading from Lamy down the hill. She said it was an outrage to improve that road. Puzzled, I was about to ask why, when a man got in ahead of me. "But Syl, I nearly broke my rear axle in one of those arroyos last week," he said. "What's the matter with you? The way it is, that road's no good for anything but carts."

"All the better," said Sylvia, a brusque, striding sort of woman. She puffed violently on her cigarette. "The harder it is to get to Santa Fe, the longer we keep it as it is, don't you see? I know what you'll say—that we're bound to lose out anyway in the end. But I say why shouldn't we do our damnedest to hold up the wheels of progress? As long as we can, anyway. If only somebody would blow up the whole Detour garage and get rid of those horrible buses and all the pesky little couriers—Oh, I'm sorry." She nodded abruptly toward me. "I forgot about your job."

Everybody went on talking about the road and the Detour and Santa Fe, not troubled about my feelings, since Sylvia had apologized. Listening, I got a new slant on things. I saw the Detour differently—I saw Santa Fe itself in a new light. I'd always, until then, accepted whatever I came upon as something that had from the beginning been just as I found it. Children do this. The house a child grows up in, his school, his parents have never been newer or younger in his mind, and will never grow older. But now I learned that Santa Fe had been an even lovelier city half a generation earlier—smaller, wilder, more innocent. I learned that some of the newly built houses were all wrong for the background, that the Indians were getting their values warped, that everything was becoming commercialized and spoiled. I was appalled, especially as they told me that I—*I*—was at least partly to blame for all this, with my Thunderbird buses and my courier sisters and dude groups.

I went home early, weighed down with guilt. Next morning, I was happily surprised to find Jane there, asleep in her bed, for she'd been doing a series of long trips to the Grand Canyon and I hadn't seen her for quite a time. I couldn't have talked to any of the other couriers, and I was longing to get it all off my chest. I made a pot of coffee for her before she woke up, and as soon as her eyelids fluttered, there I was, telling her everything about what I had heard. I failed to communicate my sense of urgency. Jane's face grew more and more impatient as I talked, until she burst out. "Oh, pooh!" she said. "I know that sort of thing—I've heard it all dozens of times. All of us get it, and it's always from one lot—that arty crowd. They give me a pain in the neck. I don't know what you see in them, honestly. I thought you'd have more sense than to take it seriously."

"But Jane, they're right," I said. "Tourists do ruin Santa Fe. Think of the herds we bring in and take around, think of the junk they buy."

"Dudes have a right to come to Santa Fe, like anybody else. Why shouldn't they buy curios? It would be hard on the storekeepers if they didn't," said Jane.

"But it's such awful stuff. Those terrible little kachina dolls. You can't find genuine ones anymore. And look at the Navajo silverwork. It's going to hell, because the Indians just don't bother when they can sell any old thing. And our uniforms are hideous." I knew I was making a mess of my argument, bringing out a mishmash of complaints I had heard the night before. Yet it was entirely clear in my mind. "The Hopi snake dance is so commercialized nobody takes it seriously anymore," I went on earnestly. "It's only a show now—no religious significance, nothing. It's all wrong, Jane."

Jane said, "When you get excited, there's no reasoning with

you. Why not look at it from the native point of view? It's their country. Indians and Mexicans were here long before your precious artists came, and they used to have a tough time, and now, when they finally make enough out of our dudes to live on, what's wrong with that? You go out and ask the first Mexican you see if he'd like to have the Detour swept away and no more dudes. What do you bet he'll say?"

I could think of no reply.

"And another thing," said Jane. "How do you imagine Santa Fe would be without us? It would be a resort for rich people and artists, and nobody else. You wouldn't be here, because there wouldn't be anything you could do. You wouldn't be here, I wouldn't be here—it would be a different place."

"But I *would* be here," I said, stubbornly. "I'd find a way."

"No, you wouldn't," said Jane, and set off to do her day's ruinous work.

Shaken but still worried, I got a horse out of the dude-ranch corral near the house and went out to ride in the hills and think. It was a very difficult subject. Did I have any right to live in Santa Fe? If the dudes were wrong, so was I. As a matter of fact, I thought, my gloom increasing, I had no right to live anywhere. I wasn't doing anything constructive. I couldn't claim to be doing anything except batten on the dude industry. I wasn't a painter or a writer. I wasn't even making money—at least not enough to put aside for appendix operations; I was earning only enough to keep myself alive. All I did was be happy.

"Oh, hell, who cares?" I asked the horse's ears.

Defiance was all very well, but I knew in spite of everything that somebody did care, and it worried me to think about that. My mother's letters never failed to express the hope that I knew what I was doing. I always assured her in reply that I did —but was I telling the truth? I took the horse back to the ranch without having answered the question.

The season drew to a close and the rush of summer tourists slackened. Jane and I had planned that at this point I should come forward and talk seriously with her employers, pleading with them to keep me on as a regular courier. I refused to do it. I wouldn't put up even a token struggle. Jane, distressed, said, "But then what *are* you going to do? You haven't saved up anything. Can you go back to that office?"

"I wouldn't ever. Never!"

"I suppose it's your own business, but I can't understand you at all," she said.

I couldn't explain, because I didn't understand myself. All I knew was that I was still determined to avoid having a future. I said, "It'll be all right. By the way, I'm going up to Taos to stay awhile with Maria."

Jane shrugged. Most of the couriers did not think highly of Taos, though they were aware that it was interesting from a tour standpoint, with its elaborate Indian pueblo and the artists who made up much of its foreign population. North of Santa Fe, and much more mountainous, Taos hadn't the capital's claim to importance, being only a little town in the shadow of a great hill. The country was beautiful, with clear streams and plenty of vegetation, but the girls said they felt depressed because of that mountain rearing up behind the town and that the canyon drive from Santa Fe was dull and dark.

I loved Taos. My friendship with a girl named Maria had come about during a weekend there, when I'd driven up with friends for a party and was allotted a bed in her house. Her father was an important businessman in the Mexican community, but her mother came from the East, and Maria hadn't been brought up as a Mexican girl but rather as an Anglo, like us. She tore around unchaperoned, and wore Levi's. The night of that party, she and I had talked until morning, or almost, about her unhappiness and discontent with Taos. I was surprised by this; I had thought that life there, with one's own horse and an unlimited time to spend in the mountains, offered all a heart could desire, but Maria suffered from the malaise common to those who live the year round in pleasure resorts. Every year when the fun and games were over and the summer people left, Maria had to remain. She had nothing to do then but think about the places her lost friends had told her about—their own places. She longed to see the East, and for some reason was particularly fascinated by Boston.

"Oh, those lovely red brick houses," she said, sighing. "The purple windowpanes, and the Common, and baked beans for Sunday breakfast!"

I protested. "You'd hate Boston. It's damp and dark, and your mother cooks beans much better than they do there."

"But you've never been to Boston yourself," Maria pointed out.

"No, and I don't particularly want to go. My own home town is depressing enough."

"I'd love to see that, too," said Maria.

She was incorrigible, but she did find me a job of just the sort I wanted—without a future. In Ranchos de Taos, about four miles from Taos itself, was a greeting-card factory run by a couple named Kirwan, in a converted ranch house. The employees lived in smaller houses that dotted the estate, and cut paper, printed, and stencilled colors. I was a stenciller. The job may sound monotonous, but in reality it was very enjoyable. The Kirwans designed their cards, and printed them on thick, vellumlike paper, and they had a small, esoteric lot of purchasers—mostly from gift shops—who bought all they could get.

Once again I was earning just about enough to get along on. I had a house to myself, with a bed, a stove, and a fireplace. Every morning, I took a pail up to the big house for my allowance of milk. At intervals, a Mexican with a cart brought me a load of firewood, and I was given kerosene for my lamps. I was also given a horse named Tom, who lived and grazed in the yard around the house. Included in his outfit was a pair of saddlebags for weekly shopping expeditions, when I would jog into Taos, hitch him to the post in the plaza, and lay in a supply of canned food. Sometimes I stabled Tom at Maria's, in Taos, for the night, so that we could go to a dance. After the party, warm under enormous eiderdowns, we would talk about Boston until her mother yelled at us to shut up. In the morning, I would jog back, clippety-clop, to Ranchos through the snow. I got awfully cold as winter came on, but the fireplace was efficient, and in the stencilling room was a red-hot stove. The other stencillers and I used to talk as we worked—about Life and Art and Right and Wrong. Sometimes we were called on to supply a verse or a motto, always in a hurry, when Mr. Kirwan dashed in from the printshop demanding two or four lines. I was proud of the verse I produced one morning:

> This little card I'm sending
> Is very small, it's true,
> But no card could be large enough
> To hold my love for you.

It was *jolly* at the card factory, and I hated to think of giving it up to go back home for Christmas. Most of our cards had Christmas subjects, and there was something about coloring one red stagecoach after another that took the spontaneous joy out of Yuletide. I spoke about my feelings one day. "I do wish I didn't have to go home," I said. "It costs such a lot to get there, and once I've arrived it will be awfully hard to get away again."

Mrs. Kirwan happened to be in the room. "Then why go?" she asked calmly.

The question surprised me, and I had to think it over. "Doesn't everybody go home for Christmas?" I asked after a pause. "Anyway, until they're married?"

"Not that I know of. I stopped going when I was seventeen," said Mrs. Kirwan.

One of the stencillers added, "I never go. It's fun here at Christmas."

So I didn't go home. I wrote a reasonable letter instead, to explain that I had outgrown childish things. Christmas was indeed fun there—everybody gave parties. I gave one myself, serving mulled wine from which, in ignorance, I had boiled most of the alcohol. I put home out of my mind completely, so that, a few weeks after the festival season, I was taken unawares when Mother arrived on a sudden visit. She said she'd merely come to see how I was getting on, and it seemed easier to believe her than not.

Once I got over the surprise, I was pleased to see her. There was no doubt that she was awfully good at taking things as she found them. She stayed with me, and didn't at all object to living in a damp, cold adobe house. When she found that I was living on cold boiled eggs and canned beans, she protested only mildly. There was a little flurry when she insisted on washing all my dirty handkerchiefs, but this was only to be expected. You couldn't say that she didn't behave well all through the days. And yet . . .

Yet I knew that sooner or later we would have to settle things. I knew she was waiting to pounce, and I tried to brace myself. I am not sure I succeeded, even for a minute; I think Mother had me licked before she started. Without trying, without malice, she did something to Taos. I don't know how. I only know that every day my house grew smaller. The work we did on the cards dwindled, too, into an amusing little stunt. All the country changed and lost its brightness. Even the mountain shrank, no longer striking me with awe in the early morning, when it threw a deep shadow as far as I could see. I felt as if I'd already gone home and was living in the playroom, and it is odd that when we came to grips at last, the night before she left, she put it almost like that.

"I can understand your fondness for this place, dear," she said. "It's a very pretty little town, lovely for playing in. I've always been fond of the West myself. But when all's said and done, a resort is no place to live permanently. Look at your little friend Maria. You told me yourself that she's miserable here."

"Yes, but—I'm not like Maria."

Mother ignored that. "In real life, people do something that matters—especially people who've had a training as good as yours," she said. I didn't reply, and she continued, "We've been so worried about you, darling."

Again I said nothing. I waited.

"I'm sure you're ready now to go back to work. Aren't you?" asked Mother.

I said, "I do work. You ask the Kirwans."

"This isn't real work, and you know it."

"Look, Mother, Taos is a hard-working community. Just because people paint or model, you can't say—"

"I know that perfectly well," said my mother. "I have every respect for artists. But you're not a real artist, now, are you? Christmas cards!"

"No, but if you hadn't made me go to college, I might have been."

"I didn't think it wise. You didn't have enough talent." Mother became brisk. "Now, what are your plans? What do you intend to do with yourself? You've had your fun for a long time, but now . . . Your father and I have talked about it, and we know it's hard to get started all over again. We're willing to help. Wouldn't you like to go back to school, perhaps, and get a Master's?"

Like a charmed cobra, I watched her. I repeated her words. "Back to school?"

"You did enjoy your science. Well, why not go on with that? We're willing to help you out with the money."

Nothing could have impressed me more than this offer. It was a fundamental law in our family that the children were sent to college and afterward were on their own. We were so imbued with the idea that we even tried to get off our parents' hands while we were still at college, taking jobs on the side when we could. My younger sister succeeded so well that on one occasion she was able to send back her entire allowance for the term. The enormity of Mother's suggested break with tradition took away most of my resistance.

I said, "You can't possibly afford it, Mother. It costs money to go on with what I like—mineralogy."

"We can manage for a while. Remember, most of you are married and gone away now," said Mother.

"No, no, you mustn't think of it. I wouldn't need money.

If I went to Columbia, for instance—they're good at mineralogy there—I'm sure I could get a job to help out. Oh, no, Mother, I wouldn't want money."

As she smiled, I realized what I had done, and added frantically, "It's just an idea, you understand. I'm not—I don't want to . . ."

She stood up, saying, "Think it over, dear. I'm sleepy. I'm going to bed." She kissed me, and left me sitting by the fire.

I tried to think it over, but it seemed to me that I couldn't even speculate about the future, or think of anything but the past. Everything I had been doing was clearly exposed in a new, glaring light. I had been wrong to work on the Detour, wrong to stencil all those greeting cards, wrong to have been happy.

"And after gladness follows pain."

The flaming end of a twig fell out of the fire onto the hearth. I leaned over and severely shoved it back where it belonged. Then I sat up and looked around the room in farewell.

KATHY, NOT ME

That year, we talked about ourselves constantly: our feelings, our actions, our pasts—though, as to that, none of us had a lot of past to talk about, and it's a wonder that we managed to fill so much time with it. There was a good deal of time to fill, too, in 1930 in New York. Today, everybody knows what that date stands for, but then we didn't realize it was significant, and this is odd when you come to think about it. When I read about some important moment or era in history, I always take it for granted that the people it happened to were aware of what was going on. In my mind's eye, I see the agricultural workers of England during the Industrial Revolution feeling the pinch and saying to each other, "Eh, lad," or whatever agricultural workers would say in those days, "what dost tha expect? It's this Industrial Revolution at the bottom of it, taking away a considerable proportion of the farming land, forcing us from our cottages and into the smoky cities, much to the detriment of our lungs. Worst of all, it makes possible that detestable phenomenon of the times, child labor." Then they go and smash the spinning jenny. Again, every schoolchild in America knows how well informed the Colonists were in the seventeen-seventies, when they fought the Redcoats. In ringing tones, they said, "Wicked British imperialists will have to learn the lesson taught by the fate of Rome. Our years of frontier life, during which we had to outwit crafty Indians and chop down trees in the primeval forest, have imbued us with the stout spirit of nationalism, so come on, boys, and get that tea moving." History is tidy. That's what makes it history. Somehow, though, New York in 1930 was different. We were living at a moment of great importance to the economics of the world, but we just went on talking about ourselves.

I knew hardly anything about the great crash in Wall Street, and if I hadn't been told the connection later I would never have known that it caused the scarcity of jobs that gave me and my friends so much leisure. Stock-market panics happened to the sort of person I had no contact with. All I knew about investments was that my mother had once, long ago, bought German marks—a transaction that had become a family joke—but why it was funny, or what turned German marks into worthless things, remained a mystery I made no attempt to solve. As a child, I hadn't an inquiring mind, and though in New York I was no longer a child, I still wasn't inquisitive about the stock market. If I'd actually seen a broker jumping out of a Wall Street window, it would possibly have meant something. I certainly hope so. As it was, life went on much as usual for a long time after the panic. Wheels slowed down, but they did it gently, and when the slowing down became noticeable at last, it seemed to have happened by itself—a natural holdup, inexplicable. As I'd always understood it, the laws of economics were simple. Once you were out of college, you got a job somewhere and supported yourself forever after. You could ring in changes to some extent. In fact, I'd already run in several, holding various jobs, and though the fundamentals remained the same, I had learned to be careful with my earnings, putting away money to tide over the periods between. Now, when the periods between stretched out until they were longer than times of employment, I fared better than many of my acquaintances, a number of whom had to leave town and go home to Oklahoma or Iowa or my home state, Illinois. This was always sad. But even so, it was a gradual ebbing away, not a sudden, dramatic exodus. I didn't look around and ask, "What's happening?" I felt merely that life was sad, and this sadness of life had become something I seemed always to have known about.

The girl with whom I shared a tiny Village apartment close to the Sixth Avenue "L"—Kathy, I'll call her—was as frugal as I. Kathy had won a scholarship to a New York dramatic school, and had come all the way from somewhere in the Middle West to use it. It amounted to the fees at the school, nothing more, but her parents sent her an allowance to live on, and she managed. Every morning, she went to school, where she was given lessons in fencing, dancing, and singing, entering a room, sitting down, standing up, and voice-throwing, and though I didn't have to get up when she did except on the rare occasions when I had a job, I did. I wasn't fond of sleeping. Besides, one of the things that made the depression so depressing was the waking moment when you remembered that there was no reason to get dressed and go out. With a job, it was very different; lying there with your eyes not quite open, you made a lot of little decisions —whether to eat one piece of toast or two, whether to take the subway or the bus, what to wear for the evening's date. To hide from myself the prospect of hours and hours of nothing, I got up and had breakfast with Kathy, though even that wasn't exactly cheering as time went on. Kathy had fallen in love with a boy I'll call Ivan, and was unhappy. This bothered me. I don't mean to imply that I was awfully fond of Kathy, because

I wasn't, though I liked her well enough. It was the unhappiness that worried me, the state itself. Anyone's unhappiness, probably, would have hurt me just as much. If you think this trait indicates something nice about my character, you are wrong. It was merely aimless sympathy, a kind of self-indulgence —sympathy gone mad. I was not nice; I was sick.

Moreover, nothing useful came out of this worry over Kathy. I didn't give her good advice. I only listened when she talked about herself—we all listened to each other by the hour, so that was nothing new—and felt sorry. I tried to feel as much sorrow as she did, as if I wanted to take on her unhappiness. I think that's how it started, but soon I began to look for more grief than Kathy's, as if some part of me wanted to feel all the misery in the world. Near our apartment house was a soup kitchen, and all day long people waited there for dishing-up time. I took on their anxieties. I don't mean that I offered to help in the kithcen; I never did anything like that, and it's one of the reasons that I know I was sick. I never even walked past the line at close quarters but crossed the street so that the people in it wouldn't be shamed by my looking at them. It was as far as any helpful impulse on my part seemed to go. That was life, I said to myself. That was how things were. I remember the weather as unremittingly dark and chilly. Though New York in other years lives in my memory as sparkling with sunlight, at that time, as I recall it, the skies were always overcast and the streets mirrored the leaden clouds in sullen, dirty puddles. I know it's not true, but that's the only way I can remember it. It was then, too, that I became vividly aware of the ornamental bridges in Central Park, when I passed by one of them on the lower level one evening just at dusk and saw throngs of people standing around or sitting on the ground underneath, holding their places until nightfall.

Now I moved into another phase of illness, and borrowed grief from the past. Nothing was too small for my brooding. I thought of an afternoon when I had baby-sat in my brother's house in Winnetka. The baby was in a playpen on the porch, and in theory I need not have stayed out there with him. In theory, I was to do my homework indoors by a window through which I could see if he was all right, but he was eager for company, and for a while I lingered with him. I picked up his Teddy bear when he threw it out of the pen, and made it growl at him, and so on. Time was wasting, however, and the books were waiting. Finally, I covered the bear over with a lot of stuff on the far side of the pen, and while he worked away at the pile to get it out I sneaked indoors. Unfortunately, I could see him perfectly well through the window. I saw him straighten up unsteadily and turn around with the bear in his arms. I saw the dismay on his face before he started to cry. Though I rushed out and comforted him, the expression had been there, and I had evidently kept it in mind ever since. Years had passed, and he had grown up, and still his dismay came back to haunt me in New York—strange company for the soup-kitchen waiters and the sleepers under the bridge, but all was of a piece; it was all unhappiness.

During this wandering and worrying, my personal problem of joblessness—which many people had to face—didn't bother me at all. The sum I had saved was diminishing, but it didn't matter. I looked for work, for a long time failing to find any, and I was quite phlegmatic about the failure. It was happening to *me*, which meant it had no importance, and I think I know why I felt that way. I was proud—too proud to be affected by a national catastrophe like the depression. When I felt fright and apprehension and grief for mankind, being ground to bits by forces beyond its control, I was plunking these disagreeable sensations down on the rest of humanity but not on me, never on me; the enemy couldn't touch *me*. And in a crazy way my feelings seemed justified when I did get jobs—three weeks here as secretary, two weeks there on a switchboard. I never felt hungry, but then why should I? Hunger was not for me but for those others. I was terribly sorry for them, and the emptier my refrigerator was, the sorrier I felt—for them.

One unemployed day, I noticed that I was walking past the door of a friend of mine named Mary, and I went in. Mary was there. She was making out, she said, in her work—she was a photographer—and there was no need to contemplate going home to her native state. While she moved around, doing something to a camera tripod, we talked—about ourselves, as usual: personalities, personal affairs, nothing large and comprehensive like the law of supply and demand. But perhaps I didn't talk in quite the same lighthearted way I usually did. I have an idea I must have gone off the rails and talked about Life. At any rate, Mary gave me a queer look and said, "You're in a dreary mood, aren't you?" She broke off to tighten a screw, and added, "Better snap out of it, my dear."

I said, with indignation, that I couldn't very well snap out of it, because I was damn well in it, and so was she, and so were all of us. I said, "That's the way things are."

"Ah, but things wouldn't look like that if you were all right." Mary put away the tripod and sat down. "Are you eating enough?" she asked abruptly.

"Of course I am. Why shouldn't I be?"

"Well, something's the matter with you. Perhaps you'd feel better if you wore decent clothes. Those shoes," she went on, looking with distaste at my feet. "Haven't you got any others? Well, you ought to get some new shoes for a beginning. Can you afford them?"

I assured her that I could manage. Privately, of course, I had no intention of buying new shoes. What—bother about petty vanity with the world in the state it was? The idea would have been funny if I hadn't got out of the habit of laughing.

When I left her, Mary gave me a little brown bottle of pills and said, "I can see you're not sleeping enough. One of these ought to fix you up. After you've had a good night, I can promise you, life'll look brighter. You can keep the whole lot—I've got more." And she called through the door after me, "Don't take more than one at a time, now."

That night, I swallowed a pill and it did make me sleep—so soundly that I didn't hear Kathy next morning. In fact, I was still asleep when the cleaning woman came in, much later. Kathy had hired her. During the depression, there was a superabundance of domestic help, and this Swedish woman, Helga, had almost wept, Kathy had said, when she asked for work. Now she was doing all the apartments in the building, twice a week. She apologized profusely for waking me, but apologies were hardly necessary at eleven o'clock, and I said so. Stumbling from one room to the other to keep out of her way, drinking Kathy's coffee warmed over, I was conscious of the mists clearing and observed myself as closely as a doctor feeling a pulse. Did the world look brighter, as Mary had said it would? Helga had squeezed out her mop for the last time and departed before I came to a decision. No, I said to myself, staring out the window, nothing was any better, but at least the pill had got me through most of the morning without the knowledge that it was passing. On the strength of that relief, I was able to write a letter to my mother—something I had put off doing for days. Often I wondered why people went home when they got discouraged in New York. Surely home was the last place imaginable for a failure. I even avoided my sister Helen, who lived in New York now that she was married; she would have understood better than Mother, but still she was family.

The days marched past, sedate as mourners at a funeral. Kathy's love affair continued to wilt, and one day she told me that she didn't expect to see Ivan anymore. She was not a demonstrative girl, and when she cried she tried to do it quietly, usually after going to bed, but now and then when I was at home I heard her. I tried not to be at home in the evenings, not only on Kathy's account but because if a day of unemployment is long an evening at home afterward is endless. Still, now and then I heard her. Between-times, I saw a lot of people—Mary and her boy friend, and an actor who'd been out of work for eighteen months, and a newspaperman, and Bernard, who is hard to classify. He'd never been a reporter or an actor or even a painter in his life. He'd never earned his living. He just went to classes at some handy university, studying one subject after another, taking examinations and getting good marks, then starting off on some quite different course of study. Bernard would always have been an oddity, but during the depression he was more than ever peculiar because of his unearned income, which he had inherited and held on to. As if this was not weird enough, he was also being psychoanalyzed, which in 1930 was so rare that I still spoke of his analyst, when occasion arose, as an "alienist." Naturally, I'd never met the analyst, but Bernard talked about him. Sometimes I had dinner with Bernard and his friends and spent an evening listening to them talk about science, literature, or philosophy, depending on what he was studying at the moment. In his way, he worked awfully hard.

One day, Kathy came home early from school, white with shock, and told me they'd withdrawn her scholarship and she wasn't to go back anymore. It was not her fault, the authorities had assured her; they were running so short of funds that they had to retrench. I could think of nothing to say but "Oh, Kathy, it's dreadful, it's awful," but it didn't matter, because she wasn't listening. Sitting upright on the edge of a chair, she gave her full attention to the thoughts clamoring in her mind, and it was out of these that she finally said, "Don't tell anybody about this for a while. I don't want it to get back to my parents, or they'll make me go home."

This sounded like sense, and I nodded, thinking I understood perfectly. Then she cried sharply, "Oh, I wish I could! I wish I could go home right now!"

"Then why don't you?"

"I can't. I'm having a baby," said Kathy.

What she meant, and did not have to explain, was that she did not intend to have it; outside of books and movies, girls in her predicament never did. Both of us knew that much but very little more, except that the operation was illegal. We discussed possible ways and means at such length that Kathy got distressed to a greater extent, and when I said that we had to get in touch with Ivan she had hysterics and had to be helped to bed. That put things off for a few hours, but in the morning nothing had changed; getting in touch with Ivan was still the first priority, and Kathy agreed at last and telephoned him.

A nasty week followed. Ivan, resentful and suspicious at the beginning, was persuaded after a while to see it as we did—a matter that involved him as well as Kathy. Once he got started, he went the whole way, anxious to get it over with so that he could resume his normal life and forget Kathy all over again. He found the abortionist, he supplied a part, at least, of the money, and he even arranged to be at the apartment on the day of the operation to make sure we got back all right—for I went with her, of course. I can see now that it all must have been a considerable strain on him as well as on Kathy, but at the time, when we got back and found him drunk, I was not inclined to make allowances. I'd found it very difficult to get Kathy up the stairs, and the sight of Ivan, staggering and foolish, was too much. Grimly, I got her to bed. She was trembling, and rather green in the face.

"There now, that's all right," said Ivan. "Let's go out and get something to eat."

At this, I drew a deep breath and let fly. All through my ranting, Kathy sobbed in the background, softly and wearily. She went on doing it even after Ivan had departed, slamming the door. She continued to be weepy for the next two weeks, until she was strong enough to go home and I saw her to the train. She cried until the last minute.

Back in the apartment, though it was quiet now, I couldn't get the sound of Kathy's sobbing out of my ears. I tried. I accepted every invitation that came along, regardless, and my dates multiplied. The telephone rang most of the time, but I couldn't forget Kathy. I was perfectly well aware that this was ridiculous, because Kathy was all right now, and had written to tell me so. But logic didn't work. What bothered me was that the thing had happened. It didn't matter that it was all over. Though it was past, and though it was Kathy, not me, someone had gone through all that cruelty. It didn't matter whether it was Kathy *or* me, and it made no difference that the cruelty was in the past, because, past or not, it was *there.* A thing like that could happen. I grieved accordingly, and the more I did, the less I wanted any part of life. Life had let me down. I knew how to get out of it, too. I'd used only three of Mary's pills and there

120

were at least twenty in the bottle—enough to kill, if taken all at once.

I had just about decided on the pills when I went to have dinner with Bernard in his apartment near N.Y.U. He had a nice place, full of bookcases. He opened a can of soup and fixed some spaghetti, and after we'd eaten he smoked a pipe while I talked about the pills, and my decision, and the rest of it. I did this not so much because I wanted to hear his opinion but out of habit. Talk, talk, talk. Bernard puffed for a while, then gave a reasoned speech of disagreement with my argument for suicide. It added up to the statement that I had a lot to be thankful for and ought to snap out of it. Just like Mary, I said to myself, and equally uncomprehending. Bernard went on to catalogue the items that he thought should cheer me up, but for all the difference it made he might as well have been talking Japanese. I had simply strengthend my resolve by talking it out.

At last, he said, "You know, I think you need the advice of an expert, like this man I go to."

"The alienist?"

"He's a psychoanalyst, as I've told you repeatedly—a very different thing—and I'm sure he could help you."

I shook my head. Everybody knew that Bernard paid ten dollars an hour for his treatment, and anyway I knew I didn't need treatment. It wasn't my fault if I could see the facts more clearly than anyone else, was it?

Bernard took me as far as the corner when I left. "Well, good night," he said, "and listen . . ." He paused, then came up with something he was sure would keep me going. "I think you're lots prettier than your sister," he said.

I went back to my quiet, empty apartment. If it had continued to be quiet, I might not have gone ahead with my intention, but the telephone rang the minute I had my shoes off, and let me in for a long talk with a friend who was depressed. Hardly had I rung off when it rang again, and I had another chat with another friend, this time a drunk one. The third time the bell shrilled, I grabbed the instrument and tried earnestly to pull it out of the wall by the roots. The cord held, but after a while the bell stopped ringing of its own accord. When I put down the telephone, I was crying.

"This has got to stop," I said aloud. I'm not sure now what I meant—what had to stop. It could have been life, or merely the crying, which embarrassed me. Anyway, I rushed for the pills. I went on crying the whole time I was swallowing them—a process that took some time, because I couldn't get more than three down at once. Afterward, though, I was able to stop crying. For some reason, I felt triumphant. I think I had the idea that I was avenging Kathy. However, the next time I knew what I was doing, there I was crying again, and the room was full of daylight. I was very sick, this time to the stomach. Somebody's arms were around me, somebody was patting my shoulder, and a voice —Helga's, of all things—was saying over and over, "Don't cry, don't cry. You mustn't. I love you," as if she were talking to a baby. She'd heard the noise from the next apartment, she said, and hurried in to find me sick. I think she must have believed that I was just very drunk, for finally she went away and left me to get over it naturally. She knew nothing about the pills—as a matter of fact, I'd forgotten them myself, I was so dopey. I went back to sleep until the telephone bell woke me again and I heard Bernard saying, "Well, how are you this morning?"

Then I remembered, and I found that I could hardly talk, because my tongue felt too big. I said, "Oh, yes. I took that stuff."

When Helen got there with a doctor, I'd gone back to sleep. I prefer to forget what happened after that, but when it was all over and he said I was rid of the stuff, I was taken to Helen's, where I went to sleep on the couch in the living room. He told Helen I'd saved myself, really, by taking so many pills that my system rejected them, and she passed on the information next day when I woke up. She asked me why I'd done it anyway, and I said, "I don't know." It was the truth. All my careful reasons had evaporated. From where I was lying, I could see the sky—a high, bright blue—and trees in delicious shades of green, all the world clear and shiny as I hadn't seen it for years. I longed to get out in it. I was full of ambition. But all was not quite well, because I was frightened by what I had done. It simply didn't make sense. It was terrifying to think I might not be quite right in the head. In those days, we still thought in terms of sanity and insanity, with a nice clear line dividing them, and I had every right to be afraid.

I was still puzzling it out when Bernard came. He waved away my thanks for what he had done—alerting Helen and so on. She'd already thanked him, he said. What he wanted to talk about was the psychoanalyst. "You must realize now that you'd better see him," he said. "You're not rational, you know."

It was so near what I had been thinking that I nodded meekly.

"You can see him as soon as you like," Bernard went on.

"Bernard, don't be ridiculous. How can I possibly—"

"And I'll pay," said Bernard.

I gaped at him, and he hurried to explain. I reminded him so much of what he'd been like before treatment, he said, that he couldn't bear to think of my going on without help. He begged me not to talk about it anymore, and then he hurried out—straight to the analyst, no doubt.

Alone, I was still in a state of shock, stunned by the scope of his offer. Why, it would run into hundreds of dollars!

What happened next was a click in my mind, and then it was as if a window blew open, letting anger flow in. I knew all about that anger, though I hadn't felt it for a long time. It was as pure as the new color of the sky, and hot as the sun. Helen came in and found me up and dressed, tying one of my shoelaces that had broken. I said to her, "Bernard wants to pay for me to be analyzed."

"Yes, he told me. It's awfully nice of him, isn't it?" said Helen. "Are you sure you feel like getting up?"

"Well, he's not going to," I said. "What does he think I am? Pay for me, indeed!" I combed my hair hard, and said over my shoulder, "Nobody pays for *me*. Who wants analysis, anyway?"

I had already packed my suitcase; now I picked it up and started out.

Helen said, "Where are you going?"

"Home," I said, "but shopping first. I've got to get new shoes. Just look at me!"

AISLE K

"The Reading-room was his true home; its warmth enwrapped him kindly; the peculiar odour of its atmosphere—at first a cause of headache—grew dear and delightful to him."

When I found this passage in George Gissing's *New Grub Street,* I felt a pleasant shock of recognition, the more so as I happened to be sitting in the Reading Room at that very moment. Both Gissing and I are referring, of course, to the Reading Room in the British Museum, in London. For a moment, I felt such kinship with the author that, though he has long been dead, I looked around half expecting to find him sitting at one of the desks in my aisle—K. I always sit in Aisle K unless it's full when I arrive. It is no use asking me why I prefer it. I don't know, because there is absolutely no difference between Aisles J and K, and any other; they all radiate like spokes from the hub, a circular counter in the center of the great circular room, surmounted by a dome inset with grimy glass. Aisle K is where I sat on my first day in the Reading Room, long ago, and I make tracks for it every morning that I go in. I went there to begin with because I had been hired to look up local color for an overworked American writer of historical romances, and, once there, immediately became, and have remained, a regular reader. We are a peculiar lot, but—with some few exceptions, such as Karl Marx—we are harmless. Though I am not sure which aisle Marx preferred, I do know that he too kept going to the same chair.

We are unobservant, too. Though I've been frequenting the Reading Room for thirty years, off and on, I recognize very few of the others, and few of them recognize me. We are too busy with our own books and thoughts to waste time frivolously summing up our neighbors. Only when a man has an *outré* beard or wears really odd clothing do I mark him in my mind and know him when I see him again. I mean, of course, when I see him in the Reading Room. Other contingencies do not arise. Though I do occasionally encounter in the Reading Room somebody from the world outside—my husband, or a friend from an out-of-town university—I have never met genuine, dyed-in-the-wool readers in shops or at theatres or restaurants, or anywhere at all but at the Museum, where they belong. Once, I bumped into a Museum guard in an Underground station—the man who usually stands at the Reading Room door in a little sentry box. In the station, he was in mufti, and though he tipped his hat politely, I didn't recognize him at first without his blue coat and peaked cap. This was disconcerting. After all, *he* knows *me*, no matter what I'm wearing, and, what's more, he always lets me go in without asking to see my ticket, which I appreciate, life being enhanced by such small triumphs. Therefore, I was ashamed of myself for having even seemed to snub him, but that's the way we readers are—absent-minded.

There is only one regular reader whom I would recognize anywhere, even at Harrods or the Zoo—not that she would ever be in either place. For a long time, I didn't speculate about her. A less regular reader—that is to say, a less self-centered person—might sometime have wasted a few minutes wondering where she goes when the Reading Room closes for the night, what aerie furnishes her shelter. But I never had. It took me twenty years to learn that her name is Stuart, and I learned that only because one day I happened to hear an attendant address her.

Yet I saw Miss Stuart the first time I ever went to the Museum. I had stopped at the outer gate to ask where to go to apply for a reader's ticket. As I paused there, she rode past me on a bicycle, through the opening in the great iron railings, and on across the courtyard toward the steps that stretch imposingly across the building's face. Idly, I watched her set up her bicycle in a rack at one side of them. She had a jaunty manner—a sort of certainty that impressed me, because I was brand-new in England and very timid—but there was more than manner to be noticed about Miss Stuart. On a cold, raw, dark day in January, in an era when women never wore bifurcated clothing for anything but the most drastic activities, she was attired in very short running shorts, a cotton sweater without sleeves, and socks. I gawked as I went after her, but by the time I had followed her to the top of the steps and into the building she had vanished. I went into the office I had been directed to, and forgot all about her in the perplexity of filling in the required form. I learned that before I could get a ticket I must be vouched for by three individuals—a property owner, a bank manager, and a clergyman. It seemed too difficult to contemplate. I was near giving up the whole idea of England and retiring to New York in disgrace. It wasn't as if I had ever passionately wanted to be there, I reminded myself. Where I wanted to be was the Belgian Congo. Naturally, I had welcomed the chance of getting out of Depression America and having my first venture abroad, but now I regretted being so impulsive. I am a chilly type, whose hands and feet remain cold even in the tropics, and I was already half stupefied with the London wintertime damp, the cold, and the dark. It was impossible to feel the emotions I knew I should be experiencing. I saw no magic in London and possessed no mysterious conviction that I had been there before. The streets did not make me think of Dickens; they were just streets. The traffic reminded me more of Brooklyn than of anywhere else. People in dirty raincoats stumped along pavements that were apparently coated with machine oil, and I could not blame them for looking as bad-tempered as they did. Henry James, I decided, must have been out of his mind.

But a trouble that went deeper than chilblains or sniffles was that I was an American and thus an object of curiosity. It may sound strange nowadays, but the fact is that at that time a lot of Londoners had never seen an American or heard American speech until they saw and heard me. Though they didn't seem particularly pleased with the experience now that it was theirs, they were curious in a dour way, and whenever I spoke in a public place, on no matter how banal a subject—asking my way, buying a newspaper—people within hearing distance would fall silent and stare at me. They were familiar with other accents, such as German or French or Scandinavian, but American was something new, and they didn't hold with it. It was weak of me to mind, but I couldn't help it. I wasn't used to being abroad and I minded awfully. So it was actually an effort to leave my lodging house in the mornings and face the city.

I felt better, though, after I had cleared the hurdle of the application form and become a reader. I did so with the help of my landlady; a property owner herself, she was good enough to supply her own bank manager and clergyman. After that, I was eager to get out of the house and into the Museum, for there, in the Reading Room, I had found peace. There all was for the most part silent, for, after all, it *was* a library. But even when circumstances did compel me to speak, nobody so much as raised an eyebrow. They were sophisticated at the British Museum. Almost every American professor or student who came to London—and there were such, even in those dark ages—went to the Reading Room. There, alone, my accent was nothing new. I suppose this relief marked the beginning of my lifelong fixation. I was the panting fox I have read about who takes refuge from the hounds in a badger's set and gets so emotionally attached to the place that he stays on, moving in on the badger for good. In the Reading Room, I found my set. I *belonged*.

Life had a regular pattern. The lodging house, in Torrington Square, was near the back of the Museum. Every morning, I dressed as fast as I could, because the room was cold, and ate breakfast from a tray, huddling close to the shilling-meter gas fire. Then I went out. I always walked fast in the morning, and the sidewalks were always wet. By the time I had rounded the Museum's flanks and reached the pillared portico, the backs of my legs were so splashed with black that they looked like a Dalmatian's. Breathlessly, I crossed the enormous entrance hall. (Everything about the Museum is outsize, as if the officials wanted always to be prepared for giants who might happen to drop in for tea.) Towered over by the roof, dwarfed and intimidated by huge stone gods, I was glad to reach the other side and the door to the Reading Room.

I felt that the Reading Room was cozy, though in general effect it is not unlike the old main hall of the Pennsylvania Station. Inside there was no further need to rush, for I was safe. The peace that descended on me, and still descends, had an even more magical effect. It convinced me that I was warm. This was an illusion. In the old days, everyone but Miss Stuart kept his coat on, and sometimes I was reduced to writing my notes wearing gloves. In those days, my feet were heavy, insentient lumps until I got home in the late afternoon and went to bed. Nevertheless, I felt warm in the Reading Room and was reluctant to go out to lunch, and as lunchtime came I envied the self-confident Miss Stuart, because she had perfected her own method of saving the trouble of going out. She always brought a bottle of milk with her in the morning, and at noon she emptied it through a straw in the Ladies' Room. It was forbidden to eat or drink in the Ladies' Room, or anywhere else in the Museum, but Miss Stuart ignored the rule. She knew the attendant, and would chatter away with her customary air of owning the place and drink her milk unquestioned.

Fixation or no fixation, illusion of warmth or not, I never went so far as to sit tight when a loud bell told us, at the end of the afternoon, to turn in our books and get out. I was always ready to go by that time. I was tired and had stored up enough reassurance to carry me through until morning. On the way back to Torrington Square, I didn't rush. The world was dark—had been dark since before teatime—and I plodded by instinct through the badly lit streets, between enormous walls and billboards. I might have been that small, featureless figure sketched in an architect's plans to show the scale of the drawing.

One evening, I was surprised to realize that my road back was not as dim as usual. There could be no doubt about it—the sun had been late in setting. Until then, I had not grasped the fact that the seasons in England bring noticeable changes, but now that I was alerted I began to check up. Sure enough, in the morning the world was lighter when I set out on my hasty journey. After that, things improved rapidly. The weather remained wet most of the time and my stockings got as spattered as ever, but the added light made a great difference to my spirits. Besides, I knew people; somehow I had gathered acquaintances. Sometimes I went out to dinner. Sometimes I would invite a friend up to have a drink in my room, though I learned that this was not always a good thing, because people didn't seem to admire the lodging house. "You ought to live in a better place than this," said one man sharply, and I was puzzled. What did he mean by better? The room was all right, I told myself. It had a row of hooks on the wall, and a chair and a bed and a little table in the corner where I kept a bottle of Black and White and a bottle of seltzer. Who needed more than that? He laughed at my bottle of Black and White, too, and said, "You Americans!" When I demanded an explanation, he said that English girls didn't drink whiskey, or gin, either. Sherry was what they drank, he said.

"And other wine as well," he added. "Wine's absolutely all right. Why don't you stick to that?"

Spring crept in. The grass in parks and squares, which had bothered me from the beginning by being green in a manner unseasonable, now grew greener and longer. The sunlight, though still watery and uncertain, was enough to plant a hint of restlessness in my winter heart. Suddenly I found my self-imposed hours in the Reading Room too long. I never became abandoned enough to stay away from the Museum in the morning, but sometimes I turned my books in early and went out into the sweet, thawing air. There was no errand to run, no meaning to it; it was only the fox putting his nose out, sniffing the wind, growing cocky.

Outside, I just mooned around looking in bookshop windows most of the time, but about once a week I took a bus and went to my new friend, Julia's, photography studio, getting there in time for tea. At that hour, as I had learned, there were always several people at the studio, who came in every day and brought things to help out when they happened to have the money—biscuits, or sugar, or tea itself. I liked to go there because being an American was not a bad thing at Julia's. If anything, it was good. She and her friends had such a dread of being insular that they would have made me welcome even if they had disliked me personally. They didn't dislike me—they teased me, but they didn't dislike me. And so I had another place to relax in, as well as the Reading Room. I seldom missed a week at Julia's, and sometimes we indulged in little extra sprees that were inexpensive—a bus trip to see the gardens at Hampton Court when the tulips were in bloom, or a meal in Soho. I didn't really enjoy long jaunts, though. I felt guilty about neglecting the Reading Room.

When summer was an accomplished fact, a blow fell on me. I finished my job. It seemed unbelievable that this could have happened so quickly, and again and again I checked the list of what I was to have read and looked at the notebooks I had filled. But there was no doubt—I had read everything I was supposed to read, and some extra books as well. Logically, I should have been glad, for there was nothing now to keep me in England; I could pack and go and leave behind the things that had so distressed me—the black-smeared pavements, the foggy air, the unfriendly faces of strangers. Yet the more I thought about it, the less I liked the idea. It had been weeks since I'd noticed the pavements, and somehow people did not seem unfriendly anymore. I had evolved a life that included Miss Stuart and her milk bottle, Julia's tea hour, even the black chimney pots outside my window, and it suited me. I simply could not face leaving the Reading Room. For the first time, I felt sympathy for those permanent undergraduates who are to be found in American universities, taking degrees in one subject after another, frantically looking for new courses until they are tottering around the campus. Indeed, I resolved to behave like them, and look for a subject that would keep me busy a while longer at the British Museum, at least until I came to the end of my money. After considering various possibilities, I selected the Royal Society of London for Promoting Natural Knowledge, an august body that, since it had received its charter from Charles II soon after the Restoration, was sure to have plenty of history. I would have a lot of fun reading about the Royal Society, I told myself, and nobody need know—nobody would care—if I was doing it for a practical purpose or not. I started on it at once.

There it is. That's my life, or, at any rate, a large part of it. I can't claim to be the British Museum's most constant reader. I've gone away from time to time, and on occasion have remained absent for protracted periods, but I have always gone back. I decided, after a bit, that absences don't matter a lot in a place like that; the years make little or no difference. When I got back the first time, after two years in the Congo, I felt as if I'd never been away. The familiar benison fell gently on my head as I went into the Reading Room and took my old place in Aisle K. At lunchtime, there was Miss Stuart in the Ladies' Room, dressed in her shorts as always, and I reflected comfortably that the Museum had borrowed timelessness from its own Elgin marbles or from the Egyptian mummies upstairs.

But I had come to this conclusion too soon. A time arrived when I overdid things, and strained the patience of even as permanent a spirit as the Reading Room's, by staying away a full decade. It was 1946 when I returned that time, and I felt a nasty little shock as soon as I set foot in the entrance room. The Museum *had* changed. Dust was everywhere—underfoot and on the cases and in the air. Wooden supports held up the ceiling, and here and there were rough screens barring the public from certain rooms. The Museum had suffered a nearly direct hit from at least one bomb, I learned, and gossip had it that consultant architects were not quite happy about the state of the Reading Room's dome. Repairs and investigations accounted for the dust, but I felt that it had really been stirred up when the bomb fell and had not yet settled, though two years had elapsed.

Not unnaturally, I assumed that after such a long absence I would have to begin the routine all over again, from the ground up. Surely my permission to use the Reading Room would have lapsed, I thought, if only because the records had been scattered, so I went to the old office and asked for an application form. The attendant, when I explained the situation, was hurt and surprised. "But Madam," he said, "if you already hold a card, all you need do is hand it in and we'll issue you a new one."

I said, "Alas, I've lost it. I know it was careless of me, but I was in China, you see, and what with the war and one thing and another—"

"Oh, I quite understand," he said. His pleasantness did not relax one tittle. "In the circumstances, we'll give you a new card even though you can't turn in the old one. Now, let's see—what was the name?"

He picked up an ancient ledger, blew off some dust, and opened it at the right letter. There my name was, just where I'd written it years before. And as I took my card I forgot the thing that had disturbed me—the dust and the bomb and the sensation of being disjointed. I was back in the Reading Room, and all was well.

There I stayed until the warning bell rang. I was going out, sunk in the old familiar stupor, when a man addressed me by name just outside the door. He was a gray man—his suit was gray, and so was his hair, and his spectacled eyes must have been gray, too, but I could scarcely see them. His glasses seemed dusty, like his hair and shoulders. He said, "We used to read next to each other in Aisle K. I remember you."

I said, I am afraid untruly, that I remembered him as well, and we shook hands. "And what are you doing now?" I asked.

There was surprised reproach in his tone as he answered, "Why, still studying for my degree, of course."

I realize now that though the Reading Room didn't really change during the years I spent away from it, changes have come while I've been right there. It occurred to me with another shock, a couple of years ago, that Miss Stuart, of all people, has altered. I noticed, God knows how belatedly, that it is impossible to tell whether or not she is still wearing shorts, because, it has slowly dawned on me, nowadays her costume is covered, winter and summer, by a frayed mackintosh. Winter or summer, rain or shine, Miss Stuart keeps that raincoat tightly belted and buckled around her, and she now wears a hat as well—a thing like a basket pulled down over her straying, pepper-and-salt hair.

I noticed this the year we readers all had to move for a couple of months into the North Library, customarily reserved for rare editions and pornography, so that the building authorities would be free to shore up the Reading Room dome. Otherwise, it was said, everything might well come crashing down on our heads. In the North Library, an oblong room, we had to work side by side at long refectory-type tables instead of at our customary sheltered, high-fronted desks, and for many this interruption of habit constituted a trauma. That was how I came to notice Miss Stuart standing in line to pick up her reserved books; I had been jolted, and was looking around as a result. Even without the new outfit, she would have seemed unfamiliar against that strange background. On her face was a fierce scowl. I suppose readers in general behaved even more peculiarly than usual during the Diaspora. One afternoon in the North Library, I was chatting sotto-voce with the Superintendent. I had turned in my chair so that I could see him, standing behind me. All seemed quiet when suddenly he looked over my head and across the room, his face showing an expression that, for him—he was a controlled man—signified extreme horror. He said, aloud and sharply, "No, no, Mr. Schmidt!" I followed his gaze. Two attendants were already hurrying toward a stocky man with bristling cropped hair who was standing at his chair, books piled on the table in front of him, arms outstretched. One hand held an unlit cigarette, in the other was a burning lighter. He was not trying to apply the lighter's flame to the cigarette, but when he was sure he had got the room's attention he said loudly, "I wish to protest. Why are we not allowed to use the Reading Room? I—" At that moment, the attendants got hold of him, one arm each, and, after extinguishing the lighter, hustled him with kindly efficiency toward the door. All the way, Mr. Schmidt kept repeating, "I protest! I protest!" until he had been ejected and the door was closed behind him. The Superintendent, taking up our conversation exactly where it had dropped, carried it on as if nothing had happened. But he was again interrupted, by one of the attendants who had taken Mr. Schmidt away. Somewhat breathless, but in a calm manner, this man asked what was to be done about Mr. Schmidt's books, and the Superintendent lifted his eyebrows, indicating that it was a question that should not have been asked.

"Are they still there at his place?" he inquired coldly.

"Yes, sir."

The Superintendent gave an impatient flick of the fingers. "Well, put them on reserve, put them on reserve for Mr. Schmidt."

Marginal notes, especially when I come upon them in a library book, are apt to startle me. One day, after we were back in the Reading Room, I found a marginal note in a Reading Room copy of Otway. In the preface, the author had spoken of Queen Elizabeth, referring to her as "the Virgin Queen," and the marginal commentator evidently had taken this amiss. Purple ink double-underlined the word "Virgin." In the margin, in the same ink, were written the words "Ha! Ha! Of such is history!"

No doubt I am foolish, but the thing haunted me. Who had done it? It must have been some other regular reader, I reflected. I reminded myself that we are a peculiar lot, and wondered how long it would be before I, too, became certifiable. I turned in the Otway without reporting my discovery—why borrow trouble?—but I went on thinking about it, and talking about it, too. I talked about it to a girl I was introduced to in a nearby lunchroom—a girl who was just starting out on her career in the Museum. She said eagerly, "Oh, I know exactly what you mean. It's quite frightening. I've been sitting in Aisle G, next to that crazy old woman in the mackintosh—you know the one? Well, yesterday I saw that she had a big book and she was spitting on it."

"Spitting?"

"Yes, that's what I said. She would spit on a page, then turn it over and spit on the next. She was very careful not to miss a single page. Well, I wondered—"

"Wait a minute," I said. "What sort of book was it?" I was aware that I had never yet tried to find out what subject Miss Stuart had been working on all those years.

The girl said, "It was some Victorian tome—*Lives of the Popes*. I didn't quite know what to do. One hates to be a tattletale, doesn't one? Besides, it's borrowing trouble. But in the end my social conscience prevailed and I knew I had to report it. To keep her from realizing what I was doing, I made the most devious trip to the desk, consulting *Who's Who* in that case over by the main entrance and then looking up something in the O.E.D. Finally, I got to the desk and told my story to one of the men. I must say, he took it very calmly, and he was awfully nice when I asked him not to give me away. He told me to go back to my desk and not to worry. I did so, and he waited a full five minutes before he did anything—*ever* so nice he was. When he got there, she was still spitting away, and he said, 'Now, Miss Stuart, you know you aren't to do that. You've been told before.' He took the book away from her and carried it off—I suppose to be fumigated. The woman just sat there without moving for a minute, and I kept my eyes on my work. Then she leaned sideways toward me and hissed, under her breath, *'Papist spy!'* " The girl paused, pondering unhappily. "Tomorrow, perhaps I'd better move to Aisle F," she said at last, and sighed.

STEWART

It would be exaggeration if I said that Stewart Cass, as I shall here call him, was responsible for my going to the Belgian Congo. I am sure I'd have got there somehow in any case, but certainly he speeded things up by listening to me as he did the evening we met at a party. I became garrulous when I learned that Stewart not only knew the Congo well but actually lived there. This, I felt, was a most fortunate encounter. Ever since my sophomore year in college, six years earlier, I had thought about the Congo and longed to see it. Africa was an unusual hobby for a young woman in the late nineteen-twenties, and, as

I had learned by painful experience, most men didn't understand my ambition to go there. But Stewart listened, and he answered questions just as if I were in my right mind, though it couldn't have been easy to cope with all I asked him. I wanted to know the sort of thing I couldn't find in books and the steel engravings that illustrated them, such as whether or not the forest was full of color, how one managed to avoid crocodiles when bathing, and if it was always necessary to hack one's way through the underbrush. Patiently and politely, Stewart set me right on these matters and on others, until, by the end of the evening, I had a definite picture of the Congo in my mind. I saw the country clearly—a region where the sky was hidden by a high, leafy roof, where tree trunks were smooth as organ pipes, and, in the absence of sunlight, all was brown and black until you tipped back your head and looked up. There, where the trees had succeeded in climbing out of the shade, they burst into rich green foliage, much, I imagined, as the *Tannhäuser* pilgrims burst into song.

Stewart talked a good deal, too, about the Africans, whom he seemed to know as well as I knew the neighbors next door in my New York apartment house. This was not surprising, for he was an anthropologist. I had learned earlier, from the general conversation, that he had long been collecting material in the Congo, preparing for a dissertation on one of the tribes there. Indeed, a friend of his, the man who had brought him, seemed to think that Stewart was taking an excessive amount of time on the job, for while we were talking he called out boisterously, "You ever going to finish that thing, Stew? Personally, I think it's all an excuse to lead the life of Riley down there. Doesn't he look like the Great White Father, with that beard?" he asked the company at large. "It would be a shame to have to shave that off."

Stewart laughed good-humoredly, stroking his beard, and as soon as the spotlight was off him I moved in again with more questions. On practical matters, as well as natural ones, he was a valuable adviser. He was informed about shipping lines, the names of towns along the Congo River, and the worth of the

Belgian franc in American money. He had been to the region I was especially determined to see—Lake Kivu—and he described it for me. I forgot no word of what he said that evening, because all of it was important to me, but the most striking aspect of our encounter was his placid acceptance of my intention to visit the Congo. Stewart, I found, was from Boston, whose women evidently did unexpected things—riding alone through the Andes, walking across the continent, teaching in China—without incurring the opprobrium or even attracting the attention of other Bostonians. I thought that clearly I must revise my ideas of New England; Boston was a better place than I had supposed.

Of course, I saw Stewart soon again. If he hadn't followed up the acquaintance himself, I would have gone against my mother's strict rule ("No young lady ever calls a man. He wouldn't respect her if she did") and telephoned him, but he saved me from that ultimate degradation, and we went out together several times. We went to the Bronx Zoo and looked at African animals. We visited the Museum of Natural History. Once, he took me to the apartment where he lived with friends, to introduce me to a young female chimpanzee he had brought home. When he was about to leave for Belgium, we had dinner and talked for hours over the coffee. I told him how my ideas about Boston had changed, and he said, "If I were you, I'd suspend judgment on that. Boston's not so bad, but it's not perfect. As a matter of fact—" Here he bit off whatever he was going to say. I couldn't make out what his expression was, because of the beard. Beards take a bit of knowing. Later, I was able to read Stewart's face in spite of his, but I was new to the game that night. He started again: "I prefer living where I do, in the Congo. Boston's all right for a visit—I enjoy seeing my family, of course. At least, I used to."

"What does that mean?" I asked.

"I think I'll tell you about it," said Stewart. "If you're really coming out to Africa, and I guess you are, you'll have to know about it anyway." I flushed with pleasure, because he had said, "and I guess you are."

He was telling me, I soon realized, the story of his life, saying that he had first gone to the Congo as a member of a university expedition, intending to remain there for one scholastic year, the term agreed upon for the party. All the young men had anthropologized to their hearts' content in the Ituri Forest, and the year drew to a close. On what was supposed to be the last day, Stewart decided to go out on one more hunting trip. His guide was leading him along an elephant track that was promisingly fresh when suddenly they came upon the elephant himself, feeding in a banana grove. The animal spotted them just as they spotted him, and came at them. The guide made his escape, but Stewart tripped on a root and fell sprawling. "The last thing I remember is the way the elephant looked, standing over me," he said. "Then he gored me, and everything's gone from my mind, because I fainted. Fortunately, he was a big fellow, and his tusks were so wide apart that one of them missed me altogether, though the other hooked me in the side. He didn't take time to trample me and finish the job—the guide made a racket and distracted him."

After the goring, Stewart hadn't been able to travel. A doctor from a mission hospital said it would be six weeks at least before he could get up. The doctor had found a woman in the village where the expedition had been camping who, he said, would do as a nurse. The other boys had to go home; examinations were in the offing.

"Abanzima took wonderful care of me," said Stewart. "She got me back on my feet before the doctor expected it. If I don't owe my life to her, exactly, I do owe my health. In short," he went on, with one of the little rushes of speech that by now I knew were characteristic, "I got very fond of the girl. And that was when the trouble started. Our crazy ideas—the crazy ideas we have in this country! If Abanzima had been white, we'd have got married. She could have come home with me. She'd have been here right now, staying with my family."

He paused for such a long time, stirring his coffee and staring into it, that I urged him on. "And as it is?"

"As it is, I'm not saying I'm beaten," said Stewart. "I may

141

marry her yet, but even so I certainly won't be able to bring her home. I realize that now, though I didn't when I was in the Ituri. I used to think that if I gave my father and mother enough time to get used to the idea— But it wouldn't have worked. I've found that out by trying to talk it over sensibly with them. I used to think they were reasonable people, but on this subject at least they aren't." He frowned. "My mother has always been a well-balanced woman, but do you know what she did after she'd heard about Abanzima? She fired the colored maid. Yes, she did, and, what's more, she said she would never have another Negro servant in the house."

We were both silent for a while. I couldn't have spoken even if I had tried to. In my eyes, Stewart was a classic figure of tragedy.

He went on. "What I'm trying to do now is arrange things so that I can spend the rest of my life in the Congo. It's not simply a matter of *deciding* to do it. The Belgians are the bosses, and they're apt to be suspicious of anyone hanging around without reasonable cause—or what they consider reasonable."

I nodded wisely. "They wouldn't approve of your staying on Abanzima's account."

"Oh, they don't mind my living with her," said Stewart. "They wouldn't understand my wanting to stay just for her, that's it. Most of the white men there, if their wives aren't with them, have black mistresses—they call them *ménagères*." He said this casually, and I attempted to look as if I, too, was taking it casually, though in fact I was badly shocked. True love like Stewart's for his Abanzima was one thing; a *ménagère* was quite another. But he was talking now about his practical plans. The Belgian government needed men to stay in the Congo as medical officers. Men were so badly wanted that the government didn't insist on fully qualified doctors for these posts but, through the Red Cross, gave a short course designed to turn out people trained to some extent who could maintain census posts in the forest and administer a certain amount of medical care. The course was given near Brussels, and Stewart had already signed up for it. If all went well, he would be back with Abanzima in three months, a Red Cross medical officer in good standing.

"But the lectures and lessons will be in French, won't they?" I asked.

"Oh, yes," said Stewart carelessly. He'd have to work that much harder, that was all. This part of his plan impressed me more than all the rest of it, which is saying a good deal. And often in the following days, after I'd said goodbye and good luck to Stewart, I thought of his story, I saw Abanzima in my imagination—a combination Undine and Madame Butterfly, wild and graceful, and prey to fears that I could hardly understand as she wondered if her alien lover would ever return. As a result of these reveries, the Congo became more than ever alluring to me.

Stewart and I kept in touch. About once a week, a letter came from Brussels saying that he was managing well in spite of the language problem. Then, a few months later, I went to England, and Stewart suggested that I go over to Belgium and visit his household. He occupied a suburban apartment, in company with his chimpanzee, Chimpo. I accepted the invitation, and as I got aboard the cross-Channel steamer I reflected that it was really, in a way, the beginning of my own trip to Africa. My breath came short at the thought.

I found the two exiles living in Continental splendor, in big rooms that filled a whole floor of a house, fitted out with massive doors and high, shuttered windows. To be sure, these rooms were practically empty, because of Chimpo's bad effect on the landlady's furniture. Chimpo had grown bigger, and was developing a mind of her own. Stewart had kept a bed and a dresser for me in a back room, the door of which could be locked, but there was nothing else in the apartment except his trunk, a mattress on the floor, and one gigantic wardrobe with handles strong enough to hold the chimpanzee when she was chained to them, as she often was. In fact, the chain padlocked around her neck was a regular part of Chimpo, because Stewart found it the only means by which he could catch or otherwise manage her. Most

143

of the time, it merely dragged along behind her. On occasion, she would gather it up as a lady gathers her train, carrying it as she ran away from some retribution or other, but even then it slowed her down.

The morning after I arrived, Stewart attached the other end of the chain to the wardrobe, padlocked it, and gave me the key before starting off to his class. "I used to leave her free when I went out, but I had to stop that," he said. "She learned to open the windows, and she climbed out and bothered the neighbors. You can let her off, of course, if you've simply got to; otherwise, I wouldn't advise it."

"What do you mean, if I've simply got to?" I asked.

Stewart's reply came after a slight hesitation. "Well, when my mother was here early last month, I had to leave her alone with Chimpo in the mornings, and Chimpo was chained up like this, and I guess she finally got bored. She got hold of Mother one day and didn't let go until I got back, in about five hours. Every time Mother felt Chimpo's grip relax, she'd start to move away, and Chimpo would bite her and hang on harder than ever. By the end of those five hours, Mother was pretty mad."

"I see." I moved out of the chimpanzee's reach.

"You'll probably be all right," Stewart called cheerfully, going out with his books.

Chimpo busied herself with her own affairs, as I with mine. I kept well clear while she chewed the corner of the wardrobe, then practiced high diving from the top of it to the floor—thump, thump, thump—over and over. Everything was all right until I went to fetch the newspaper on the far side of the room. I tried to slip by at a distance I considered safe, but the chimpanzee, who was lying on the floor in what appeared to be a pensive mood, suddenly whirled around on her bottom and, stretching out, reached my skirt with her foot. Before I could get out of the skirt, she had pulled me over and was holding me fast by the leg, and Mrs. Cass's experience would have been repeated if I hadn't had the padlock key in my pocket. As it was, I unlocked the chain. One good turn deserves another. Chimpo immediately released me. For the rest of the day, we were on friendly terms.

144

I even allowed her to open the door for the grocery boy. I had hoped to surprise him, but he didn't turn a hair. He addressed Chimpo in her own language, a coughing grunt, and walked in, unconcerned, to put down the groceries.

"Ah, yes," he said when I expressed surprise, "I've done my time in the Congo." He tousled Chimpo's head on the way out.

After Brussels, being back in London seemed very dull, and I wasted much time daydreaming about leopards, palm trees, and rivers sluggish in the sun. Stewart passed his examinations, and when I next heard from him he was reunited with Abanzima and working in a village called Tange, on the Ituri River. His letters were heavy, but in tissue-paper envelopes on which the ink was often smeared by water. As the time of my departure grew nearer, he wrote every few days with last-minute requests for purchases he wanted me to make. He wanted hair clippers, for one thing, and a certain kind of tinned butter—one tin only, so that he could experiment with its staying qualities before ordering crates of it. The list grew enormously long. In return for getting these things, he sent me lots of information on ships and advice about supplies. It was through Stewart that I found a French shipping line that offered remarkably cheap third-class passage from Bordeaux to Boma, on the west coast of Africa, and I went straight off to buy my ticket. Economy was important to me. I was taking along enough money—jut enough, as it turned out—to get me there, and leaving behind the rest of what I had saved, which was to follow me in three months. In the line's office, I had a long argument with a clerk, and then with the manager. In all their years of experience, said these gentle-men, they had never heard a woman of any color propose to travel third class on their ships. When pressed, however, the manager admitted that there was no written rule against it, and he had to give in.

There were further arguments when I bought my supplies. In an elegant Bond Street shop that supplied everything in the world for big-game hunters in tropical countries. I gave my order along the lines advised by Stewart. The frock-coated salesman—

himself as soft-footed as any wild thing of the forest—was startled into raising his voice. Only twelve tin chests? So few pairs of khaki shorts? What about a tent and a bathtub? He declared it sheer suicide to venture into Africa without what he considered the proper accoutrements. But I resisted. I had been advised by an expert. One didn't need a tent, I told the salesman. Quoting Stewart, I declared that a traveller in the forest simply paused in a village before night fell, and paid a few francs for the loan of one of the native houses. As for the bathtub, the Congo was full of rivers, not to mention Lake Kivu. "It's a mistake to carry a lot of stuff," I said severely. "It means more porters, and that means more food for them—a lot more expense all around. Haven't you found yourself that it's best to keep things simple on safari?"

"I?" said the salesman, suddenly thawing. "Miss, the furthest I've ever been from London is Brighton."

Tange was nearer the Congo River, on which I was to make most of the trip from Boma, than Lake Kivu was. Kivu was southeast, at the border of Ruanda-Urundi. It therefore seemed logical, if the word "logical" can be applied to my journey at all, to stop off with Stewart's household first, and so I planned it. I was seven or eight weeks getting to Tange, and ran many gantlets, from the European end, where the Bordeaux porters were rude about my tin trunks (each to carry no more than thirty pounds, the approved weight for an African bearer), through the voyage itself.

Third class was comfortable enough. As a matter of fact, there was a fourth class, too—a fact I hadn't realized when I booked, or I'd have had a shot at it. Fourth class was full of African troops and chickens; third class, except for me, was occupied by noncommissioned officers on their way to the French Congo— swarthy, undersized men from Marseille and Corsica, with deep voices and five-o'clock shadow. They were polite to me but often quarrelled with each other, and most nights were noisy after I had gone to bed. During the trip, I picked up a Midi accent and a number of idioms I hadn't been taught in high school. Bordeaux was raw, rainy, and generally depressing, and after we were at sea I was sick for a while, but when we had paused at Madeira and were making for Casablanca, summer was suddenly upon us. Every day the sea was more blue, the sun yellower. Here and there, we third-class passengers had a bit of deck space the size of a man's handkerchief, and in one of these clearings at the stern of the ship I would lean on the rail for hours, staring down at a shark that followed us faithfully the whole way.

I think I was stupefied for the first fortnight. Not until we anchored offshore at Dakar, in Senegal, did I realize where I was. A line of palm trees like green sentinels stood at attention back of the harshly bright yellow sand of the beach, and all of a sudden I knew I was there, in Africa—that I wasn't looking at a picture in an atlas, or reading Conrad. I myself was there. The women walking along the beach with babies slung on their backs, in dresses of cotton printed with huge blobs of color—they were real. Somewhere over there on the other side of the palm trees were their houses. I wondered if Abanzima wore clothes like theirs, and if any of them resembled her. Now I felt impatient of the ship, anxious to get off it and into the country. The rest of the voyage seemed very long until I disembarked at Boma.

Then came a train, a paddle-wheeler up the Congo, Stanley-ville, where I stayed for several days, and a truck that took me up the last bit of road, leading to the roadless forest. There I was unloaded at a dock on the bank of the Ituri River, and found the canoe Stewart had sent for his mail and me—a long, heavy craft that even English-speaking Congolese called a pi-rogue. It was poled or paddled, depending on necessity, by tattooed men in loincloths. For a long day, they and I moved upriver toward Tange, and I had the strange sensation all along that I just wasn't there at all. They couldn't communicate with me nor I with them, so they took the tactful way out by pretend-ing I was part of the mail, nothing more. When they spoke to each other, their voices were resonant. Often they burst into song, hitting the side of the pirogue with the paddles to stress a beat. Now and then we passed another boat going in the opposite direction, and then all the boatmen chatted back and forth until they were far out of sight of each other. They could make their voices carry, somehow, without raising them.

We moved on oily black water between banks where the forest crowded to the brink, trees jostling for foothold. Here and there, infrequently, a clearing moved into view—a space, open for about twenty yards, in which a path could be seen leading to the water, and in the distance a little jumble of clay-walled houses. Sometimes there were women and children playing in the water. They, too, carried on long conversations with my boatmen. Often everyone shouted with laughter, so that I longed to know the joke. We stopped for a rest at one of these places. People stood around and stared as I ate the box lunch I'd brought from the Stanleyville hotel. In such circumstances, it was hard to chew in a natural manner. Eventually, I fought back by staring at them, especially the women, asking myself if any of them were like Abanzima. I didn't think they could be. I could see no beauty in any of these females, hair twisted into rows of tiny topknots like coiled wire, some of the bodies bare above the waist. So many pairs of naked breasts abashed me, especially as few of them were up to Greek or Balinese standards.

It was dark when we reached Tange. Long before the pirogue turned in toward the bank, the boatmen called out and received a reply in that effortless conversational tone of voice that seemed able to travel any distance. As we approached, a line of little lights moved through the dark, tracing a zigzag pathway down what appeared to be a steep slope. The boat was beached, and I climbed out, moving stiffly. A familiar coughing noise warned me of what to expect just before Chimpo hurtled out of the darkness to embrace me. Stewart appeared in her wake, teeth showing through his beard in the torchlight, and we shook hands. Commandingly, he said over his shoulder, "Abanzima!"

She approached, giggling in a shy way, and I took her outstretched hand. My gesture was mechanical; I was overcome with surprise and dismay. Though it was dark on the beach, I could see that my Undine, my maiden of classic tragedy, was no beauty. Why, she was an old woman! The teeth now showing in a welcoming smile were filed to points, her bare breasts were shrivelled, and her head—this was the worst shock of all—was shaved smooth as a billiard ball. In a daze, I walked up the bluff with the others, in single file, quite forgetting to observe that my tin boxes had at last found the mode of carriage they had been made for; they were all neatly balanced on African heads.

We came to a large house—large, that is, by Congo standards—and went into a room with many books and boxes in it, a wooden table for a desk, camp chairs, and a cot with sheets and a mosquito net. A pressure lamp threw a bright light over everything.

"You're to sleep here a night or so," Stewart explained, as Abanzima went out one of the back doors on an errand. "Until I was positive you were on the way, I didn't get the boys to work building your house."

"A house for me?" I asked in amazement. "But I'm only visiting, not staying here."

"There's not that much labor involved, and when you go—if you go—I'll be able to use it," he said. "Now you're here, though, it would be foolish to hurry off. People make long visits in Africa, you know."

Members of the household filed in to put down the luggage, and when it was all there we started opening some of the things Stewart had ordered. Chimpo kept getting in the way until Stewart took her to the veranda, a wide, roofed affair that ran all around the house, and chained her. By this time, I realized that we were being watched by a large, rapt audience out in the dark. We were actors on a bright stage. The audience was quiet, but I could hear some sounds—heavy breathing, a soft whisper, an occasional inadvertent squeal of wonder. Stewart did not seem at all self-conscious about the watchers. Imperturbably, he went on opening crates, and I, in loyal imitation, unpacked. While I was at Tange, I imitated Stewart in every way I could, until near the end.

Abanzima came back with a tray, followed by two more women similarly laden. They cleared off part of the table and set down food for us to eat. Evidently, it was for Stewart and me alone. When I asked if Abanzima wasn't going to eat with us, he shook his head and said she didn't, except on special occasions. The Congolese were very casual about their food, he explained. Abanzima stood watching me, her small brown eyes attentive as a lip reader's. When she caught my eye, she burst into a high cackle of laughter, covering her mouth and rocking her body. Stewart smiled—a thing he didn't do often or easily—saying, "She likes you."

Oh, well, perhaps she wasn't so very ugly after all, I decided. Nor was she as old as I had thought. It was cicatrization that marked her face and her chest, not wrinkles, as I'd at first supposed, and I was getting used to it. She'd cut her hair, Stewart explained, to make it grow better. Eating chicken and rice with palm oil, I took stock of the two other girls, each of whom had come forward as soon as she set down her tray to offer her hand. The taller, Nambedru, had a strangely shaped head—elongated, with hair parted and plaited in strips, or stripes, that ran from front to back like marks on a melon. In fact, her head would have looked exactly like a melon if it hadn't been for her eyes. They were beautiful—enormous, set very wide apart, and slightly tilted at the outer corners above high cheekbones. Sissy, the other girl, was small and had a pleasant, rather scared smile. Both were cicatrized and both had filed teeth, like Abanzima's—another feature that I had learned by the end of supper to take for granted.

Nambedru brought a teapot and filled our cups, serving Stewart first, as she had done all through the meal. "They always serve the men first," he explained. "It would only confuse them if I tried to change the custom."

Nambedru looked critically at the table and leaned over to take away a ketchup bottle, and Stewart tugged playfully at her ear and said something that made her giggle wildly. She retreated in a coltish stumble, and he watched kindly, saying, "She'll learn. She's still pretty young—just came from her village a month or two ago."

"How old is she?"

"Oh, they never know, but I should guess she's about fourteen. She and Abanzima are Mangbetu, you know—they're cousins of some sort. It's a very interesting tribe. Its region is farther north. You don't find many around here. They have a custom of wrapping their babies' heads with tight bandages as soon as they're born, and the skull is deformed while it's still soft. You've noticed how long her head is? I don't know why Abanzima's isn't the same, but her mother died in childbirth and probably nobody else took the trouble to wrap her head." I said that was a good thing, naturally assuming that a man would not care for a melon-headed wife, but Stewart didn't understand. He merely shrugged, and said that the practice didn't seem to affect Mangbetu faculties in any way.

"And is Sissy also a Mangbetu?" I asked.

"No," said Stewart. "Sissy comes from this village, in a way. Her father's from the local tribe and her mother's a pygmy. You could see it if you knew pygmies—those turned-out lips and the lighter color of her hair. I only got her last week."

At the moment, the implication of that speech was lost on me, for I supposed it was merely my host's way of referring to servant hiring. At any rate, I was too sleepy to go out of my way to find implications. Stewart suggested that I go to bed, and said that I was obviously so sleepy that I wouldn't mind if he went on working at his letters across the room at the desk. So that I might undress alone, in the dark, he carried out the lamp for a few minutes, giving rise to disappointed murmurs outside.

My little house was soon ready, and I became part of the establishment. I fitted into the somewhat wacky routine as smoothly as if I'd always been there, and the local people called me "the doctor's sister." Each morning, I went along with Stewart to the hospital, as the consultation building was called, and watched him deal with people who had malaria, or yaws, or stomach ailments, or festering wounds. He gave injections for VD, and filled in an endless series of forms for the authorities in Brussels. I learned how to bandage and take blood samples and remove chigoes from under toenails, how to label bottles and apportion medicine. The first Swahili words that I picked up were medical. I learned not to go to the outhouse at night without a sentry—as we called the watchman—who brought along a lantern, for fear of leopards. I learned how to sit inert in a pirogue when it was near crocodiles. I made a contribution to the general welfare by figuring out a way to feed Chimpo only the stuff we wanted her to eat and keep her from stealing our delicacies. If I wrapped her food carefully, with furtive looks over the shoulder, and carried it to the cupboard and made a great show of hiding it, Chimpo would rush over and snatch it out of my hand. Then she would gallop out-of-doors, chortling, while I chased her and shouted. I felt it obligatory to chase her. With the prize clutched in one foot, she would climb her favorite tree, perch on a branch just out of reach, and eat the food as fast as she could stuff it in, watching with satisfaction as I yelled and shook my fist. It was a long procedure, but why not? We had all the time in the world in Tange.

One way and another, I acquired a good education in Ituri ways, though an important part of my training was surprisingly delayed—my realization that Nambedru and Sissy were not merely domestics. I tumbled at last when Stewart and I were shopping in the market and he paid for a length of printed cotton, saying idly, "It's a funny thing how much three wives can cost a man, even in the Congo."

I was terribly shocked; in fact, I felt as if I'd been slapped in the face. What of that beautiful love story now? I simply could not understand how a man could claim to love a woman, as Stewart had said he loved Abanzima, and yet take on another girl— no, *two* other girls. No doubt I could have asked him these questions without giving offense; perhaps he even expected me to. If I had, he would have replied in his most detached manner that these women were used to polygamy and would have felt out of place in a monogamous society. But I was too staggered to discuss the thing at all. For weeks, I scrupulously avoided any mention of these relationships. If Stewart caressed any of the girls, even Abanzima, in my presence, I averted my eyes. Yet somehow or other, in time, I got used to the situation.

After all, it was the way everybody around us lived. The chief of the village had six or seven wives, and every male who could afford the bride price of goats and spears and money had at least one or two extra. Abanzima never showed any resentment; she would get angry at other things quite often and pout for hours while Stewart tried gently to coax her back into laughter, but she didn't seem jealous. In fact, as I reflected sadly, it was I who was out of step. Whenever I made some new male acquaintance in the villages round about, he invariably asked me severely, "Where is your master?," or, in another version, "Where is your husband?," for both ideas were expressed by the same word in the vernacular. So I did get used to the situation, but there is a difference between accepting the status quo and approving it. For one thing, no matter what Stewart said, I couldn't believe that the girls really liked the setup. Most of the time, Abanzima and Nambedru got along pretty well, because, Stewart said, they were related and called each other "sister." He said, "They'd naturally look out for each other, but they regard anybody from another tribe as an intruder and a threat."

"Then how do they feel about Sissy?" I asked.

"Oh, of course they hate Sissy. I've got to keep an eye on things in that quarter, or they'd take advantage of her. As it is, Abanzima never misses a chance to tell me awful things about her." He chuckled—fatuously, it seemed to me.

"I think it's hard on her then," I said.

"Do you?" His air of certainty irritated yet intimidated me. "It isn't really. Sissy's in her home town, she's got relatives here —but the others aren't native to this part of the forest. I guess it evens itself out."

More weeks passed. Even before I learned that there would be a long delay in getting my second stipend—the sum I'd intended would take me back to America, after Kivu—I had become so much a part of Tange, or vice versa, that I made no firm plans for going away. Once or twice, I proposed a departure date, but Stewart always had objections, and finally we agreed that I might as well count on a year, or even two, at Tange. As he said, things

153

sounded pretty depressing back in New York. Actually, we didn't want to alter the state of affairs, simply because to do so was too much trouble. The air had that effect. There were no seasonal changes as we know them in America—no bracing autumn breezes, only the rainy and the dry months, and in Tange even these weren't clearly separated; I recall wet days and dry days, but no pattern. Once in a great while, some Belgian official or other would come along, on a tour of inspection or doing a little hunting. Usually these men were accompanied by *ménagères*, who were entertained by Stewart's wives while the gentlemen talked. Such guests never stayed more than a night or two, but even that short a visit seemed to me an interruption rather than a wistful reminder of life outside. Letters from home didn't bother me in the same way—I could enjoy them because I was free to choose my own time to reply—but visitors called for effort. Not that I was lazy. I wasn't. In Tange fashion, I lived strenuously, making expeditions by pirogue to other villages and busying myself with the clinic, as well as with a variety of animals— a baby wild pig, a very young baboon and about eight others who were older, five or six goats, other monkeys, a parrot, and a deer. But I didn't like social effort. I liked peaceful afternoons when nothing happened, when Chimpo slept in a cool spot, her arms outflung, and chickens strutted and pecked, when somebody down on the riverbank conversed gently with somebody else hundreds of yards away on the other side, and the goats bleated, and the girls did each other's hair. At such times, all three of them got on well, gathered on that part of the veranda that overlooked the yard where they cooked. Our European meals were prepared by a man, but each girl had her own fire and cooking pot.

On one such afternoon, sitting on my own porch nearby, it dawned on me that Abanzima's head was now covered with hair like those of her co-wives. This meant that I had been in Tange a long time, I reflected comfortably, and I realized also that I'd got used to Abanzima's looks. I could even see prettiness in her, and I thought back to a recent evening when she had seemed quite charming. All the women gave themselves a lot of baths.

Two or three times a day, a girl would carry a bucket of water out to a clump of bushes near the house, strip, and pour water over herself. That evening, Abanzima had gone out with her bucket, only to find, after she had taken off her dress, that she'd forgotten to bring any soap, so she went back to the house to get it without dressing again. Being stark-naked didn't bother her, of course, since clothing in the Congo, at least for people at home there, was a status symbol rather than a modesty preserver. However, one of the occasional visiting Belgians had dropped in a few minutes earlier, unbeknownst to Abanzima, and he was on the front stoop, having a drink with Stewart and me, just as Abanzima ran across the lawn. A stranger was not the same thing as a member of the household, so Abanzima, in the posture of the Capitoline Venus, shielded herself with both hands as she passed us, smiling her best society smile. Yes, Abanzima was pretty, I told myself; time disposes of aesthetic prejudices.

Time had taught me a great deal more, I reflected, now thinking of Melina, who came occasionally to visit me. She was an ex-wife of Saidi, the village chieftain, and she had been his favorite until the astonishing day when she left him. In the Congo, girls did not usually walk out on chiefs. When they did, it was for love of somebody else. But Melina hadn't run away with a lover. Nor had she been kicked out. She had simply left, calmly and definitely. When I asked her why, she said, "I didn't like him."

That Melina didn't like Saidi was hardly surprising—he was a wretched little man, without beauty or common sense—but merely disliking one's husband wasn't a reasonable excuse, by Congo standards, for a woman's doing such an extraordinary thing. Furthermore, her parents refused to let her come home to them—they were understandably afraid of being embroiled in a quarrel with the royal house—so Melina lived alone. It was an unheard-of situation. "What does she *do*?" I once asked Sabani, one of our servants. "What does she live on?"

He said, "She walks and walks by the river."

It was a poetic expression, and it pleased me. I liked to think of Melina walking by the water like a dreamy, calm Ophelia. But Sabani hadn't answered my question; I still didn't know how Melina fitted into the village economic system. Finally, Stewart explained. Melina had become a streetwalker, he said, though, strictly speaking, Tange had no streets. Sabani hadn't been able to put the situation into the right words because there were as yet no words in the language to describe Melina's profession. She had had no predecessors.

On another afternoon, a few days later, I sat on my veranda feeling hungry and wondering why the dinner bell hadn't rung. Usually Nambedru rang it, running around the house and calling "Food! Food!," but today I had heard nothing, though the sun was setting and it was past dinnertime. At last, I walked over to the other side of the house and found a group of women —Abanzima, Sissy, and a couple of friends—gathered around Nambedru, who was crouching on a stool and sniffling. Her head was freshly bald. The other girls were plainly furious. I asked what the matter was, and Abanzima replied bitterly only that it was Stewart's fault.

I went in search of him. He was working quietly in his office. When I asked what was going on, he answered impatiently, like a man with more important matters on his mind than women. "I shaved Nambedru's head," he said. "Her hair was getting too long. That is, I clipped it. There was some row with Sissy over plaiting it, so I put an end to that."

Shock took away my breath for a moment, and then I said, "She's crying out there, Stewart. You told me they don't mind having their heads shaved, but—"

"Well, it seems I was mistaken," said Stewart, bored, and then he shouted for dinner.

Though I was hungry, I hoped it wouldn't come. I wanted the girls to rebel. But it did come, almost immediately, and Nambedru carried her tray in with the others, though her brow, under her naked head, was wrinkled with resentment and grief.

That night, in bed, I expended much indignant thought on the subject and lost a good deal of sleep over it, so it was not as gratifying as it should have been when, next morning, Nambedru appeared in her normal happy mood, laughing and chattering with the other girls just as if there had been no crisis at all. Once again, I reflected, I had let emotion outrun reason. I had applied my American prejudices and principles to a culture wholly different from my own. Even so, my feelings toward Stewart had changed. That afternoon, when the whole household went swimming and divided as he ordered, women in one bend of the river and himself and the boatmen in another, I heard him expounding something, and the sound of his voice, heavily authoritative, made the skin on the back of my neck prickle unpleasantly.

The prickling returned often after that, and it was a relief when one of our Belgian acquaintances arrived a little later on a tour. He was planning to hunt elephants a day's journey from Tange, and when he suggested that I go along I leaped at the invitation. Stewart, surprised, pointed out that I had often expressed abhorrence for big-game shooting, and I had to say, lamely, that everybody ought to do a thing at least once before condemning it.

So I went hunting. The official habitually travelled by tipoye, the native sedan chair carried by four men. I had always been opposed to tipoyes, because Stewart was, and I often quoted him to the effect that anyone not crippled ought to walk in the forest, especially on a hunting safari. But the official, naturally, objected to riding while I walked, and as he also objected to walking, I had to ride. It was a bumpy business. Clearly, tipoye-riding was not only wrong in principle but uncomfortable. By the time *Monsieur*, aided by a local chief and any number of trackers, had got his elephant, I was heartily sorry I had ever gone along. The thought of Tange seemed good once more, and my liverish dislike of Stewart was sweated out. I left the Belgian official before the next leg of his trip and went home to Tange by pirogue.

The landing was deserted when I arrived. Nobody was in sight even at the top of the bluff, and as I climbed I wondered why. At the top, I saw some sort of activity near the house, but I couldn't make it out until I had got there and stepped up on

157

the porch. "Hi!" I called. Chimpo answered from somewhere with a burst of coughing, but there was no glad rush to embrace me, not even a jangle of chains, so I presumed she was tied up. I walked along the veranda and around the corner, where I stopped short. Under the branches of a large tree in the middle of the lawn stood Abanzima, her head hanging. She lifted it and glanced at me, and then it drooped again. A collar like Chimpo's was padlocked around her neck, and a chain tethered her to the tree's trunk. The male cook was squatting close by, chopping something in a bowl. He gave me a furtive look, said, "Salaam, Madamu," and bent again to his work. Around the corner came Sissy, who stopped when she saw me and rapidly reversed, disappearing.

I went to the office and found Stewart, working as usual at his papers. He looked as if he had been suffering one of his periodic bouts of malaria. "Oh, hello," he said. "Back, are you?"

I fell into a chair opposite him and said, "Now what?"

He told me. He had caught Abanzima *in flagrante delicto* with one of the local men, he said in a voice shaking with rage, and this was part of her punishment. Unable to bring himself to send her away, he had tied her bed to her back and made her walk through the village. Now, to expiate her sin further, she must spend every day for a week tied to the tree from sunrise to sunset.

Nobody could have argued with Stewart at that moment. Certainly I didn't. I merely asked where Nambedru was, and he said that as she had been in on the affair, he'd packed her off home to her native village. "What's more, I'm demanding the bride price back from her parents," he said. "Not that I've got a hope in hell of getting it."

I suppose I might have argued. I could have reminded him that he had often told me of unfaithful wives in the neighborhood and of the freedom of Congo morals. I might have, but I didn't. Going to my house to unpack, I took the back road, so that I wouldn't have to observe Abanzima's disgrace again. For the rest of the week, I did the same thing. I didn't discuss the situation with anyone, not even Sabani or Melina. Melina didn't come near the house anyway. Then, one day, Abanzima wasn't tied up anymore but came into the house and was just as she had been before, except that she was quieter now that there was no Nambedru to laugh with. Stewart was quieter as well, and none of us went out of our way to start conversations with him.

Nothing is static, and little by little the house grew noisy again. Chimpo stole food from the kitchen, Abanzima shouted curses at her, we all laughed, and the great silence was over. Melina called on me again. There was a lot of work at the clinic. A band of pygmies arrived and set up their little leaf houses at the village outskirts, where they stayed for a few weeks and then moved on. I did a lot of thinking about Stewart during the long afternoons, sitting on my porch, looking at the river. Once again I wondered if I shouldn't have taken a firm stand. But Abanzima's punishment had been none of my affair. She had submitted, hadn't she? I was no anthropologist, to know what was and wasn't correct in African lives. I had to admit to myself that I hadn't the slightest idea what went on in the girls' minds and hearts. Oh, I got on all right with them; we laughed and talked together and gave each other little presents, but that was all— and probably all that was possible. And it was obvious that Stewart and Abanzima were on good terms again. I was very glad.

Then, one evening, brushing my hair before dinner, I noticed that it was getting long. I liked to keep it almost as short as a boy's, and I had been cutting it wherever I could, getting Nambedru to snip it off in back. Stewart would have to do it now, I thought, or one of the other girls, and I took a pair of scissors with me to the big house, where Stewart was sitting out-of-doors with his before-dinner drink. Sissy and Abanzima stood beside his chair, one on each side, like a couple of guards. Genially, he asked, "What are you doing with those shears?"

I explained, and asked, "So will you cut the back for me?" and pulled up a chair of my own, ready for a drink.

Stewart said, "No."

"No, what?"

"I mean I won't help you with your hair," he said. "It's silly to fuss around with it the way you women are always doing. Why don't you let it grow?"

I said, "Because it's much too hot here for long hair."

I was smiling, but Stewart wasn't. His eyes were shining coldly. "All right then, cut it all off," he said. "I'll use the clippers on you if you'll do that."

I stopped smiling. "Oh, don't be such an idiot. Sissy or Abanzima can trim me if you won't."

"No, they won't," said Stewart. "No member of my family is going to use halfway measures on her head anymore. And that goes for you as well as the other girls." He repeated the order to Abanzima and Sissy in Swahili, and they nodded solemnly, Abanzima making a little clucking noise in her throat to confirm the agreement. Bewildered, I looked from one dark face to the other. They looked back with identical expressions—sympathetic, wary, warning. Solemn and inflexible, Stewart sat on his throne. No member of his family . . . "Clippers or nothing," he said.

Next morning, I left Tange.

PAWPAW PIE

When I first arrived in Africa, I had been afraid of lots of things. The sight of a crocodile's nostrils and eyes lying just clear of the river water set me trembling. Walking, I would make myself dizzy watching the ground for snakes and at the same time watching the trees for leopards. Then, there was that mouth-drying crossing of ravines and creeks on slippery single-log bridges. At night, I dreamed about falling off those bridges, and when I woke I would lie in the dark wondering endlessly what the strange noises that fill a Congo night might signify. I was deeply ashamed of myself for being so feminine, and did my best to conceal the true state of affairs from everybody—from Stewart Cass, above all, for he had great contempt for any weakness. But I didn't want the Africans to know about it, either.

Fortunately, these anxieties—excepting the log-bridge nightmare—bothered me for only a few weeks. I am adaptable, and the other fears soon died out. It helped that the Africans I met were even more timid than I; there is nothing more reassuring than to be surrounded by cowards. They would start and tremble at the most harmless things—a rooster crowing before dawn, or a lizard of the wrong color. I was kept particularly well informed of these imaginary perils by a five-year-old orphan named Matope, who, in the eyes of Tange, belonged to me, or at least didn't belong to anybody else. He had come into the clinic to get treatment for an infected foot; after he was cured he just stayed on, sleeping on my porch and eating meals with me, though most of the time, like any small boy, he preferred hanging around the men of the village. Matope was a good watchdog, especially against dangers I knew nothing of. Once, coming into the room when I was cutting my toenails, he warned me sharply against letting the bits fly just anywhere. He picked up those he could find and handed them back, explaining that an enemy, if he got hold of such leavings, could do me a lot of harm.

By this time, I didn't at all mind the idea of striking out by myself for Lake Kivu and the east coast of Africa, especially as I wouldn't really be by myself at all. I planned to be accompanied by bearers, as well as by Sabani—the man who cooked and washed for me—and Matope. Even a pet baby baboon, Angélique, was to come along. I hadn't yet made up my mind what to do about Matope when we reached the end of the trip and it came time to pay off the party. In that region of the Congo, every boy, when he reached the age of eighteen or so, had to put in two years' work in the government mines, and Stewart had told me that the experience was bad for them and often ruined their health. I wanted to get Matope away from that and take him back with me to the States. I pictured him growing up in my house—wherever my house was going to be; my imagination wasn't yet ready to conjure it up in detail—as an adopted son, going to school every day, wearing shoes, being a credit to me generally and a comfort in my old age. It was a nice picture, but there were difficulties. Doubtless to discourage the wholesale export of native labor, the government demanded a bond of ten thousand francs—about two hundred and fifty dollars—for every Congolese leaving the region. Moreover, our own authorities, when I wrote to Washington for information, replied that they couldn't guarantee to let Matope in until he passed a physical examination at Ellis Island. I had already decided that with careful managing I could pay the bond money, and if we both went steerage I'd be able to buy our passage. But what if Matope should have some unexpected ailment and be turned back at the last border? I'd done a lot of thinking on this subject. Of course, if he didn't go with me he would be all right in Stewart's household, at any rate until he was eighteen and had to go into the mines. But just then I was not inclined to leave anyone I loved in Stewart's care.

Stewart and I had not quarrelled outright, because this would have made a scandal in Tange, and Stewart, a thorough Bostonian, had a healthy respect for appearances. It was fortunate for me that he was so conventional, for otherwise, in his annoyance with me for having dared to criticize him and for walking out, he might well have blocked my request to the village chief for the loan of twelve porters, and I wouldn't have been able to get away.

As it was, my departure was seemly enough, but I must admit it wasn't well thought out. Details are awfully important in the Ituri, and in collecting supplies I neglected several important items. I took no sugar, no butter and no other cooking fat of any sort, because to get these rare commodities I would have had to ask Stewart to give me some. Except for these things, however, I had everything I needed; I was used to travelling light. To be sure, I wasn't very clear as to my immediate destination, but I knew that I wanted to go east and then south. I had come into the Congo from the west, and my overall aim was to cross Africa by way of Lake Kivu, which was southeast, at the border of Ruanda-Urundi.

163

The chief, when I talked to him about the porters and about where I wanted to go, was surprised and then dubious. Nobody ever went east from Tange, he said. Nobody knew anything about the country there except that there was no road. By "road" he meant the single foot track, about six inches wide, that connected the villages in the forest; such a road was as important to the Congolese as the New Jersey Turnpike is to drivers in New Jersey. When the chief had protested for a while, Sabani, who was there also, interrupted to put in his own argument. To the east, the forest was unpleasantly wet and swampy, he declared, and for years no man had tried to go through it. The only roads to be found were elephant tracks, and they might lead anywhere. Warming up, he painted a dismal picture of what might happen even if we did get to the other side. The people over there weren't of the same tribe as our villagers, and they might refuse to sell us meat. Worse, there might not be any game at all, so there would be no meat to sell. Porters expected a meat ration every day, and sulked when they didn't get it. They might even run away and leave me helpless with all my boxes heaped up somewhere in the middle of the forest.

All this I ignored, because, in the Congo of those days, if you listened to local warnings you never got anything done. You had to possess a strong conceit. If you didn't believe down to the marrow of your bones that you always knew best, and that Nature was sure to smile on *your* undertakings, whatever she might do to those of others, you would have to give up. With my usual sublime self-confidence, therefore, I rode roughshod over the objections, just as the chief and Sabani had known I would; the whole conference was a kind of formality and nothing more. I did, however, accept Sabani's suggestion that we hire as guide a pygmy who happened to be staying near Tange for a season. I talked to him myself. He said he would lead us through the maze of elephant tracks, and that it should take about two days to get to the other side of that swampy part of the forest. Like all pygmies, he was incapable of getting lost.

Single file, then, we set out, a number of the porters balancing tin boxes on their heads. One, however, carried my bamboo bedstead and roll of mats, and another had a crate with cooking implements in it and two chickens slung head downward off his shoulder, according to custom, legs tied together in a bunch. The cook box held my supply of staple foods—a bag of rice, tea leaves, and a bottle of syrup. The syrup, I felt, would take the place of sugar. The men had their own kind of food; one of them carried a bunch of plantains—those enormous green bananas that are a substitute for bread when they are boiled or fried—and each man had his own dried meat or fish and a supply of evil-smelling oil. I find that now I tend to harp on the subject of food, but at the time I scarcely gave it a thought.

According to Stewart's *Encyclopædia Britannica,* we had about a hundred miles to traverse before we got near the Uganda border, in the plains. In that district, there would probably be motor roads and even a town, where I might arrange a lift south, toward Lake Kivu. But the motor-road business seemed so far in the future that I couldn't waste time pondering it. Sufficient unto the day—that was how I felt after a year sitting on the banks of the Ituri River. The flowing water seemed to have wiped out of my thoughts every vestige of time sense. What interested me was the log bridges I might be called upon to cross. Fortunately, the first day was free of these hazards. Instead of crossing rivers and ravines, we wallowed through miles of flat mud and rotting leaves, following our pygmy along a zigzag path. Elephants, it seemed, walk in the most erratic way imaginable, but we had to follow them because they had picked solid ground, of which there was not much. I slipped and slid and spattered myself, and couldn't wipe the sweat off my face for fear of rubbing mud on, but at least there were no bridges—as I reminded myself when the atmosphere grew oppressive.

It is never exactly bright and gay in the forest, but usually there are places where the sun breaks through in little medallions. And in the part of the country I had known, every so often on a walk I had come upon a clearing where Africans had planted a garden and sun filled the whole place. In the haunts of the elephant, we were too deep down under the trees to see any real light at all. There were flies, too. To keep my spirits up, I had to depend on the men's singing. In the afternoon, we came to the deepest, darkest place of all; there had been a lot of stamping and general wallowing, and small trees lay trampled and rotting in a black pool. "This is where the elephants dance," said the pygmy, beaming. "On the other side we will soon come to higher ground."

We did, but we hadn't reached a village by nightfall, and that meant we would have to camp out. In a village, I would have borrowed a house to spend the night in. I had no tent, but the men made me a little lean-to out of branches, and built their fire nearby, where they cooked their food and talked and talked and talked. After my meal of chicken, grilled on a stick, and boiled rice, I lay on the bamboo bed and wondered how far we had managed to walk. I had planned on a minimum of ten miles every day, but I doubted if we'd done that much. Still, what difference did it make? I was beholden to no one. I fell asleep.

Next day, I knew we were getting out of the swamp even before we saw the sun, because we had to cross a long, slender log under which there was water that was not stagnant. The porters cheered at the sight of it. I had no desire to cheer, but clenched my teeth as I made my timid way across, moving sidewise. The only times I disliked Matope were when he would run along one of those bridges ahead of me, never sliding. On the other side of this one, the country was less thickly forested, and after another hour or so we heard people's voices. They must have heard us much sooner, because the porters sang nearly all the time, making up the words as they went. Usually, the burden of the song was something about me, or some rudimentary form of social comment, like this:

Oh, we are tired.
Oh, we are tired.
Oh, Madamu makes us work hard.
Oh, it will be nice to rest.

The men who soon met us proved, in spite of Sabani's warnings, to be much like our own people in Tange, ready to make friends and sell food to the porters. I was even able to buy some food myself: a pawpaw, or, as it is usually called in the States, a papaya melon—orange-fleshed, soft, and rather insipid, but very welcome in the otherwise fruitless forest. It wasn't always easy to get.

There was a pattern to be followed at such meetings. The village chief came first, wearing an Arab robe to show that he was a civilized man, and lesser dignitaries followed in his wake. We all shook hands, and I asked if I could have a house for the night. Then we marched together solemnly to the village clearing, where I, with my boxes and gear, was put into a house, while old ladies, bent double to sweep out the mud floor with tiny brooms, shouted an exchange of pleasantries with the porters. Somebody turned up with a chicken to sell. Sabani chaffered, bought the chicken, then opened my mats and spread them over the floor so that I wouldn't get chigoes. The bamboo bed was set on the mats and covered with fresh banana leaves—the springiest mattress imaginable. I didn't have a bathtub, but I washed in a bucket while Sabani cooked my chicken and rice and a concoction of plantains and syrup. After the first two nights, I had to do without this dessert, because Angélique got hold of the syrup bottle and emptied it on the ground, licking up all that didn't soak into the earth.

The villagers went away while we ate, but afterward the chief came back. Now was the moment, if I'd been a government official on tour, to offer him a drink, but I didn't have any drink. I explained and apologized, telling him that I wasn't an official at all. Graciously, he waved away my words and asked if I was ready for the *baraza*. It was a question that mystified me. I knew, of course, what a *baraza* was. Literally, it meant "front porch," but after many years during which colonial officials had dispensed justice from their porches—presumably because a porch was a handy platform—the word had come to be applied to any court or hearing.

"What *baraza*?" I asked.

The chief bowed apologetically. He said he was sorry to trouble me, but it had been such a time since anyone had come along that the cases had piled up a bit. Sabani shoved my arm, whispering, "Go along, go along!," so in the end I went.

In front of the chief's house and porch, most of the adult population of the village stood waiting, leaving a little circle of bare ground in the middle. The chief led me up to the porch and gave me a chair. It was not until two men had set up a bare table in front of me that I realized what was going on. *I* was to be the judge. "Oh, now, look here!" I protested. "I can't—I'm not—"

They had made a natural mistake. All their lives, they had been taught not to take the law into their own hands but to wait until the great white boss came along. Lately, as the chief had said, nobody had come for quite a time. Now here I was, travelling the way white people always did, with a lot of people in my retinue, and, what was more, coming through that elephants' swamp where only Europeans would be silly enough to go. Of course I was fit to dispense justice. "I'm not the government," I said.

The chief just laughed. Words, words! He wanted to get on with the business at hand. He gave a signal, at which a man leaped to his feet and began to state his case. Willy-nilly, I listened, and, as the speech went on, was hypnotized. He was an excellent orator, and he took a long time. His grievance was that his wife had left him and gone to live with another man. He demanded her return or, failing that, payment either from the other man or from her parents. Now and then, as his passionate, smooth, full voice rolled on, the crowd made little grunting noises of assent or amusement. Finally, he finished the speech and stepped back, and the other man got out into the middle to state *his* case. He, too, was an accomplished speaker. Such periods! Such stirring appeals to reason! The woman, he said, had never been the other man's wife in the proper sense of the term; he hadn't paid her parents the full bride price. He himself, given a little time, was willing to pay her family the arrears. After much more of the same, he also stepped back into the crowd, and now everybody looked at me.

"What do you say, Bwana?" asked the chief.

I said, "Where is the woman? Let's hear what she has to say."

There was an approving, if surprised, murmur, and the girl stepped out. She talked pretty well herself, though not at such length, about how the first man was bad and beat her, and hadn't paid enough for her. I didn't know whether she was telling the truth or not. I suspected her of exaggeration, but she made her point—she wanted to stay with the second man.

Now it was my turn to speak. I knew better than to sum it up simply, so I put it this way: What was the use of hanging on to a woman who didn't want to stay? She would only run away again and again. There was no comfort or good to be had of such a woman. Therefore, I thought they had better negotiate a deal about the money, so that in the course of time the first man got back most of what he had already paid, after which the girl's parents would get some, at least, of the sum outstanding. "You can arrange it among yourselves, I'm sure," I said.

That was the main case of the evening. As time wore on, I gathered confidence, and by the end of the proceedings was laying down the law like a veteran. Nevertheless, it was a relief when everything was over and I could go to bed.

The classic Belgian pattern of safari was based on the idea that toward midday the sun was far too cruel for walking under, so the travellers would start out before sunrise, at four or five in the morning, and walk until eleven, when everybody stopped and rested until midafternoon. Then, when presumably shadows began to lengthen, they walked again for a while. Actually, there was hardly enough sun in the forest to throw a shadow of any size, and we could have walked the whole day if we'd wanted to. We didn't, of course. Rather than aim at a quota of miles, we would set a certain village as a limit and carry on until we reached it, when we would stop no matter what time it happened to be. Often our choice was made for us, when there was no suitable village at just the right spot. Sometimes we had to cut short our walk, and at other times we made an extra-long day of it, on one occasion covering more than twenty miles. All in all, we had a good time, with plenty of meat to buy along the way. I couldn't eat it myself, half cured as it was and full of maggots—I stuck to chicken—but Matope loved it.

Matope was having a ball. He would walk all day without once complaining that he was tired, and at night he sat up like a man among men, listening to the porters swapping lies with the locals. Angélique was his particular charge. During the march, she ran about as she liked, because a baboon, once tamed, never runs away very far, but in the villages she had to be kept on a tether, and it was Matope's job to see that she stayed out of mischief. I didn't want to annoy our hosts, and baboons are not exactly what everybody loves.

Yes, we were getting along fine. There were only one or two drawbacks—at mealtimes I found myself less and less able to choke down my dry chicken and rice, and there were still those damned log bridges, though Sabani had worked out a method of getting me over them that saved time, even though it shamed me. Whenever we came to a bridge, half the party went ahead and spaced themselves along it like a bucket squad, the last one holding out his hand for me. I would then inch cautiously across, clutching with my other hand that of the first member of the rear party, solemnly following. It worked every time but one. That was toward the end of a long day's march. The log was unusually fat, and perhaps I was overconfident that I could negotiate it. Across the creek was a welcoming committee from the next village, waiting for us. I was carrying Angélique on my shoulder. There had been a sharp rainfall a few minutes earlier, and I guess the log was slimier than I expected. Anyway, halfway over my foot slipped and it happened. Down I went into a stream bed that was more than half mud, Angélique throttling me and yelling in terror.

"Don't laugh! Don't laugh!" I heard Sabani shouting to the spectators as I stood up. Nobody did.

The forest thinned out, and we passed through more and more clearings. The land rose, too. We hadn't yet reached the plains, but we were now in a country where people ate rice rather than plantains. Fortunately, this made no difficulty for the men, who were sophisticated enough to eat rice when they had to. For me, of course, it made no change; I'd been on rice all along. Indeed, I felt as if I'd been on rice and chicken my whole life. It didn't nauseate me—yet—and I seemed to be doing all right as far as strength went. I kept up with the others, and I wasn't hungry, exactly, but I began to dream of desserts. Every night, I gobbled sundaes, angel cake, crisp pies that oozed sweetness and were all, without exception, absolutely enormous. They were a child's vision of pleasure; not once did I conjure up pheasant or filet mignon. When I woke in the morning, all I had was the memory and a slight uneasiness in the stomach, which went away with my cup of sugarless tea.

Then came a time when I could admit to myself that we were definitely out of the forest. Bare country could be seen ahead of us, full of sunlight; the bush had dwindled to scattered shrubs, and under our feet the ground was rocky. The porters had never seen land like this, and they didn't like it. They felt exposed, and as a result felt cold, though it was really warm. But they weren't used to noontime glare, so, for the first time, we halted in the middle of the day and rested. We started again, and soon came into sight of a range of stony hills that would have to be crossed, and again the men began to complain. That night, we slept in a village like none we had yet seen, high on a hill. Its houses were made of stone instead of the mud we were used to, and wind howled around them.

It had been a long time since I'd heard wind so close to my ears. In the forest, it was visible, moving the tops of the trees, but, except on the river, you never felt it. I, too, was cold, and lay shivering all night. We were thankful when we got off the hills and onto the plains, strange though the open land still seemed to our forest eyes, but now I was inclined to lag, because of something disturbing that the village chief had said—that we weren't far from a settlement of Europeans, who lived on a motor road. Cars meant that this phase of my journey was ended, that I'd have to give up the retinue and go on by myself, at vastly greater expense. I had no option, for the government had ruled that if any other method of transport was available nobody could travel on foot, with porters. I dreaded the change. I shrank from the thought of living in a white world again, where I would have to talk to people. For months I hadn't had to make conversation, and I felt that I'd lost the knack. It was all too much effort—problems to grapple with, uncomfortable clothes, and practical arrangements to make. What, for example, was I to do about Matope?

After a couple of hours, I plucked up heart. I could see no signs of white occupation. The scattered bush, the occasional planted clearing, the log bridges were still completely African. I grew cheerful—until suddenly we came to the crest of a bluff and looked down on what was undeniably civilization in the shallow valley ahead. Everywhere, trees had been cut down. Two large buildings of some kind of gray material dominated the scene, surrounded by a level pavement. A rusty-looking truck stood at the door of the larger building, and I could see, all too clearly, the road by which it had travelled, snaking around the hills across the valley. I knew this was not a missionary's establishment, even before I took in the narrow-gauge railway track and the group of native huts near it, and the ragged men carrying earth in baskets. Apparently, there was some sort of mining activity going on.

Singing, the porters wound down the hill behind me, toward the buildings, while the workers with their baskets halted to stare at us. A tall white man wearing a topee came out of a door and peered up the road at us. One could tell, even at a distance, that he was puzzled, and then, as he stood waiting with folded arms, he seemed belligerent. When I got closer, I saw that I was not mistaken. He looked angry, but his first question, oddly enough, was the same one I had always got from African village chiefs: "Where is your husband, Madame?"

Mechanically, I gave the same reply I had used all along: "I have no husband. I'm alone."

I gave him my name and he gave me his—de Blank. Politeness required such an exchange, but it wasn't politely that he then asked, "What are you doing here?"

The chiefs had never asked that, but I told him, explaining

172

that I was on my way to Lake Kivu and the east coast. I asked my own question: Could he please tell me where on the map we were? Scowling, he muttered a name. He was now looking over my porters, obviously in the hope of finding something incriminating. What could be the matter with him? Had a war been declared while I was out of touch with the civilized world?

"You have been hunting?" he asked after a pause, and then I thought I understood his attitude. He must suspect me of having sneaked into the territory to shoot big game without a license. Such poaching was not unknown, since licenses to shoot big game were expensive. But he could see for himself, I reflected, that we weren't carrying ivory or bulky skins. He did see this, and his manner didn't thaw perceptibly, though he stepped back and invited me into the building.

Indoors was a modern office, full of file cases, with geological maps on the walls and rock specimens on the desks. There I was introduced to another man, a Mr. Vandevell, a silent and spectacled Belgian, younger than de Blank. He bowed, and quickly looked at Mr. de Blank, who shouted to an African clerk, asking for tea. I sank into the chair offered me, took off my helmet, and wiped my forehead. It was odd, I thought, how different everything was all of a sudden. I had got up in the morning in an Ituri state of mind, placid and self-contained, in a world I could manage. Yet now, only a few hours later, among white people, I was frantically trying to think of a dozen things at once. Moreover, I was nervous, imagining enmity where probably none existed. It was just that I'd forgotten how Europeans behave, I told myself. I'd forgotten how rude and abrupt they can seem.

De Blank, seated behind his desk, held out his hand and said, "Your passport, Mademoiselle."

Well, really! But perhaps he was some sort of policeman. I handed my passport to him, and he began to study it page by page, while a fly droned up near the ceiling, sweat dripped off my nose, and Mr. Vandevell sat staring straight ahead at nothing. Suddenly Mr. de Blank gave an exclamation and slammed the passport down in front of me, though he kept a grip on it. "I thought so! Here it is, in black and white," he said, running his finger back and forth on the page. "You can't deny it, Mademoiselle."

Strictly speaking, it was blue and white—what I had written in the space marked "Occupation." "Mining engineer," it said proudly.

"Yes," I said. "That's what I was at the time I got the passport." I looked at him wonderingly. "I was a mining engineer working for an oil company, but I stopped working at it. Why? What's the matter?"

"You came here as a mining engineer," said de Blank. "You are an American engineer, spying on us. You heard about our gold mines, and it is not unknown in Washington that uranium is sometimes associated with gold." He slapped the passport triumphantly and snatched it back. "*Now* what have you to say?"

I didn't have anything to say for a minute. I had met another Belgian, I recalled, with the same notion—that every American he met was trying to get hold of the Belgian Congo's uranium. "Well, it isn't true," I said at last.

The very weakness of my protest must have given him second thoughts. Why on earth, he probably mused, should a rich country like America send a female nitwit to do a delicate job of espionage? The severity of his glance abated, and he sat back. Then he jumped up. "For all that, you've been trespassing for days. You must have known it was forbidden to come on our concession without special permission," he said. Ignoring my protest that I hadn't the slightest idea what a concession was, he took out a map of that region of the Congo and motioned to me to come and look at it as it lay spread out on the desk. "Now, let's see where you came in, according to your statement," he said. "You started here and came like this."

I was glad to see that the line of our route was admirably straight. Considering our obstacles—rivers and hills—it was a job to be proud of. "Did I really walk all that way?" I asked, enraptured.

"So you say, Mademoiselle. And regard. All of it, except perhaps your first two marches, was on our land—our concession. We have the right to explore all this tract, Mademoiselle, and you've been trespassing." He folded the map and shoved it into a drawer as if he couldn't trust me in its vicinity. He brandished my passport. "I'm sorry, but I shall have to keep this until we've investigated you. I'm sending a messenger off immediately to town, where one of our representatives can telephone the nearest American consul."

"That'll be all right," I said. "How long is it going to take?"

"A couple of days. I'll put you up, of course. But where?" Perplexed, he looked over toward the other building, evidently living quarters for both men.

"Tent?" suggested Mr. Vandevell. It was the first time he had spoken.

Yes, Mr. de Blank said, a tent would be admirable. He gave orders to the clerk. Catching sight through the window of the little throng of squatting porters, he went on, "My men can take care of yours."

"Can I buy food for them for a couple of days?" I asked. "After that, when they've had a rest, I'm sending them back home. I suppose I can go on in a truck from here?"

Yes, he said, the supply truck would be able to take me as soon as he had my *bona fides*. By this time, his tone was, for him, positively pleasant, and we drank our cooling tea in an atmosphere of relief.

The tent, when I took possession of it, was already furnished in a splendor to which I was no longer accustomed, with a rug on the ground, a dressing table, a cot, and a chair. Sabani was there, unpacking the one dress I still possessed and scattering my other things around. He admired the tent's furnishings. "Nice," he kept saying, touching them. "Nice."

Matope came in with Angélique, properly tethered, and listened while I told Sabani of the plans I had made. Sabani went out to report all this to the head porter, but Matope remained. It struck me that he was looking very downcast. "What's the matter, Matope?" I asked.

"What about me?" he asked in return.

Yes, indeed, what about him? I was no nearer a solution to his problem than I'd been when we started out, and I paused to think it over. I was sitting in the chair, a halfway-reclining model, and, in response to a gesture, he climbed into my lap and cuddled down, and we sat comfortably, as we had often done before, back in Tange, when it was time for him to go to bed. I said, "I'm feeling sad, Matope, about going away," and he grunted. For the first time since I'd started out for Africa, all those months before, I felt adrift. It didn't make sense; after all, I was on my way home, wasn't I? Still, I felt it.

"Well, *what* about you?" I asked in cheerful tones. Having come to grips with the question, I felt a flow of determination. I was ready to settle problems—Matope's and my own as well. I said, "You can come along with me, Matope. We'll manage. My family will be very glad if you come, and I'll always look after you."

His skinny little body, which had been so warm and reassuring, did not exactly stiffen, but I felt it jump, and then, astonishingly, he burst into tears. "I don't want to come!" he wailed. "I'm afraid!"

In a jumble of words, he told me why. He hadn't the slightest desire to leave home to go to a strange country on the other side of the world. Yet he didn't want to part from me, either. His heart was heavy because I was going, but he was terrified of coming along. I tried to reason with him, but he didn't listen.

"What will happen to me over there in Bulaya?" he demanded —"Bulaya" being a Kingwana word the Congolese used for Europe and any other white man's country. "Look at Angélique. At home, she runs around wherever she wants, but now that you're with the white men, you keep her on a rope. In Bulaya, you'd have to keep *me* on a rope, like Angélique." He thought of an even worse peril. "In Bulaya, they'll cut me up into pieces and put them into cans and sell me for meat."

I began to talk, to correct these misapprehensions, to explain. Then I stopped. He'd heard all this nonsense from the porters, during those long sessions at night. Who was I, an alien and a woman, to convince him against such a tremendous weight of authority? I surrendered. "All right, you silly boy, you don't have to go if you don't want to," I said. "You can take Angélique back to Tange instead."

"Oh, Madamu!" he said, still mournful. He hugged me, then scrambled out of my lap and ran to tell the news to the others.

I heard them all on the far side of the yard, in the mine workers' quarters, settling in. They felt fine. The job was over, and they could rest and eat before starting back. They called and joked and laughed. I heard the preliminary thump of a drum, like a throat clearing; as soon as it was dark, they would be dancing. Taking a deep breath, I got out of the chair and picked up my crumpled, moldy dress.

Most Belgians in the Congo lived in as elaborate and ceremonious a way as possible. The Englishman in the jungle, with his dinner jacket—that proverbial figure—had nothing on them. The mining men weren't in dinner jackets, but they had put on white coats and neckties, and the meal moved solemnly on and on. Mr. de Blank led the conversation along stilted lines—the weather, the Depression, European royalty. Mr. Vandevell listened, assenting where assent was needed. The talk was so slow that between sentences one could hear noises from outside, the singing and laughing in the African quarter. But I listened to none of it—neither to Mr. de Blank nor to the merriment out-of-doors. I was concentrating on the food. Each time the servant appeared with a fresh course, I held my breath for fear he might drop the dish before it was served. Except in my dreams, I had forgotten food was like this, juicy and savory; I had forgotten that white people really ate anything besides dry chicken and drier rice. My whole being was obsessed with the delightful sensation of eating.

"And what are Mademoiselle's plans, back in America?" asked my host with rusty geniality.

I was at a loss to reply. Plans? I had none beyond those for the day after tomorrow, when I could leave. Nevertheless, I had started to say something when the servant appeared bearing the dessert. My eyes fell on it as it hovered in the air and descended in all its beauty to the table, and I stopped even pretending to

177

join in the talk. The dessert was a pie, covered to towering height with meringue. I had never in my life seen anything more lovely. Mr. de Blank cut into it in slow motion and served the slices. The filling was of pawpaw—orange, and sweet. One slice was not nearly enough—I knew *that* before I started—and I gobbled it. And then I was taken by a fit of the shakes. I sat there, humiliated but shaking with pure lust, waiting for the offer of another piece, clutching the chair seat to keep my hands from snatching.

Mr. de Blank looked at me, grinned, picked up the pie plate, and put the whole thing down in front of me. "At your service, Mademoiselle," he said.

CHRISTMAS
WITH THE WALKERS

Whenever I think of the Christmas season I spent in the eastern reaches of the Belgian Congo, in 1932, I experience a floating sense of unreality. A number of questions occur to me and are unanswered. For example, where exactly was I? I can't be certain, though I remember the house all right—a pleasantly big, rambling bungalow set among coffee plantations—and I have a vivid recollection of the country, the unfenced miles of red soil open to a brilliantly sunny sky. Far off, mountains crouched like blue tigers. The air was never oppressive, even at noon, from which I deduce that I was fairly high up. The reason I am so vague about

179

the location and altitude of the bungalow is that I never asked anybody any such questions; at the time, it didn't seem important. My hosts, whom I'll call Ron and Peggy Walker, agreeable as they were, seemed mere incidents along my way. Later, when I began to think back, I was surprised at how clearly I could recall that visit. It was as if I had been at a theatre watching a play in which the Walkers were the actors—a play that went on and on, like one of those traditional Chinese dramas. The same stagy exaggeration is there, the heightened color of everything, the glare. Only one thought mars this simile. I cannot ignore the fact that I, too, was there on the stage, and that I hammed it up as badly as the others.

I had never heard of the Walkers until just before I met them. There was no reason that I should have—they were miles away from Tange. If I hadn't chosen to follow an eccentric path going back to America, the meeting would never have taken place. Actually, I was in no desperate hurry to get home at all. If I'd been able to follow my inclination, I would have stayed in Africa, but I didn't see how I could. Quite apart from other considerations—my mother's wrath, for one—I didn't have enough money to keep going. Before my hoard disappeared altogether, I would have to get to the coast and buy passage.

In the forest, I'd travelled on foot. Now, on the other side of the mining camp, I was in open country, where there was a motor road of sorts, and the law of the land—as well as common sense—prohibited walking safaris. I had duly dismissed my retinue at the mining camp, and there I was, alone in a government rest house. I'd expected to find buses, but the African watchman at the rest house said there weren't any. The few Europeans of the district had their own cars, he said, but there *was* one form of transport, satisfactory, if irregular—the SEDEC trucks. At these words, I nodded and relaxed, because I was familiar with the system. SEDEC, the Belgian branch of the great Lever firm, had a monopoly of trading posts in a large portion of the Congo. Hardly any area was without such a post, or store, to which the Africans brought their peanuts, or skins, or palm nuts, or whatever, and bartered them for SEDEC trade goods such as kerosene and Manchester cotton, dried fish and whitewash, salt and knives. The SEDEC trucks, or lorries, as the British called them, constantly traversed the main roads carrying replenishments to the posts and bringing back native produce to headquarters. SEDEC drivers also gave travellers a lift now and then, but they weren't obliged to do this. SEDEC had no formal license to operate a bus company, probably for the good reason that there weren't enough potential passengers to make it pay, but I had never heard of a driver turning down a reasonable request for passage. Admittedly, there was no rush on them. Few white people needed such conveyance, and the Africans hadn't yet become travel-minded. But I'd hitched a ride myself on a SEDEC truck to get to Tange from Stanleyville, on my way in from the west.

As I say, I relaxed. It should have been easy to do this after all the practice I'd had in the Ituri, where I had sat for idle hours on my veranda looking at nothing. And there was nothing, or less than nothing, to look at from the rest-house veranda—just a stretch of dusty red road and then sandy, rubbled waste. Yet, after a day of inactivity, I felt uneasy. I think it was because the Africans who straggled past in occasional groups, raggedly clothed, never spoke to me, even to say "Salaam." Any stranger in the Ituri would have said "Salaam" and have followed it up with a flood of conversation. This indifference hurt my feelings, and I was doubly glad when, on the second day, the SEDEC truck arrived. Two cheerful young Englishmen, Peter and John, who were in charge of it, readily agreed over a bottle of Beck's Beer to take me along south. The senior of the two, Peter, said it was a jolly good idea. When they heard I'd made a journey through the forest, they declared it a jolly good effort, but they were frankly puzzled about my object in having done it—my object, for that matter, in being in Africa at all.

"You're not a missionary, by any chance?" asked Peter in some alarm.

No, I said, I was not a missionary.

"But you aren't doing any shooting, I think you said."

No, I was not after game. "I just wanted to see Africa," I said, and his face cleared.

"Oh. Now I take your meaning. Well, jolly good." He raised his glass, John raised his glass, I raised my glass. The bottle was empty, so we got into the truck and drove off.

"It does seem a pity that you haven't had any shooting, though," Peter said. "What's everyone going to say when you get home with nothing to show for it?"

John said, "It's not too late, you know."

"That's true. You can still get a bit of it in." Peter was relieved. Clearly, I had outraged some deep sense of the fitness of things. "I'll tell you what we can do. You write out an application for a permit—a general permit, you know, which doesn't include elephant. Elephant comes high, fifty pounds a head, and even then you've got to hand over the ivory to the government—it's a fearful ramp. We'll ignore the elephant, but I'll take your application along and turn it in at Isuru or wherever my next port of call may be, and we'll get you that permit in no time. Now, I've got a friend who can outfit you on the cheap, and take you out after lion. Splendid chap he is—Ron Walker, the white hunter. You must have heard of him."

"No, I haven't. I'm sorry."

"He's a great old boy," said John eagerly. "He's got ninety-nine lions to his credit. Think of it. Ninety-nine! He says when he's got the hundredth he'll be ready to pack it in and call it a day."

"I doubt that," Peter said.

I was stirred by curiosity. "There seem to be a lot of British around here. How does that happen? Or have we left the Belgian Congo? I expected to see Belgians."

"Belgians? Oh yes, there are plenty of those about." Peter dismissed the Belgians. "It's quite true, there do tend to be quite a few English in this part of the country. It's being so near Uganda and all, I suppose. The Walkers have a place—it's not so extensive as most. They raise coffee, and they've been doing it for donkey's years. You see, Ron can't make a go of it anymore as a hunter, because there simply isn't the demand. Your beastly American Depression stopped the millionaires coming."

He smiled to take the sting out of the words, but I couldn't possibly have felt offended anyway; I was too happy and exhilarated. The road was absorbingly lovely, sometimes taking us high up over valleys of scattered bush or clumps of irrigated trees, sometimes plunging into narrow passages between rock walls. The old euphoria of the traveller, a sensation I'd almost forgotten in the forest, was stealing over me—that keen expectation of something happening soon, something fascinating.

"I know what we'll do," said Peter. "You have no set plans as to where you've got to be tonight, I take it. It makes no odds? Then we'll go straight along to the Walkers'. I'd have been going there in any case; when I'm in the vicinity, I like to stop by and spend the night. They'd love to meet you."

"Sure it's all right?" I asked the question merely out of politeness and not because I had any hesitation. In Africa, people never objected to unexpected guests. The guest should not impose on his hosts by staying too long, but to visit for one night, or two or three, was not considered an imposition.

"Peggy'll enjoy a bit of a natter with another woman," Peter assured me. "It's not often she gets the chance way out here."

John added, "You're sure to like her."

John was right. At tea in the Walkers' sprawling bungalow, I liked Peggy more with every bite of shortbread. Ron wasn't home, but she said he wouldn't be long. Peggy might be rather sallow, I reflected, but European women tend to lose their complexions in Africa. To be sure, she was elderly—I think now that she was probably thirty-eight at most—but, to give her her due, she cooked like an angel. I was still ravening for sweets, and while Peggy and Peter and John talked gaily about people unknown to me (with names like Poppet and Bunty and Chris and Tiny Tim) I munched silently, contentedly, and continuously on iced cakes. From the talk, I gathered that the Walkers, in spite of what Peter had said about Mrs. Walker's loneliness, lived in a social whirl. Almost every month, it seemed, somebody they knew would drop in—Peter, or Tim, or Old Gaffer—and, compared with my existence on the Ituri River, this was living it up.

Good old Ron now made his appearance, greeted with cries of pleasure. Smiling, though evidently exhausted, he laid aside his rifle, took off his wide-brimmed hat, mopped his face, and shouted in Swahili, ordering somebody to bring in something. He was tall and lean and handsome in his elderly way—he was about forty—with white hair and a military mustache. In reply to the shout, an African man carried in a dead antelope to show us. It seemed Ron had just shot it. The boys asked Ron where he'd found it and where the bullet had hit it, and all that, while the African, who had been along with Ron on the outing, stood stiffly at attention. Nobody spoke to him, which suprised me a little. I hadn't exactly expected to be formally introduced to the Walkers' domestics, but this complete ignoring of a man's presence was disconcerting. Though I wasn't a newcomer to Africa, I felt something alien in this part of the country—a cool little wind, blowing between the life I'd known in the forest and that of the eastern plains. Here, without conscious intent or malice, Africa seemed to be kept out-of-doors, at far more than arm's length. The attitude of the Walkers and their friends was never put into words. I don't suppose they could have expressed it in words. It just existed.

Next day, the SEDEC youths left at sunrise without me. I'd been invited to stay on for Christmas, and had not merely accepted the invitation but jumped at it after Peggy showed me the larder. It was full of cakes, pies, and puddings she and the cook had made ready for the coming holidays, when the Walkers, following a long-established custom, gave a party for all the British for miles around. I was glad to stay—my mouth was already watering—but how was I to get away afterward?

Peter told me just before he left. "You can't depend on one of our fellows coming along, I'm afraid," he said. "Whenever *I'm* driving this way, I stop in, but that doesn't apply to the others, and this place isn't on the regular route, so what you'd best do is arrange in advance. Write to the central office in Stanleyville and put it up to them. Just say as soon as possible after Christmas, and everything will be all right."

I wrote the letter that day. One other matter had to be attended to—my clothes. I had nothing to wear for the party, nothing at all but bush shorts and shirts. Peggy suggested that we drive the twelve miles to the nearest SEDEC post that afternoon and buy a length of cotton. "Something not too African, you know. They must have a good selection for the Christmas season, now that Peter's brought a load."

We did this, and when we got back Peggy spread the cloth on the floor and cut it to paper patterns. After that, we spent the sunny hours sewing, while Ron made his rounds of the estate or busied himself with the livestock. All around us in the house, African servants cleaned, polished, cooked, or laundered, always maintaining the reserve I'd noticed in Ron's gun boy. It could not be accurately described as silence, because now and then one of them would talk to Peggy about something connected with his task, and when they were outside the room where we were I would hear them talking and laughing just like Tange people. It was our presence that kept them buttoned down, and *their* presence, in turn, had an effect on Peggy, though she would have scoffed if I'd said so. Whenever she had to address the cook or the laundress, her voice sounded different—higher-pitched, more stilted.

But even in Swahili Peggy had a lovely voice, full and musical, and perhaps it was this that invested the next days with the drama I remember, because everything she said sounded intense. She said a lot, and so did I. Naturally, what with cutting things out together and trying on and pinning, we chattered as we worked. I'm always voluble when I'm at ease, but I don't recall what I talked about. What is fixed in my mind is the thing Peggy told me about Ron and herself, because it startled me so. The burden of it was that they weren't happy together—a fact I would never have suspected. Certainly they appeared to get on all right.

"No doubt," said Peggy when I said this. "But that's all on the surface. You see, Ron did a dreadful thing to me, the worst a man can ever do to a woman. He was unfaithful"—here she pulled out a basting thread—"with a woman who lived on one of the farms up there in the north." She paused to bite off a fresh length of sewing thread. "He'd probably kill me for telling you, but I've got to talk about it to somebody."

"And is it still going on?" I asked.

She shook her head. "She's gone back to England."

"I can't believe it," I said. "Are you sure? I can't believe it of Ron, of all people."

I was thoroughly sincere, but I don't know, now, why I should have been surprised. I was quite old enough to know better. I suppose it was because I'd grown to think of the Walkers together, as a cozy couple. My heart sank at the thought of how perfidy dwells in the hearts of men—a fact brought home to me all the more strongly because of Peggy's voice, full of passion and pain.

Sewing with tiny, even stitches, though her eyes were wet, she told me she'd discovered the affair accidentally, when Ron had left a letter from the woman in his bush-shirt pocket and the laundress, in all innocence, brought it to her. "It nearly killed me," she said in a voice so low it was almost a whisper, and my eyes, too, filled with tears. Oh, she said, Ron had been terribly sorry at first—really full of remorse. He couldn't do enough to show it. But time had drawn the sting out of his self-reproach and blunted the effect of her admonitions as well. "He seems to think I can forget all about it and carry on as if it had never happened," she said. "Really, men are incredible, aren't they?"

Flattered by this appeal to my worldliness, I first shook my head in wonder at men's incredibility, then nodded in agreement, but the gestures were lost on Peggy. She kept her eyes on her sewing and her attention on her inner self. "What's more," she said, "he saw her in London when we were on leave. I just know in my bones he did."

"Well, but—when did it all happen?" I asked.

"It must be nearly three years now," said Peggy, "but it nearly killed me. My heart isn't strong, you know."

"Peggy," I said, "I'm so *awfully* sorry."

I was. There was so much pity in me, as a matter of fact, that some of it spilled over on Ron. Men couldn't help themselves, I reflected; men were made that way. It was a law of nature that my mother had imparted to me in early youth, at which time I'd furiously denied the truth of it. Now I decided that Mother was right, after all. Nothing else could account for masculine behavior. I said timidly, "It might help to remember that there are times when men can't help themselves. They're different."

"My dear, you can't tell me anything about men." Peggy's voice grew crisp. "Of course they're different, the dirty pigs. And I must say for Ron that the woman made a dead set at him. Only, as I ask myself, why should *I* be the one to do all the forgiving and forgetting? Just because I was hurt—and who wouldn't be?—and wanted to be by myself for a bit, he resented it. He's been sulking now for months. You'd hardly believe it, but it's been a year, ever since we came back from leave, that he hasn't come to my room." She paused to look at me; I was embarrassed, and didn't meet her eyes. "A woman can stand just so much neglect, my dear," she went on. "It's not as if *I* haven't plenty of chances to misbehave. Sauce for the gander, you know. Someday I'm going to surprise that fine gentleman."

I could no longer hold up my end of the conversation like a woman of the world, because I was afraid I might be blushing. Everything had suddenly become all wrong. Surely a woman of Peggy's age should not even think about misbehavior with men. It was grotesque; it was unseemly. I marvelled at her blindness. Finally, I told myself that people tend to get silly as they grow older and I must try to understand. Into my thoughts, to bolster this resolve, popped an incident, hitherto banished from my mind, which had to do with Mr. Barlow, transport manager at the Stanleyville SEDEC office. I had met him when I'd gone in to fix things up about riding on the truck to the Ituri, and I had thought him a nice old man. Then I discovered that he wasn't nice at all—and a married man, at that. For a moment now, I toyed with the notion of telling Peggy this tidbit to distract her, but I decided not to. It wasn't much of a story anyway.

Christmas approached. On the surface, the Walkers were much as usual, giving no hint of the secret consuming Peggy's vitals, though now and then she would send me a glance fraught with significance. "See how beautifully I behave? See how martyred I am?" said her eyes.

I helped her cut colored paper into strips, which we then pasted into linked circles, making chains. Ron, commanded to loop these things around the rooms, obeyed with grumbling good humor. Once, as I passed through a room where he stood on a high stepladder, he turned toward me and made a helpless gesture, paper chains fluttering daintily from his big, suntanned hands. "Ninety-nine lions, and then this!" he said.

Peggy said tenderly, "Poor old boy. Get on with it." Her eyes said to me, "See how well I can behave, even when my heart is broken?"

Yet I *liked* Ron. I couldn't help it. There was the morning before Christmas Eve, when I woke up early, too hungry to wait for breakfast, and went into the larder for something to eat. I was emerging, chewing away, when I met Ron, and I was just thinking how seedy he looked at that hour when he shouted at me, "God damn it, woman! So help me God, if I ever again catch you eating cakes with green icing before noon, I'll kill you!"

Came Christmas and the party, at which I met Tiny Tim, Bunty, and all the rest of that merry crew. At least I am sure they were merry, though I can't remember any of them, or anything about the party, either, except that somebody brought a Victrola, and there was singing and dancing and drinking and a lot of loud laughter. Everybody talked about animals they had killed. We had put up lots of camp cots, and most of the guests stayed the night and the next day. I do remember that after the last one had gone and we were eating a late supper, I found myself viewing the plum pudding with a lacklustre eye. I didn't want another mince pie, either. A milestone had been reached, apparently—my sweet tooth was gone at last. As a natural sequence to the discovery, I said, "It's funny I don't hear from Stanleyville."

Not at all funny, the Walkers said. The mails were always late during the Christmas season. "And so are the lorries," Peggy added. "I doubt if you've missed even one at this date."

Next day, my letter arrived with the Walkers' mail, at breakfast. I remember how peaceful it all was as I slit the envelope, the shutters half drawn against the sun but the table shining in reflected light. Our teacups cooled as we read, and one fly buzzed around the toast. I was a long time with my letter. I had to read it twice before I could believe it. The signature was Mr. Barlow's—Mr. Barlow, my half-forgotten acquaintance of Stanleyville, to whom my request for a place on a SEDEC truck had apparently been referred. It was a very nasty letter. Mr. Barlow had written that he would certainly *not* send a SEDEC lorry to pick me up at the Walkers' or any other spot. Considering everything, he continued, he was astonished at my effrontery in making such a request. Furthermore, he was issuing orders to all concerned that no SEDEC lorry in future was to give me a lift in any circumstances whatsoever, and he ended the letter with a polite message to the Walkers, wishing them a happy New Year and expressing the confident hope that they and I would all get on nicely together in the years to come.

Having brought myself at last to admit that all this was really there on the page, I uttered a sharp cry of anger. The Walkers, interrupted in their own reading, were alarmed to find me crimson with emotion, fighting back tears of rage.

"My dear, what ever is it?" Peggy cried.

Wordlessly, I handed her the letter, and she read it and passed it on to Ron, saying, "Cad!" Peggy could say things like that. Besides, in that house, "cad" was not a laughable word. It sounded right. And Ron, too, sounded right as he demanded in stentorian tones, "What's the matter with the fellow? What's behind all this?"

I told them all about it—the pass Mr. Barlow had made, the rebuff, and now, as a result, the reckoning. The air quivered with our indignation, and if one should ask why we didn't merely roar with laughter, the only answer is that white people in

Africa just didn't laugh things off. Life wasn't a laughing matter. It may have been the climate that affected us, but I'm not sure one should always blame that. More likely, it was that the Walkers and all the others—and I, too, at the time—didn't see other white people often enough. The Africans weren't in our world; we were isolated, so we played charades. Mr. Barlow was a case in point. Back in Bournemouth, where he came from, he would never in a month of Sundays have behaved as he was doing in Stanleyville. Nor would Ron have carried on in his native Huntingdon as he now did on the coffee farm. Nor would I have been alarmed in St. Louis, as I was in that breakfast room, when he ranted and raved. He called Barlow a splendid lot of names, of which "cad" was merely the beginning—kindergarten stuff. The oration ended on a high note. "An Englishman's house, by God, is his castle!" roared Ron. Then, striding splendidly to the wall, he pulled his rifle from its perch over the mantel and marched out of the house.

"Oh, God!" I said, tears running down my face. I went down on my knees by Peggy's chair—yes, I did—to say imploringly, "What's he going to do, Peggy? Where is he going?" I must have had some notion that he was going to march to Barlow's office, hundreds of miles away, and shoot him through the heart.

Peggy soothed me. "Don't be afraid. He's coming back. He's probably going out to get a deer, because we're running short of meat. You poor child! You know, somebody ought to horsewhip Barlow, at that."

My feet were on the ground again. I said, "But what am I going to do now about getting away?"

"We'll figure out something," said Peggy. "Perhaps one of the neighbors. Or if only our old car was trustworthy . . ."

That evening, Peter drove up in a SEDEC truck, accompanied by an African assistant. He clasped our hands as he came in, saying, "What ho! Now tell me all about it. What have you been doing to our Mr. Barlow?"

"Tell him," said Peggy grimly, her arms folded.

So I went over the story again.

Peter clicked his tongue. "That's bad. Barlow's overdue for leave, that's about the size of it. Someday, when he looks back on all this, he won't be able to credit it."

"Never mind Barlow," I said impatiently. "What about me? How am I going to get out?"

Peter hesitated, and we knew what was going on in his mind. He'd had his orders. They were ridiculous orders, but did he dare to disobey them? Finally, he patted my shoulder and said, "We'll think of something, now don't you fret," and we all went to have a drink.

In the end, it was Ron who thought of something. He came home, just as Peggy had predicted, with a dead animal. He was calm and cheerful, greeted Peter cordially, and made himself a drink. "Just in time, old boy. In the very nick of time," he said. "I don't doubt the girls have brought you up to date on the outrage. It seems to me a council of war is called for." He took a deep draught of his whiskey and suddenly spluttered into the glass. "What sort of a load are you carrying this trip?" he asked.

Peter said, "I'm travelling light, actually—came down here to see what was what as soon as I got that directive, of course, and I'm afraid we didn't have time to take on a full cargo, but I expect I'll make it up coming back. Why do you ask?"

"I've just had a look at our storehouse," said Ron. "Remember that axle you brought in for us last March? Well, it so happens we've still got the crate it came in, cover and all. There's plenty of room in it to hide a body."

Everybody cheered. Peggy went over and kissed her husband. His face flushed, he kissed her in return, quite heartily, while Peter assured me it would all be easy. "You won't have to stay in your coffin more than an hour. Just until I'm well out of sight of the post. I could do it faster, but I wouldn't want to shake you to bits. From then on, it's plain sailing. You can sit up on the front seat with me the whole way to the bus line, and nobody'll be the wiser."

"What about that man with you?" I asked.

"My boy? I'll fix him, I can assure you of that. I'm telling him that I'll pay him a good tip on the day I go on leave, on condition nobody hears about this. By the time I come back, old Barlow will have had his holiday and come to his senses. Everything's going to be all right."

Ron and Peggy, occupying the same chair, smilingly agreed with Peter.

It was a lovely sunrise the next day, clear and still, and so early that the Walkers, emerging from Peggy's bedroom and standing on the veranda to wish us Godspeed, were still in their dressing gowns. The empty crate was in the truck, with the African—a beaming smile on his face—standing guard over it.

"You won't be able to wave goodbye," Peggy complained as we embraced and kissed.

Ron pecked my cheek and said, "Goodbye, my dear. God bless."

I lay down in the crate, and Peter fitted the top over me and filled the box with darkness. I was laughing in the dark, but my mind wasn't on the ridiculous present; I was feeling the old expectancy, the excitement of things to be. I felt the truck's engine start up, and there was a jolt. My blind, voiceless body was carried cautiously, slowly to the bottom of the drive, bumpety-bump across the cattle drive, grindingly around the bend, and on toward Kivu. Kivu! Everything else was blotted out, and already I might as well never have spent Christmas with the Walkers.

DAR

I am trying to remember how it happened that I took a first-class train ticket from that town on Lake Tanganyika where the boat stops—Ujiji?—to Dar es Salaam. I shouldn't be blamed, perhaps, if such details are forgotten, but I think I can safely hazard a guess that it was because white people would not have been permitted to travel by any lower class. Otherwise I would certainly have saved as much money as I could. Funds were low, and I still had to buy a steamship ticket—to Europe, as there was no other way to do it—and then return to America. There were two British army officers in uniform sharing my first-class carriage, talking volubly and with much laughter about friends and old school days. It suited me that they should be happy with each other because I was preoccupied and had no wish to be interrupted. I had a lot of moping to do. The train was running through country that looked much the same in all directions—dry and nearly bare of brush and trees. Nothing distracting. I was free to be as gloomy as I liked while I reflected that the adventure was all but over. I told myself that it was like coming down after one has climbed a mountain; it was anticlimax the whole way. I'd done what I'd wanted to do, and had finally put the seal on the whole thing by seeing Lake Kivu. Actually, Kivu had been almost too picturesque, too pretty, but I could not yet bring myself to admit it.

And now, what next? Nothing, nothing. There remained mere formalities and the end. I was resolved to stay as short a time as possible in Dar es Salaam—only long enough to ship out—and that would be that. Far off, in Chicago, Illinois, were my parents, and, very likely, a few odd sisters and cousins as well, but I thought of home exclusively in terms of my mother. In my mind's eye she was sitting there grimly waiting for me. That was all she was doing—waiting. It did not alter matters that I was perfectly well aware, really, that this mental picture was a gross misrepresentation of my mother's way of life, that in truth she had a busy nature and was interested in all six of her children and even more in her grandchildren. The truth made no difference; through the past months, her letters had built up in me a stubborn conviction to the contrary. The year was 1933, and each letter, as I recalled, had contained a passage that went more or less like this: "Things are very bad. So-and-so hasn't been able to find work, though he's been trying for three months. Such-and-such is clerking in a store downtown, but it's only a temporary job. Goodness knows when things will be better. *Why* don't you come home?"

"Dreadful, isn't it?"

I jumped nervously. One of the British officers, ready now to make friends with a stranger, had spoken to me. "Hot, isn't it?" he added.

I agreed that it was hot, and they ordered drinks for all three of us and settled down for a chat. There was no more time for moping. My companions remained voluble for the rest of the ride. Having found out, in the customary roundabout method of the British, who I was and where I was going, they described Dar es Salaam reassuringly as a very nice place. For themselves, they didn't live right in town; they were in barracks somewhere outside, but they often got in for an afternoon at the Club. Dar was pretty quiet, just at the moment, they admitted—"Your American depression has hit it, you know. It's very hard on trade and shipping"—but still, it was good enough. I asked about hotels, and one of the men told me that there was only one but that I'd find it quite satisfactory. "A very decent little pub, as a matter of fact," he said. "A widow woman runs it—Mrs. Blenkinsop. Her husband was in trade out here for years, and when he died she decided she'd try to go it alone, so she opened this hotel and she's made a good job of it."

"Brave little woman," said the other one, lighting his pipe.

"I suppose it costs quite a lot to stay there?" I asked nervously.

No, no, they said—the prices were reasonable. In any case, it was the only hotel in town.

We pulled into Dar es Salaam station at dusk. My friends were in a hurry to get to their post, but they found the hotel car for me—a battered, rusty vehicle—and put me into it and waved goodbye. I liked what I saw of the town on the way to the hotel. The train had made an abrupt descent from the highland into an appealingly lush, tropical country, full of flowers and trees and big white-plastered houses and smaller adobe ones. There were palms along the coast road, and I caught a strong whiff of the sea. It was a true port city, full of shops and people of all sorts. After months of living in a backwoods community where everyone was a member of a neighborhood tribe, I was stirred with sudden delight at the sight of so many different people—Indian, African, Arab, European, even Chinese—sauntering about to catch the evening breeze. Then I remembered that I would have to leave all this almost as soon as I'd discovered it, and the old regret rushed in once more.

But I had no more time for emotion; it was just one thing afer another in Dar. Half an hour later, booked in at the hotel of the English widow, Blenkinsop, I didn't stop long enough to unpack my pajamas in the flimsy cubicle of a room. I wanted to get out and think, because it looked very much as if I was in trouble. Mrs. Blenkinsop had not been visible; a bored Indian clerk had taken my signature and told me what my room and meals would cost, which was more than I had feared even at my most pessimistic. Even so, it wouldn't have mattered acutely if there had been a ship in a day or two, but the clerk had told me that the next northbound vessel wasn't due for another two weeks. He had explained, "The crisis, you know. There is very little business for the ships to call in for, and many of them have been cancelled for more than a year. Times are very hard in Dar es Salaam. Never mind. You can book in the next one. It's an Italian liner, very comfortable, and you are sure to find plenty of accommodation. Business is dead."

What worried me, as I paced the road outside, was that fourteen days of paying the hotel's price would probably use up so much of my money that I couldn't buy a ticket, even for third class. At any rate, it would cut things pretty fine. I walked along, my thoughts stewing. The road seemed quieter than I had expected, and I thought that it might be because night had fallen, or perhaps the lull was owing to the hotel's position, well away from the commercial streets and above a strip of beach. I saw an informal promenade by the sea, where a few people, some of them Arabs in long robes, were walking, and I made my way down the path and joined them. There was a moon. The beach, the houses in the distance, and the clothes of the walkers all gleamed pure white. Here and there on the water, a shallow arc of foam appeared and disappeared, to appear again a few feet away. Absently I noticed a man walking toward me briskly among the saunterers, his heels beating a rapid rhythm. As he passed me, his little brown eyes glanced at me and lit up with a recognition that puzzled me. He swung around and came back to me. "Didn't I see you this afternoon at the railway station?" he asked. He talked with a quick, clipped accent.

I said, "You might have. I was there."

He fell into step beside me. "I go every day to meet the train," he said. "I have a hotel, and I go there to pick up people to stay in it. I was going to ask you, but you were with those two Englishmen, and they put you into the car, and I knew you must have reserved your room in advance. Most of the officers' families go to the English hotel. You are an officer's wife?"

"No, I'm nobody's wife," I said. "But I thought there *was* only the one hotel."

George—he was George Something, a long Greek name—made a scornful gesture. He told me that there were quite a few hotels in town—his own family, for example, owned and operated two of them, and had done so for years. But the British officers wouldn't have told an innocent stranger this because they were on the side of their compatriot, Mrs. Blenkinsop. "She will cheat you, that woman, so look out," he added. "Her prices are very high. How much are you paying?"

I told him, and he shook his head as if he could scarcely believe in such wickedness. "You see? Ah, it is a pity I didn't talk to you when I saw you on the station. I could have given you a better room and better meals, and for half that sum."

Hope had dawned. I said eagerly, "I can move, can't I?"

George seemed not to have thought of that. He gave a great start of surprise, and looked at me with admiration. "Why, yes, you could," he said.

I could hardly walk out on Mrs. Blenkinsop that night—not without paying for the room anyway—so I waited until morning. Then, by prearrangement, George came with a couple of porters to carry my luggage out to his hotel car, while the Indian clerk looked at us from heights of superiority. Only when I was going out the door did he remember that he had a letter for me. It was an invitation to tea at Government House a few days later, and I realized that my officer friends had been at work on my behalf.

In itself, George's hotel was practically indistinguishable from the one I had deserted, but its position, on one of the town's main streets, was less smart. It didn't matter; Dar es Salaam wasn't very urban anyway, and there was little traffic. The bar, a large shady room, was obviously popular. The bead curtain that shielded it from the view of passersby hardly ever stopped swinging from the time I went through it, late in the morning, until lunch. A procession of men passed in and out—small, swarthy men, mostly, who bore a sort of resemblance to George —but one or two Englishmen came in too. There seemed to be some Portuguese and Lebanese drinking beer at the tables, but most of the patrons were Greek. I had met some of these Greeks of East Africa before. Few of them had ever seen Greece, nor did they show any desire or curiosity to do so. They had been born in East Africa, or Cairo, or—in George's case—Istanbul. Their fathers and grandfathers had been traders, and so were they.

I was in the bar because, before I had even finished unpacking, a boy had come to say I had a caller waiting downstairs. Evidently the British officers had broadcast the news of my arrival throughout the community as well as up at Government House. I went down and found a young Englishman waiting for me in the bar. He introduced himself as a reporter. He said, "I understand you've walked right across the continent, unaccompanied. Pretty good effort, and it ought to make a good story."

I agreed. It would have made a wonderful story if it had been true. "But the fact is, I didn't walk across," I said. "I travelled by paddle steamer and train and truck and the lake boat on Tanganyika, as well as on foot. Anybody could do that. I don't see how you could write it up, do you?"

"No, I don't suppose I could," he said. "Didn't you even do any shooting? We can always use a big-game story, especially if it's about a woman."

"Not even that."

"Oh, well." He pocketed his notebook. "It all goes to show how anecdotes can be puffed up in this town. Have a drink, won't you?"

Malcolm was his name. We talked about Dar es Salaam,

where he had been living for the past year. He wasn't at all like any newspaperman I'd ever met before. He was stuffier. But he admitted to a liking for Dar es Salaam. "It's not exactly go-ahead, obviously, but one couldn't expect it to be considering the financial situation of the world," he said. "It was never wildly exciting, I daresay. Now it's slowing down, nearly to a halt. Still, we progress in some ways. Do you know, we've actually got the cinema with sound? You wouldn't have believed that, would you? I shouldn't think any other city in Africa has it."

Noncommittally, I murmured something; I had already heard the news from George.

"They're opening tonight, for the first time," Malcolm went on. "They're showing some sort of operetta, I believe, with your American black-face comedian Al Johnson."

"Al Jolson," I said. "Yes, I heard about the talkies even before I left for Africa."

"Shall we go tonight? Everybody in town will be there."

I shook my head. "Thanks, I would like to, but I can't. I've already told George I would go with him."

"George?" demanded Malcolm. He sounded shocked. "Forgive me, but you don't mean *George*, do you? The proprietor of this hotel?"

"Yes. Why? What's the matter?"

For a moment, Malcolm looked down at his hands, which he had clasped, then he stood up and became energetic. "Well, that's all right, it's not too late to fix things. We'll have him in, and you can tell him a mistake's been made, that you're sorry, but of course you can't go with him. Don't worry, he'll understand." He reached for the bell.

"Wait a minute," I said. "Perhaps George would understand, but I don't. You'd better explain it to me before you do anything."

Malcolm hesitated, and when he spoke it was with caution. "I'm afraid I couldn't make it clear to you. You see, you've just arrived, you're full of the notions people do have when they're new out here. It takes time to understand our point of view. You

199

must take my word for it, I'm afraid, when I tell you that one simply doesn't go to the theatre with George. One simply doesn't, that's all."

"Why not? Surely you can put it into words?"

"Oh well, if you must have it—George is a Greek."

"Yes, I know that."

"Greeks are not considered white in Dar es Salaam. That's all."

We stared at each other. It may sound odd, but there was something innocent about Malcolm, never more so than when he was being offensive. I was full of words, but couldn't bring myself to say any of them.

"You can't do it, my dear girl," said Malcolm.

I said, foolishly, "Want to bet?"

Then I thanked him for the drink, and he went away.

That evening, at the cinema palace, George and I were staggered by the wonder of it all—the enormous voices and the music that seemed to come not so much from the screen as from everywhere around us, the words nearly, if not quite, matching the movement of the actors' lips. Whatever would they do next? We foreigners in the audience applauded everything and anything because we were happy and proud of the miracle. The Africans up in the gallery, however, remained calm. They liked the picture; they liked all pictures. But the talking they accepted because it was just another clever thing that had been dreamed up by white people, and they had become blasé about clever inventions. In the Ituri, I remembered, the Africans had behaved the same way the first time an airplane flew over. They'd been interested, in a mild way; they had admitted that it was a wonderful thing to have accomplished, but there was no awe-struck amazement, and after that first time they didn't bother to look up when other planes flew over. They had seen outboard motors, and some of them had even seen motorcars. Why not, then, a mechanized bird as well?

All in all, I enjoyed my first date in Dar very much, even though I got another letter from Government House next day—

a polite note of regret that the tea party had been called off. Malcolm, however, did not stay away. He turned up that afternoon and managed not to speak about Greeks and white people for quite a long time. Finally, though, we were at it again, embroiled in a silly argument during which he kept using incredible phrases: "Of course it's very splendid and American of you, but—" "What you don't realize is that we've got to maintain—" "You simply don't appreciate our problems." Every day, after that, he came over, and every day we argued. I don't think I quite believed that Malcolm existed. He must have had the same doubts about me, but he kept on dropping in, and sometimes we went out in his car for a drive. Not often, though—I was too busy with other social engagements; I was all dated up with the Greeks.

They entertained me in their houses. They showed me around the city—the shops where Indians sold silks and jewels, or ivory cutters made chessmen and little elephants; they showed me old Arab houses with carved doors. Often I went out for walks by myself, early in the morning before anyone I knew was awake. On one such excursion, I came by accident on a little square that I hadn't seen before. In it was a ring of men in headdresses and long robes, slowly dancing to drums and flourishing curved knives at each other. I drew back into the shadows of a side street, but they didn't care whether I watched or not. On another morning, I found a group of camels, loaded with bundles tied up in rough brown cloth, each camel led by an African. They were marching toward the outskirts of town. As it happened, I had never before seen camels outside a circus. I followed them, though it was a very hot day, until they stopped in a palm grove.

Most of the time, though, I fooled around with George's crowd. They weren't all Greeks. There was a Mrs. Mueller, who was Swiss, I think, and Fernandez, an Argentine, and a few other foreigners. We sailed, or lounged on the beach, or danced in the hotel to the music of a Victrola. One night we wore our bathing suits and went driving a long way, in a cavalcade of cars, to a spot on the coast that was new to me, where we swam in warm, shallow, phosphorescent water. It was a strange place. There were pools that shone like silver, and beyond them a line of palm trees was outlined in strokes of India ink against the stars. On the way back, I said idly that I couldn't understand why other people didn't throng to that lovely beach.

"Oh, they're afraid of the sharks," said George cheerfully. "I'm not, because I have a theory that sharks never come inshore at low tide."

The Italian ship didn't turn up on the day she was supposed to. This, they told me, was nothing out of the ordinary. But when I went down the next morning to check up, there was still no news. The morning after that was dreadful. A rumor spread all through the hotel that the ship was not coming in at all; it had sailed right by, said the gossips, and would put in at Zanzibar instead of Dar. This story rapidly gained supporting detail. I was told the kind of cargo the captain preferred, and that a load was waiting in Zanzibar; there was none in Dar. I was told that this sort of thing happened so often that it was scarcely worth remarking. I was told that I would probably have to wait at least another month for the next ship. It was appalling. All I could do was count money in my mind. Then, all at once, there the ship was, on the horizon, drawing nearer and nearer. After the first burst of relief, I had only the old, true worry to battle —the thoughts of going home.

I packed the afternoon before I was to sail at daybreak. Mrs. Mueller came to see me—a cheering influence with her large presence, broad smile, and cotton dress figured with enormous, brilliant flowers. She was busy, she said, arranging a farewell party for me, and wanted my ideas on the guest list. All the usual crowd, of course, had been invited and were coming— George, with his entourage of relatives, Mr. Fernandez from South America, and so on. Wasn't there anybody else I would like to ask?

I said, "It's awfully nice of you, Mrs. Mueller, and it all sounds lovely. Really, everyone's so kind in Dar es Salaam, I hate to go. No, I can't think of anybody else."

"Are you sure?" Mrs. Mueller looked sidewise at me. "Well, *I* can think of one person you've forgotten—that nice boy Malcolm. Surely you'd like to ask him to your sendoff party? Oh, yes, I've seen you together." She shook a finger at me, and laughed loudly. "It's a small village, Dar is," she said.

As a matter of fact, I didn't at all want to ask Malcolm, but I could hardly explain my reluctance to Mrs. Mueller, of all people. He had been very snooty about her: "Mrs. Mueller? Really, my dear girl, where *do* you pick them up? That woman used to run a laundry, did you know that? I'm quite sure of the facts."

No, of course I couldn't tell her. I decided just to invite him, because he was sure to refuse. That afternoon, when he came to pay his respects, I conveyed the message, and to my surprise he did not immediately and scornfully reject the idea.

"Well, I might manage it," he said thoughtfully. "Who's going to be there, do you know?"

"Oh, you wouldn't like it. There'll be George, for one."

"Oh, I get along with old George. We're the best of friends," said Malcolm. "Who else?"

I began to name them. When I came to Fernandez, he stopped me with uplifted hand, and shook his head vigorously. "That's enough," he said. "Sorry, but I couldn't possibly meet Fernandez socially."

Fernandez had seemed to me quite inoffensive. I said, curiously, "Now, would you mind telling me what's wrong with *him*?"

"Oh, he's an Argentine," said Malcolm, pronouncing it to rhyme with "wine." "Here in Dar, you see, Argentines aren't considered white."

"Well . . ." Somehow I could think of nothing to say. It would have meant starting a long way back, well before Malcolm's expressed thoughts began. I would have had to ask him why people *must* be considered white, anyway, and there was no use posing a question like that to Malcolm.

EDDYCHAN

Some time ago, we had a considerable outcry in England over a book of memoirs by a Japanese officer. He wrote of the regiment in which he served during the Second World War as the Glorious Regiment, and he claimed a splendid record of chivalry for his brother officers—and, indirectly, for himself—in their treatment of European prisoners of war. In particular, these were the men who had to work on the Burma-Siam Railway, and, according to the author, the Japanese officers were so tender of their captives' health that they cut their own rations so that the laborers might not go hungry. To put it as politely as possible, the British survivors of the episode do not agree with this account.

An enraged Briton does not paw the ground, he writes to the papers, and for a good while the correspondence columns of the daily press were pretty crowded. And the whole incident started me thinking once again—about memory, hatred, and the hangovers of wars generally. During the Japanese occupation of Hong Kong in the forties, while I was there, I suppose I did as much hating as anybody in town, yet today I can't work up even a lukewarm passion against the former objects of that feeling. Often, I can't recall what they did that was so awful. Apparently, whether I like it or not, I have a selective memory, and it's not only selective, it arranges. Like a tactful hostess seating a dinner party—or a Japanese army officer writing his memoirs—it keeps hostile items well separated. Only once have I succeeded in bringing a kind of unity and reason into play along with my arranging memory, forcing myself to see a subject whole, and I am sure I'm all the better for the exercise. By a coincidence, that subject is Japan.

Just after New Year's Day, 1935, my sister Helen and I sailed from San Francisco for Yokohama on a Japanese ship, en route to China. I am puzzled to account for the fact that we travelled first class. It wasn't my customary style. Possibly I had insisted that Helen, on this her first trip abroad, was too effete to face discomfort—I was like that—but it is more reasonable to suppose that the Something Maru was a one-class ship. Whatever the reason, it was fortunate that we weren't tucked away in tourist or steerage, because there we wouldn't have met Eddychan. As it was, we noticed him almost right away, when the ship was scarcely out of the Golden Gate. We were in an excited state, staring at everybody and everything, thrilled by the exotic look of the public rooms, by the puzzling little cubicle where the floor was raised about eight inches from the surrounding deck and carpeted with matting—a place, as we were to discover, for Japanese to sit on their legs and relax in homelike conditions—and by the preponderantly Japanese passengers. The man we later learned to call Eddychan stood out like the Rock of Gibraltar as he paced around the deck; he was obviously American—white-haired, Western-suited, pince-nezed—but he was always among Japanese companions in kimonos. The man he walked beside was a sturdy, scowling type in sandals and gunmetal silk tied in by a sort of sash with an ivory carving hanging on it. We thought him very attractive. Three other Japanese followed the pair, speaking if spoken to. The American spoke fluent Japanese—an accomplishment that appeared to us, with our Middle West background, far more impressive than a similar fluency in French or German. We wanted very much to know more about the group, and were delighted when the American finally came around the deck alone and paused to talk to us.

One of us asked, "Who is that old man in the wonderful clothes? Are you his interpreter?"

"You might call me that," he said gravely. In fact, as we soon found out, he was being modest. He was an important businessman travelling as one of a delegation of industrialists who had just completed a world tour and were now on their way home. He spoke Japanese because he'd been born in Japan, the son of a missionary, and was completely accustomed to the country. His friends, he said, called him Eddychan, a Japanese diminutive of Edward, his Christian name. As for the old man in the wonderful clothes, his name was Mr. Kuroda, and he was head of a leading textile works. His costume was one that any conservative Japanese gentleman might wear. "Kuroda-san doesn't believe in Westernization," Eddychan said. "He's not anti-Western, but he's satisfied to stay the way he is. He's a wonderful old man, full of life. You'll like him, and he'll like you. It's been great fun travelling with him—it's been a good trip altogether. I was able to look up a lot of old friends and a few relatives in the States." He smiled. "Still, it's going to be good to get home."

We asked a lot of questions about Japan. We knew very little about it, beyond the nursery stories we'd read as children and a collection of prints owned by Helen's husband. Eddychan set to work to make up for the gap in our education. As earnest as his father must have been with Sunday-school pupils, he gave us our first lecture on Japanese philosophy, and assured us that there would be more. Later, we were introduced to Kuroda-san, and from that moment on we were members of the party. We played Ping-Pong with the followers, or bathed with them in the pool, and every afternoon, at three o'clock, we had a Japanese lesson with Eddychan in the little *tatami room* (which, we now learned, was what the cubicle was called), trying to sit on our unshod heels as we repeated phrases after him: "This is ours. Those are yours. What is this? That is a lady. Thank you very much." American passengers glanced curiously into the room as they walked by, and looked amused. In the evening, we would meet the others for drinks in Kuroda-san's private suite. The old man tried to converse with us, chuckling richly when communication broke down. It all seemed to please Eddychan. One night, we attempted to entertain the company by singing in harmony, but stopped short at sight of Kuroda-san's expression of distaste. "He isn't used to chords," Eddychan explained. "Japanese music is always simple, with one melody and no harmony." Rallying, Kuroda-san sang a Japanese drinking song to show us what music ought to be, and spent the next hour teaching it to us.

That night, in our cabin, Helen said, "I can't believe that stuff we heard in Honolulu. If you ask me, it's applesauce."

I rubbed my aching ankles—it was a *sukiyaki* night when everyone had sat on his heels, on deck—and wondered what she meant. Honolulu? We had stopped there but, like many incidents in our pre-ship life, it was already dim. "What did they say?" I asked.

"Oh, a lot of stuff about spying, and how we'd have to be careful of the Japanese. You must remember."

"Oh, yes, that. I don't believe it," I said. I unfolded the blanket at the foot of my berth and carefully pulled it up to a point just over the breastbone. Pulling it higher left the feet exposed. Everything about the cabin was just a bit too small, too low, or too scanty, and gave me a generally oversized feeling that I liked. At home, nobody considered me a big person. "It can't be true," I continued. "If they really hated us so much, would they advertise for tourists the way they do? All those posters about cherry-blossom time, and Fujiyama—it must cost millions of dollars."

Helen said, "I'm going to ask Eddychan. He'll know."

Eddychan did know, and told us all about it. Now and then there was a tiny unpleasantness, he admitted, in some Japanese official's treatment of a Westerner. It was because a few of them, a very few, were extreme in their dislike of the West, but we shouldn't give it a thought. We would not have a bit of trouble, he assured us. The Japanese character was basically sound and opposed to violence. Japanese had a deep appreciation of beauty, and above all things they admired moderation. It was an aesthetic question, really. Before we knew it, we were listening to an Eddychan lecture on something far removed from the little vexations of officious customs inspectors—Japanese frugality. "They hate anything that seems to be showing off," he said. "They carry this idea to great lengths. A Japanese is so averse to making himself conspicuous that he wears the dullest possible colors and tries to look as if he'd dressed carelessly. A rich man may buy himself an expensive watch, but he'll have the works transferred to an old case, just to avoid ostentation."

This was hard to believe, but we tried. After he had gone, we spoke to each other of Eddychan's devotion to his adopted country. He was a wonderful character, we agreed—learned, kindly, and idealistic, even if somewhat preachy. I said that he ought to live in a monastery.

Helen and I were standing on deck the day before we were to land at Yokohama, watching the brisk business going on in the ship's shop, where passengers were investing heavily in perfume and stockings, when Kuroda-san came along and joined us. He, too, peered in, then turned to us and gestured toward the interior. Following the gesture with our eyes, we saw Eddychan among the shoppers, buying what looked very much like a lipstick. "Hah!" said Kuroda-san, and we could tell from the congested look of his face that he was about to speak English. He went on, in a heavily insinuating voice, "Eddychan, she have friend. Kamakura friend. Big girl, big!" To illustrate, he made an imaginary mark high up on an imaginary wall. Then he walked off, leaving us silent. Finally, Helen said loyally, "I'm *glad* he has a girl."

Of the landing I remember only a few details, such as the deputation that greeted Kuroda-san. Among a lot of smiling little men who bowed and bowed stood a little woman in brown. Tears rolled down from behind her spectacles. From the fact that Kuroda-san spoke to her only briefly and then ignored her, we knew she was his wife. Eddychan had told us quite a lot about domestic habits in Japan, and had recited to us what he said was an old proverb: "The Japanese gentleman beats his wife in public but kisses her behind the screen." Conscientiously, but without notable success, I was standing there trying to appreciate this point of view when another Japanese woman appeared and hurried up to Eddychan, beaming. I was glad to see that, for once, he didn't behave like a Japanese gentleman— he nearly kissed her, though that would have been shocking— and then he introduced her to us as Kazuko. As Kuroda-san had said, Kazuko was taller than the average. She wore a hat and a Western-style navy two-piece suit.

I had warned Helen that we would have to shake hands with our shipboard companions and say goodbye as soon as we landed. "Friendships you make on board never last afterward," I said, out of my wealth of experience—but this time I was wrong, for Eddychan had no intention of letting us go. With Kazuko, he chaperoned us into Tokyo and saw us settled at the Imperial Hotel—or, as Kazuko called it, the Teigoku Hoteru— and, as I remember, we spent practically all our time in Japan with them. I have an idea they persuaded us to stay a good deal longer than we'd planned, too. Certainly we saw many things— the holiday resort of Enoshima; Atami, with its hot baths; and various mountaintop vistas—but my most vivid recollection is of their house. Yes, their house. Helen and I were startled to find that Eddychan and Kazuko seemed to be living together like a regularly married couple, openly and without apparent shame. In the course of time, we gathered that they couldn't be married because Eddychan had a wife back in America who was estranged from him but didn't want a divorce. The Japanese, including Kazuko's relatives, seemed to take the arrangement for granted, so Helen and I did, too. The house stood on a small hill above the beach at a fishing village, Jijima, not far from Kamakura. We stayed there only one night; there wasn't much room. We had reservations at an inn in Kamakura, where we moved next day, but I remember the house best.

There Helen and I dressed up in Kazuko's kimonos, though she refused to go along with us and put one on, saying that she was too tall to wear it. Eddychan translated her explanation that she'd always been a problem to her family because she took up so much room. She was sensitive about it, especially as they evidently blamed her height on the fact that she took kindly to Western culture and sat on chairs, thus stretching her legs. Yet there were no chairs in Eddychan's house. It was all empty and clear, with nothing to break the smoothness of walls and floor but one alcove, where a scroll hung above a vase of catkin twigs. Kazuko opened a hidden cupboard door along the bottom of a wall to bring out a short-legged table and some drinks, while Eddychan showed us how carefully the house had been put together—with pegs, not nails, and with one special post of fine-grained wood. A large round window looked out to the sea over a hanging garden. Back of this big room, hidden away, were the kitchen and a Japanese bathroom with a tank of water over a fire. We boiled ourselves in that, and then ate seafood with chopsticks. People came in to be introduced: the servant—a little maid—and, later, a number of Kazuko's relatives, ranging from very young to ancient, who lived in a house nearby.

At bedtime, Kazuko and the maid turned the long room into two by pulling a screen across the middle. They brought out bedding from the cupboards and made up our bed, with large cushions for mattresses and fluffy quilts on top. We slept to the roaring, surging sound of waves below, but next morning, under a sky colored like a pigeon's neck, the sea was calm and reflected the sunrise. From the window, Helen and I watched people bathing naked in the shallows. Then we thought we had gone crazy.

A man in armor rode by on a white horse, cantering heavily and silently on the sand. "Eddychan!" we shouted, and Eddychan ran in, wearing a short kimono kind of garment. He soothed us, laughing. Yes, we had really seen it, he said—the rider was an eccentric neighbor who paraded in his father's samurai clothing every morning. None of the local people paid him any attention.

One can understand why I should remember the samurai, but it is more puzzling that other details should have survived in my mind through the years, though they have no apparent meaning. Why shouldn't I have forgotten about my toothbrush? There is nothing to remember about it except that I found it neatly lined up with the toothpaste tube, side by side, at the head of my bed at the very minute I needed them. I hadn't put them there myself. In the same way, I've hung on to Eddychan's story about the fact that Japanese reading styles—or, rather, printing styles—were changing. "You never know whether to go the old way, from right to left, or the new way, from left to right," he complained. "For a long time, I was puzzled by a certain sign I saw on my way into Tokyo every morning. It said 'Chiri dogu,' which meant nothing in either language, Japanese or English. Chilly dog? I'd heard of hot dogs, but not chilly. Then all of a sudden I caught on that I was reading it backward. It was 'Goodrich.' "

From Kamakura, we returned to the Teigoku—six strong this time, because Kazuko's small niece and nephew accompanied us. The room we took was communal—a long chamber, much plainer than the one Helen and I had occupied earlier, filled with iron cots. All of us, Eddychan included, slept there. Evidently, the hotel kept rooms like this for Japanese families. It was much cheaper than several smaller rooms would have been. The next morning, we all took the train from Tokyo into the countryside, where a group of student friends of Kazuko's met us and took us on foot to a temple. They had brought bags of mandarin oranges to share with us. Kazuko ate a lot of oranges, telling us that in the season when they were plentiful she always ate so many that her skin turned bright yellow. But at the end of our outing she was taken ill, not from eating oranges but with tonsillitis, and the doctor she went to sent her to stay for a few days in a Tokyo hospital.

Just at this time, there were great preparations all over town. Decorations appeared everywhere, and the streets were full of men in uniform. Helen and I learned that there was to be a grand procession in which the Emperor would participate. Along the parade route, all upstairs window shades were pulled down, by order, so that nobody might commit the offense of looking down on His Majesty. People were pretty edgy about everything, and Eddychan suggested delicately that we make no attempt to watch the procession, so we didn't. Instead, we stayed indoors all morning, and in the afternoon went to visit Kazuko in her hospital. She lay in a Western bed, with legs, but it was set up in a Japanese room carpeted with matting. She said she was feeling much better. Without Eddychan, conversation was necessarily limited, but we'd learned a little Japanese by that time, and we managed. After a while, another visitor arrived, an army officer splendid with gold braid and a sword at his side. Being in his socks, he was somewhat shorter than he would have been out-of-doors, so that the sword trailed behind him. I think Kazuko said that he was a student doing his military service, but I'm not sure. He had brought her a present of a large sketch pad and some paints, and after a while he unbuckled his sword, squatted down on the floor, and painted a picture of a cherry-blossom spray.

In Shanghai, Helen and I didn't talk much about Japan, and this was to be expected. The mind of a traveller has only one spotlight, and it is always trained on the present scene. Only later, in tranquillity, can he sort out what he remembers, and life in Shanghai, though it was many things, was not tranquil. Of course, even in all the racket and crash of that city, we wrote sometimes to Eddychan, but between letters we were too busy to think of Jijima. Eddychan knew this, and must have told Kuroda-san. The old man, too, wrote us a letter, translated in advance by his office interpreter: "To think that you are living in

China and your heart is no longer Japanese—behold me sunk in deepest desolation!"

When Helen began her packing to go home and we sorted out the things we had bought—pictures and carvings and lacquer—we came upon a kimono we had selected, with the help of Eddy-chan and Kazuko, in a big shop on the Ginza. That day, we'd been crazy about its colors—tender blues and greens that glowed like the flames of burning driftwood—but now the pattern looked strangely insignificant. Now the blues and greens were just colors. The glow was gone.

"Why, it's faded," I said.

Helen said, "It's the light. I've noticed when I'm painting how different things look here. Over there, we saw everything in a misty light. Here, it's all much more harsh. There are things you can't take with you." She folded the garment and put it away.

In the same manner, I folded up Japan, and did a thorough job of putting it away. There seemed nothing else to do, with history developing as it did. The Japanese I read about in the Shanghai papers, careering around North China, grabbing one privilege after another, sending peremptory threats to Nanking, were so far removed from the Japanese I knew that I began thinking of their country as a place I'd never seen. My Japan was an entirely different land, a land where one saw soft, nacreous colors at sunrise and everyone was devoted to philosophy. As the years passed and those other Japanese moved in on Chinese territory, robbing and sacking the cities, the illusion of this duality grew easier to maintain. The small, hairy men in uniform and split-toe rubber boots who overran the Chinese city of Shanghai bore no relation to the people who had fished and bathed in the waters below Jijima and took their children to play at Enoshima. It was simpler not to think at all about Eddy-chan and Kazuko, especially after Pearl Harbor.

Early in the fifties, I went to the East again and spent some time in Taiwan. The records say that the Taiwanese derive from

Chinese stock. Perhaps by now they have remembered this fact and behave accordingly, but when I was there they were still very resentful of Chiang and his followers, who had recently taken refuge on their island after fleeing across the Formosa Strait. The Taiwanese clung like barnacles to the Japanese customs with which they had grown up. It was puzzling to see those tall islanders slopping about in sandals and kimonos, and doubling up to sit on the matting-covered floors of their tiny houses. They were like a big dog I once had who would never believe he wasn't a Pekinese. At any rate, the people of Taiwan naturally reminded me of Japan. Japan was close, up to the north, beyond Okinawa. I felt its nearness as a sort of challenge. The feeling grew stronger and stronger, until, finally, I boarded a plane and flew to Tokyo.

It was a stupid thing to have done, I reflected a few hours later in my room at the Imperial Hotel. I was out of temper. Nothing was the same—I had seen that much from the window of the bus during the long, cluttered drive from the airport. This wasn't a return to the past but a meaningless venture into a strange city. Prewar streets had been obliterated and replaced by roads that led in new directions, so that I was lost before I started anywhere, and Tokyo was enormous beyond my power to have imagined it—a great, haphazard collection of buildings without a nucleus. Although the outside of the hotel still looked as I remembered it, like the base of a dark-red pyramid, inside all had been changed—at least, as far as I could see through the crowd of tourists struggling to make their way through the lobby. I asked myself what in the world I was doing there. I would have been tired and depressed in any case, because I'd come by night flight and it was the middle of the morning. As things were, there seemed nothing to do about the debacle but book a passage out as soon as possible. However, after a bath, I reminded myself that I knew people in the city—not friends of the old days but acquaintances from Hong Kong—and I thought I might as well telephone some of them and fill the time. One of them, an Englishman, asked me to join him at lunch. "That is, if you don't mind meeting a couple of other people," he said. "They're Japanese business contacts, and I can't very well cancel them out."

Five minutes after we sat down to eat, the man on my right asked me if I'd looked up Eddychan as yet.

I squealed and dropped my spoon in the soup. "Do you mean he's still alive? I never thought—"

My neighbor, smiling broadly, assured me that Eddychan was still alive, still living at Jijima and working in Tokyo. "I spoke because I remembered meeting you once with him. You were with another lady—your sister, I believe? Oh, Eddychan will be delighted to hear that you are in Tokyo. I had better telephone the news to his office. Excuse me." He hurried from the table to make the call.

When I got back to the hotel after lunch, Eddychan was there.

Everyone knows what it is like to see a friend after long absence. There is a moment of non-recognition, like that experienced when you catch sight of yourself in a triple mirror at an unaccustomed angle. Then it is gone and you are once again looking at a familiar face. For that moment, Eddychan was a strange, shrunken old man with bitter wrinkles around his mouth, but the old man vanished in the next moment, and I never saw him again. That was Eddychan hugging me and smiling with joy. I was in Japan again, and everything was all right.

"Of course you're coming out to Jijima with me, right now," he said. "Hurry up. Pack a bag."

Without waiting for my answer, he telephoned Kazuko. I heard her exclamation when he told her I was there. Eddychan hung up and said, "She wasn't sure she wanted you to come, but I talked her into it." I suppose I must have looked distressed, for he laughed. "She had to ask what you look like first. Specifically, she wanted to know if you're any fatter than you used to be."

"Oh, yes, I—"

"That's what I told her," said Eddychan, "and she said, 'In that case, hurry up and bring her.' Kazuko's awfully worried be-

215

cause she's put on weight. I really think she'd have refused to welcome you if you'd been slim." He beamed, delighted, as always, with women's foibles.

I said, rather resentfully, "Then how can she bear having *you* around? You're so thin I hardly recognized you. What's happened to you?"

Eddychan stopped laughing and said, "I'll tell you all about it when we get home."

I didn't know Kazuko, either, for just a minute, when she came running in clogs along the Jijima street to meet us. She hadn't aged—at least, not to my Western eyes—but she was indeed heavier, and she was wearing Japanese dress besides. But she was Kazuko, and the house, when we got there, was the same house. Contentedly, I wandered around it, pausing at the window, saying, "Just the same, just the same."

"Alas, not quite the same," Eddychan answered. He was getting the little table out of the wall, and the glasses and a bottle "If you look really closely, you'll find it is all pretty shabby, I'm afraid. Poor old place, it's badly run down. The wood ought to be renewed every so often, and we haven't had it done. I'm afraid the roof may blow off in the next bad storm. It's almost impossible to get work done these days, you see. The real workmen don't exist anymore. Kazuko's got one devoted helper who tries, but it's not the same. He's just the village idiot, and you need a real artist for a house."

He seemed about to embark on one of his old lectures about the Japanese sense of beauty, but instead he broke off to talk to Kazuko about dinner. There were no servants, he explained; Kazuko did the cooking. I refrained from asking about the relatives and their children, thinking that they must have died or gone away.

It wasn't until we had eaten and put the bowls away that Eddychan talked about the years between. I started it with a question.

"Oh, yes, I saw it coming," he replied. "One couldn't help but know it was in the cards. What I didn't foresee—and nobody else

216

did, either—was the way the military-slanted group would behave once they'd got what they wanted and we were at war. For a while, after Pearl Harbor, things went on quite calmly—surprisingly calmly. We lived much as we'd always done, though, of course, we didn't go into Tokyo. Then, little by little, things happened. Young people disappeared into the services or prison, banks shut—I don't remember all of it. I'd always intended to make arrangements about money—transfer funds to America for safety—before a crash came, but I didn't. At the beginning, I expected to be interned, and when I wasn't we began to think they'd decided to overlook me. I'd been here all my life, and I knew so many people. I'd even thought seriously of taking Japanese nationality at one time, but decided against it because I had commitments in the States. Sometimes I've wondered if it would have made any difference if I'd done that, but I don't think it would. They had the bit in their teeth." He poured drinks. "Kazuko, here, was full of plans. She'd get a job even if I couldn't, and keep us both going." He looked fondly at her. "Then, one day, they came to the door and told me to come along. I was put into a camp in Tokyo for a while, and then sent to another place way up in the mountains—you don't know the district. It was pretty rough."

"What about Kazuko?" I asked. Kazuko looked brightly at me, and back at Eddychan. She was listening closely, understanding most of it.

"She nearly went crazy," said Eddychan. "She couldn't find out where I was. It took her two weeks before she tracked me down."

Kazuko said something to him, and he shook his head, but after a little argument he said, "She wants me to go into details about how they treated us, but what's the use? We were set to digging for a new road. Then I got sick, but they wouldn't let me off. They were pretty brutal."

It was dark now, and the only highlights in the room were our glasses. In the dusk, I saw Eddychan reach out to a place on the mat, without looking. His fingers closed on his pipe exactly where Kazuko had put it, where he knew it would be, and I remembered my toothbrush.

"This girl," said Eddychan, and shook his head a little. "She dropped everything. Left her family and came up to the mountains to be nearby. She got herself a job, and every day, after work, she walked to the camp. It was several miles each way from the town. She brought extra food and comforts—everything she could get—and tried to bully the guards into passing them in to me. Sometimes they did, but sometimes they beat her up and drove her away."

Kazuko said something again, and he added, "Oh, yes. When it was all over and I got out, I was considerably reduced in importance. I weighed eighty-four pounds. We had a good laugh the first time I put on the clothes she'd saved for me all that time."

It was several years after that evening that I got a letter from Helen asking me for news of Eddychan and Kazuko. She'd been corresponding with them ever since my visit, but then, she said, Eddychan had stopped writing and she had heard a rumor that he was dead. She wanted me to find out what I could, so I wrote to the man at whose luncheon party I had met Eddychan's friend. He answered, "Sorry to give you such bad news of your friends, but I've just had the report from my people here that he and his girl friend are dead, done in by one of the locals. Apparently, the murderer was the village idiot. They'd befriended him, and he had the run of the house, doing repairs and odd jobs. He must have had a brainstorm. At any rate, he stabbed them both to death."

Not long ago, I had occasion to revisit Japan. This time, there were no moods, no nostalgia. I had a good, practical reason for being there, errands to run, people to see. I wouldn't have had time to look up old friends even if there had been any. One morning, I started for a luncheon appointment a long way out of Tokyo, down the peninsula past Yokohama, by car. There were two Japanese with me, besides the driver. Countryside motoring in Japan is no longer the ordeal it used to be, for splendid new roads were built for the Olympics. Our chauffeur was a steady character, not addicted to sounding his horn in the old, tempestuous way. In short, there was nothing to remind me of prewar days, and I didn't give them a thought until, unexpectedly, something rose up ahead of us—mountain and island in one, close to the shore. Its sides were circled by paths and staircases. Houses and shops balanced on the slopes. Up and down the stairs and along the paths went people, the children carrying pails and spades and other seaside gear. It was decidedly a holiday scene, and I recognized it.

"Enoshima!" I cried.

My companions assented, pleased by my excitement. "Have you been to Japan before?"

I said that I had. "It was long ago," I went on. "I was staying with friends, and they brought me to see Enoshima. They had a lovely house at Jijima."

"Where did you say?" asked the other man.

"Jijima," I repeated.

They looked blank. I wrote the name in a notebook I was carrying and showed it to them. "It's that fishing village, you know, on the bay quite near Kamakura," I said. "You can see Fuji from the front window, most days."

"Jijima." They said it over to each other softly, in perplexed tones. The first man turned to me. "There's been much building in this part of Japan. Boundaries, villages—many of them disappear. Still, perhaps—" He leaned forward and asked the driver, but the driver didn't know about Jijima, either. None of them had ever heard of it.

And I suppose that may be what I mean about seeing a subject whole. In the end, there are death, disappearance—and completion.

THE BIG SMOKE

Though I had always wanted to be an opium addict, I can't claim that as the reason I went to China. The opium ambition dates back to that obscure period of childhood when I wanted to be a lot of other things, too—the greatest expert on ghosts, the world's best ice skater, the champion lion tamer, you know the kind of thing. But by the time I went to China I was grown up, and all those dreams were forgotten.

Helen kept saying that she would go home to California, where her husband was waiting, as soon as she'd seen Japan, but as the time for her departure drew near she grew reluctant and looked around for a good excuse to prolong the tour. As she pointed out to me, China was awfully close by and we knew that an old friend was living in Shanghai. It would be such a waste to let the chance slip. Why shouldn't we go over and take just one look, for a weekend? I was quite amenable, especially as, for my part, I didn't have to go back to America. My intention was to move on south in leisurely fashion, after Helen had gone home, and land someday in the Belgian Congo, where I planned to find a job. All this wasn't going to have to be done with speed, because I still had enough money to live on for a while. My sister accepted these plans as natural, for she knew that a man had thrown me over. Officially, as it were, I was going to the Congo to forget that my heart was broken; it was the proper thing to do in the circumstances. My attitude toward her was equally easy-going. If she didn't want to go home just yet, I felt, it was none of my business. So when she suggested China I said, "Sure, why not?"

We went. We loved Shanghai. Helen shut up her conscience for another two months, staying on and cramming in a tremend-ous variety of activities—parties, temples, curio shops, having dresses made to order overnight, a trip to Peiping, embassy recep-tions, races. I didn't try to keep up with her. It had become clear to me from the first day in China that I was going to stay for-ever, so I had plenty of time. Without a struggle, I shelved the Congo and hired a language teacher, and before Helen left I had found a job teaching English at a Chinese college. It was quite a while before I recollected that old ambition to be an opium smoker.

As a newcomer, I couldn't have known that a lot of the drug was being used here, there, and everywhere in town. I had no way of recognizing the smell, though it pervaded the poorer districts. I assumed that the odor, something like burning cara-mel or those herbal cigarettes smoked by asthmatics, was just part of the mysterious effluvia produced in Chinese cookhouses. Walking happily through side streets and alleys, pausing here and there to let a rickshaw or a cart trundle by, I would sniff and move on, unaware that someone close at hand was indulging in what the books called that vile, accursed drug. Naturally I never saw a culprit, since even in permissive Shanghai opium smoking was supposed to be illegal.

It was through a Chinese friend, Pan Heh-ven, that I learned at last what the smell denoted. I had been at a dinner party in a restaurant with him, and had met a number of his friends who were poets and teachers. Parties at restaurants in China used to end when the last dish and the rice were cold and the guests had drunk their farewell cup of tea at a clean table. That night, though, the group still had a lot to say after that—they always did—and we stood around on the pavement outside carrying on a discussion of modern literature that had started at table. We were in that part of town called the Chinese city, across Soochow Creek, outside the boundaries of the foreign concessions. It was hot. A crumpled old paper made a scraping little sound like autumn leaves along the gutter, and the skirts of the men's long gowns stirred in the same wind. During dinner, they had spoken English out of courtesy, but now, in their excitement, they had long since switched to the Chinese language, and I stood there waiting for somebody to remember me and help me find a taxi, until Heh-ven said, "Oh, excuse us for forgetting our foreign guest. We are all going now to my house. Will you come?"

Of course I would. I'd been curious about his domestic life, which he seldom mentioned. So we all moved off and walked to the house—an old one of Victorian style, with more grounds than I was used to seeing around city houses in America. I say Victorian, but that was only from the outside, where gables and a roughcast front made it look like the kind of building I knew. Indoors was very different. It was bare, as one could see at a glance because the doors stood open between rooms—no carpets, no wallpaper, very little furniture. Such chairs and sofas and tables as stood around the bare floor seemed as impersonal as lost articles in a vacant shop. Yet the house wasn't deserted. A few people were there in the rooms—a man who lounged, as if defiantly, on the unyielding curve of a sofa, four or five children scampering and giggling in whispers, an old woman in the blue blouse and trousers of a servant, and a young woman in a plain dark dress.

This last, it appeared, was Heh-ven's wife, and at least some of the children were theirs. I was embarrassed because the whole household gawked at me; one small boy who looked like a miniature Heh-ven said something that made the others giggle louder. Heh-ven spoke briefly to his family and told us to follow him upstairs, where we emerged on a cozier scene. Here the rooms were papered, and though everything still seemed stark to my Western eyes, there was more furniture around. We trooped into a bedroom where two hard, flat couches had been pushed together, heads against a wall and a heap of small pillows on each. In the center of the square expanse of white sheet that covered them was a tray that held several unfamiliar objects—a little silver oil lamp with a shade like an inverted glass tumbler, small boxes, and a number of other small things I didn't recognize. I sat on a stiff, spindly chair, and the men disposed themselves here and there in the room, very much at home as they chattered away, picked up books and riffled through them, and paid no attention to what was going on on the double couch. I found the proceedings there very odd, however, and stared in fascination.

Heh-ven had lain down on his left side, alongside the tray and facing it. He lit the lamp. One of his friends, a plump little man named Hua-ching, lay on his right side on the other side of the tray, facing Heh-ven, each with head and shoulders propped on the pillows. Heh-ven never stopped conversing, but his hands were busy and his eyes were fixed on what he was doing—knitting, I thought at first, wondering why nobody had ever mentioned that this craft was practiced by Chinese men. Then I saw that what I had taken for yarn between the two needles he manipulated was actually a kind of gummy stuff, dark and thick. As he rotated the needle ends about each other, the stuff behaved like taffy in the act of setting; it changed color, too, slowly evolving from its earlier dark brown to tan. At a certain moment, just as it seemed about to stiffen, he wrapped the

223

whole wad around one needle end and picked up a pottery object about as big around as a teacup. It looked rather like a cup, except that it was closed across the top, wtih a rimmed hole in the middle of this fixed lid. Heh-ven plunged the wadded needle into this hole, withdrew it, leaving the wad sticking up from the hole, and modelled the rapidly hardening stuff so that it sat on the cup like a tiny volcano. He then picked up a piece of polished bamboo that had a large hole near one end, edged with a band of chased sliver. Into this he fixed the cup, put the opposite end of the bamboo into his mouth, held the cup with the tiny cone suspended above the lamp flame, and inhaled deeply. The stuff bubbled and evaporated as he did so, until nothing of it was left. A blue smoke rose from his mouth, and the air was suddenly full of that smell I had encountered in the streets of Shanghai. Truth lit up in my mind.

"You're smoking opium!" I cried. Everybody jumped, for they had forgotten I was there.

Heh-ven said, "Yes, of course I am. Haven't you ever seen it done before?"

"No. I'm *so* interested."

"Would you like to try it?"

"Oh, yes."

Nobody protested, or acted shocked or anything. In fact, nobody but Hua-ching paid any attention. At Heh-ven's request, he smoked a pipe to demonstrate how it was done, then relaxed against the pillows for a few minutes. "If you get up immediately, you are dizzy," explained Heh-ven. I observed his technique carefully and, by the time I took my place on the couch, had a reasonable notion of how it was done. You sucked in as deeply as possible, and held the smoke there as long as you could before exhaling. Remembering that I'd never been able to inhale cigarette smoke, I was worried that the world of the opium addict might be closed to me. In daydreams, as in night dreams, one doesn't take into account the real self and the failings of the flesh. The romantic is always being confronted by this dilemma, but that night I was spared it. When I breathed in I felt *almost* sick, but my throat didn't close, and after a moment I was fine.

I couldn't dispose of the tiny volcano all in one mighty pull, as the others had done, but for a beginner I didn't do badly—not at all. Absorbed in the triumph of not coughing, I failed to take notice of the first effects, and even started to stand up, but Heh-ven told me not to. "Just stay quiet and let's talk," he suggested.

We all talked—about books, and books, and Chinese politics. That I knew nothing about politics didn't put me off in the least. I listened with keen interest to everything the others had to say in English, and when they branched off into Chinese I didn't mind. It left me to my thoughts. I wouldn't have minded anything. The world was fascinating and benevolent as I lay there against the cushions, watching Heh-ven rolling pipes for himself. Pipes—that's what they called the little cones as well as the tube, I suppose because it is easier to say than pipefuls. Anyway, the word "pipeful" is not really accurate, either. Only once, when Hua-ching asked me how I was, did I recollect the full significance of the situation. Good heavens, I was smoking opium! It was hard to believe, especially as I didn't seem to be any different.

"I don't feel a thing," I told him. "I mean, I'm enjoying myself with all of you, of course, but I don't feel any different. Perhaps opium has no effect on me?"

Heh-ven pulled at the tiny beard he wore and smiled slightly. He said, "Look at your watch." I cried out in surprise; it was three o'clock in the morning.

"Well, there it is," Heh-ven said. "And you have stayed in one position for several hours, you know—you haven't moved your arms or your head. That's opium. We call it Ta Yen, the Big Smoke."

"But it was only one pipe I had. And look at you, you've smoked four or five, but you're still all right."

"That's opium, too," said Heh-ven cryptically.

Later that morning, in my own bed, I tried to remember if I'd had drug-sodden dreams, but as far as I could recall there hadn't been dreams at all, which was disappointing. I didn't feel any craving, either. I simply wasn't an addict. I almost decided that

225

the whole thing was just a carefully nurtured myth. Still, I gave it another chance a few days later, and again a third time, and so on. To make a surprisingly long story short, a year of earnest endeavor went by. It's impossible now to pinpoint the moment in time when I could honestly claim to be an addict, but I do remember the evening when Heh-ven's wife, Pei-yu, said I was. I had arrived at their house about six in the evening, when most of the family was in the smoking room. It was a nice domestic scene, the children playing on the floor, Pei-yu sitting on the edge of the couch really knitting, with wool, and Heh-ven lying on his side in the familiar position, idly stocking up opium pellets to save time later, now and then rolling a wad on his second finger to test the texture. A good pellet should be of just the right color, and not too dry, but not too sticky, either. These refinements added a lot to one's pleasure. I suppose people who are fussy about their tea have the same impulse.

I was feeling awful that evening. I had a cold and I'd been up too late the night before. I was also in a tearing rage with Heh-ven. By this time, I was publishing a Chinese-English magazine at a press he owned in the Chinese city—or, rather, I was trying to publish it, and Heh-ven was maddeningly unbusinesslike about the printing. That day, I'd waited at home in vain for hours because he had faithfully promised that some proofs would be delivered before three o'clock. When I marched in on the peaceful scene in the smoking room, only a fit of sneezing prevented my delivering him a stinging scolding. At the sound of the sneezes, Pei-yu looked up at me sharply. Then *she* started scolding Heh-ven. I hadn't learned any of the Shanghai dialect— it was Mandarin I was studying—but the spirit of her speech was clear enough.

"Pei-yu says you are an addict and it's my fault," interpreted Heh-ven cheerfully.

I felt rather flattered, but my feelings about Heh-ven's lack of performance on the press made me sound surly as I replied, "Why should she say that?" I lay down in the accustomed place as I spoke, and reached for the pipe.

"Because your eyes and nose are running."

"So? Is that a symptom?" I looked at Pei-yu, who nodded hard. I inhaled a pipe and continued, "But that isn't why my nose is running. I've got the most awful cold."

"Oh yes, opium smokers always have colds." Heh-ven prepared another pipe. "When you don't get the Big Smoke, you weep. Still, in your case, I think my wife is mistaken. You are not yet an addict. Even *I* am not an addict, really—not very much addicted, though I smoke more than you. People like us, who have so much to do, are not the type to become addicted."

No, I reflected, Pei-yu was certainly exaggerating to a ridiculous degree. Of course I could do without it. I liked it, of course —I liked it. I had learned what was so pleasant about opium. Gone were the old romantic notions of wild drug orgies and heavily flavored dreams, but I didn't regret them, because the truth was much better. To lie in a quiet room talking and smoking—or, to put things in their proper order, smoking and talking—was delightfully restful and pleasant. I wasn't addicted, I told myself, but you had to have a bit of a habit to appreciate the thing. One used a good deal of time smoking, but, after all, one had a good deal of time. The night clubs, the cocktail and dinner parties beloved of foreign residents in Shanghai would have palled on me even if I'd kept up drink for drink with my companions. Now I hardly ever bothered to go to these gatherings. Opium put me off drinking, and people who didn't smoke seemed more and more remote, whereas smokers always seemed to have tastes and ideas compatible with mine. We would read aloud to each other a good deal—poetry, mostly. Reading and music and painting were enough to keep us happy. We didn't care for eating or drinking or voluptuous pleasures. . . . I seem to fall into a kind of *fin-de-siècle* language when I talk about opium, probably because it was rather a *fin-de-siècle* life I led when I was smoking it, and in a social as well as a literary sense. The modern, Westernized Chinese of Shanghai frowned on smoking—not on moral grounds but because it was considered so lamentably old-fashioned. My friends, in their traditional long gowns, were deliberately, self-consciously reactionary, and opium was a part of this attitude, whereas modern people preferred to stun themselves with whiskey or brandy. Opium was decadent. Opium was for grandfathers.

We used to read Cocteau's book on opium and discuss it. Hua-ching loved the drawings that represent the feelings of a man under cure, in which the pipe grows progressively larger and the man smaller. Then the pipe proliferates—his limbs turn into pipes—until at last he is built up completely of pipes. During such talks, Heh-ven sometimes spoke of himself frankly as an addict but at other times he still said he wasn't. I never knew what sort of statement he was going to make on the subject. "My asthma caused it, you know," he said once. "My father is asthmatic, so he smokes. I, too, am asthmatic, and so is Pei-yu. Now and then, when hers is very bad, she will take a pipe, because it is a good medicine for that disease."

One day, after he had been even more contradictory than was his custom, I drew up a table of the smoker's creed:

1. I will never be an addict.
2. I can't become addicted. I am one of those people who take it or let it alone.
3. I'm not badly addicted.
4. It's a matter of will power, and I can stop any time.

Any time. Time. That was something that had lost its grip on me. It was amazing how watches varied their rate of running, sometimes galloping, at other times standing still. To keep up with my job, I had to look at my watch often; it had a trick of running away when I didn't notice, causing me to forget dates or arrive at appointments incredibly late. I appeared sleepy. I know this from what outsiders told me about myself—"You need sleep," they would say—but I never *felt* sleepy, exactly; inside, my mind was unusually clear, and I could spend a whole night talking without feeling the need of rest. This was because I was an addict. I admitted it now, and was pleased that I could feel detached. We opium smokers, I reflected, *are* detached, and that is one of our advantages. We aren't troubled with unpleasant emotions. The alcoholic indulges in great bouts of weeping sentiment, but the smoker doesn't. You never find a smoker blubber-

228

ing and blabbing his secrets to the opium seller. We are proud and reserved. Other people might think us drowsy and dull; we know better. The first reaction to a good long pull at the pipe is a stimulating one. I would be full of ideas, and as I lay there I would make plans for all sorts of activity. Drowsiness of a sort came on later, but even then, inside my head, behind my drooping eyes, my mind seethed with exciting thoughts.

Still, I couldn't ignore the disadvantages. If I had, I would have been unworthy of the adjective "detached." Being an addict was awfully inconvenient. I couldn't stay away from my opium tray, or Heh-ven's, without beginning to feel homesick. I would think of the lamp in the shaded room, the coziness, the peace and comfort with great longing. Then my nose would start to run and I was afraid somebody from outside would have the sense to understand what was the matter with me. When I say afraid, that is what I mean—for some reason, there was dread in the idea of being spotted. This was strange. True, smoking was against the law in Shanghai, but only mild penalties were likely to have been visited on me. Still, I was afraid. I think it may have been a physical symptom, like the running nose.

All of these little points we discussed at great length, lying around the tray. Hua-ching had a theory that addiction lay not so much in the smoking itself as in the time pattern one got used to. "If you vary your smoking every day, you have far less strong a habit," he assured us earnestly. "The great mistake is to do it at the same hour day after day. I'm careful to vary my smoking times. You see, it's all in the head."

Jan, a Polish friend who sometimes joined us, disputed this. "It's the drug itself," he said. "If it's all in the head, why do I feel it in my body?" The argument tailed off in a welter of definitions. A smoker loves semantics. However, I resolved one day to test myself and see who was master, opium or me, and I accepted an invitation to spend the weekend on a houseboat up-river with an English group. In the country, among foreigners, it would be impossible to get opium.

Well, it wasn't as bad as I'd expected. I was bored, and I couldn't keep my mind on the bridge they insisted that I play, but then I never can. I had an awful cold, and didn't sleep much. My stomach was upset and my legs hurt. Still, it wasn't so bad. I didn't want to lie down and scream—it could be borne. On the way home, my cold got rapidly worse—but why not? People do catch cold. The only really bad thing was the terror I felt of being lost, astray, naked, shivering in a world that seemed imminently brutal. . . . Half an hour after I got back, I was at Heh-ven's, the cronies listening to my blow-by-blow report, expressing, according to their characters, admiration, skepticism, or envy. I was glad that none of them failed to understand my impulse to flee the habit. Every one of them, it seemed, had had such moments, but not everyone was as stubborn as I.

"You could have given her pills," said Hua-ching reproachfully to Heh-ven. I asked what he meant, and he said that addicts who had to leave the orbit of the lamp for a while usually took along little pellets of opium to swallow when things got bad. A pellet wasn't the same thing as smoking, but it alleviated some of the discomfort.

Heh-ven said, "I didn't give them on purpose. She wanted to see what it was like, and the pills would have spoiled the full effect. Besides, they are somewhat poisonous. Still, if she wants them, next time she can have them."

Snuggling luxuriously on a pillow, I said, "There won't be a next time."

Some weeks later, I got sick. I must have smoked too much. In a relatively mild case of overindulgence, one merely gets nightmares, but this wasn't mild. I vomited on the way home from Heh-ven's, and went on doing it when I got in, until the houseboy called the doctor. This doctor was an American who had worked for years in the community, but I didn't know him well. Of course, I had no intention of telling him what might be wrong, and I was silent as he felt my pulse and looked at my tongue and took my temperature. Finally, he delivered judgment. "Jaundice. Haven't you noticed that you're yellow?"

"No."

"Well, you are—yellow as an orange," he said. "How many pipes do you smoke in a day?"

I was startled, but if he could play it calm, so could I. "Oh, ten, eleven, something like that," I said airily, and he nodded and wrote out a prescription, and left. No lecture, no phone call to the police, nothing. I ought to have appreciated his forbearance, but I was angry, and said to Heh-ven next day, "He doesn't know as much as he thinks he does. People don't count pipes— one man's pipe might make two of another's." The truth was that I resented the doctor's having stuck his foot in the door of my exclusive domain.

All in all, if I'd been asked how I was faring I would have said I was getting on fine. I had no desire to change the way I was living. Except for the doctor, foreign outsiders didn't seem to guess about me; they must have thought I looked sallow, and certainly they would have put me down as absentminded, but nobody guessed. The Chinese, of course, were different, because they'd seen it all before. I annoyed one or two people, but I managed to pass, especially when the war between China and Japan flared up just outside the foreign-occupied part of the city. Shells fell all around our little island of safety, and sometimes missed their mark and bounced inside it. It is no wonder that the American doctor didn't take any steps about me—he had a lot of other things to occupy his mind. The war didn't bother me too much. I soon got used to the idea of it. Opium went up in price —that was all that mattered.

But the war cut me off definitely from the old world, and so, little by little, I stopped caring who knew or didn't know. People who came calling, even when they weren't smokers, were shown straight into the room where I smoked. I now behaved very much like Heh-ven; there was even an oily smudge on my left forefinger, like the one on his, that wouldn't easily wash off. It came from testing opium pellets as they cooled. Heh-ven, amused by the smudge, used to call the attention of friends to it. "Look," he would say, "have you ever before seen a white girl with that mark on her finger?"

231

I wasn't the only foreign opium smoker in Shanghai. Apart from Jan, there were several others I knew. One was connected with the French diplomatic service. He and his wife had picked up their habit in Indo-China. It was through them that I met Bobby—a German refugee, a doctor who had built up enough of a practice in Shanghai to live on it. He wasn't an addict—I don't think I ever saw him touch a pipe—but he seemed to spend a lot of time with addicts. Sometimes I wondered why he dropped in at Heh-ven's so often. I rather wished he wouldn't, because he was dull. Still, it didn't matter much whether outsiders were dull or bright, and as he happened to call on me one afternoon when I had received a shattering letter, I confided in him.

"It's about this silly magazine I've been publishing," I said. "They want to expand its circulation—the people who own it, that is—and they say I've got to go to Chungking to talk to them."

"And you can't go, of course," said Bobby.

"I can, too," I lifted myself up on my elbow and spoke indignantly. "Certainly I can go. What do you mean, I can't? Only, it's a bother." I lay down again and started rolling a pellet fast. My mind buzzed with all the things that would have to be done —arranging about my house, getting a permit to travel. And I'd have to go through Hong Kong, taking a boat down there and then flying inland. It was tiring just to think about it, and here was Bobby talking again.

"Listen to me. Listen carefully. You can't do it—*you* can't."

This time he managed to worry me. "Why not?"

"Because of the opium. Your habit," said Bobby.

I laughed. "Oh, that's what it is, is it? No, that'll be all right." The pellet was ready, shaped into a cone, and I smoked it, then said, "I can stop whenever I want to. You don't know me well, but I assure you I can stop any time."

"How recently have you tried?" he demanded, and paused. I didn't reply because I was trying to reckon it. He went on, "It's been some time, I'm sure. I've known you myself for a year, and you've never stopped during that period. I think you'll find you can't do it, young lady."

"You're wrong," I said violently. "I tell you, you're all wrong —you don't know me."

"And in the interior it's not so funny if you're caught using it, you know. If you're caught, you know what happens." He sliced a stiff hand across his throat. He meant that the Kuomintang had put a new law into effect; people they caught smoking were to be decapitated. But surely that couldn't happen to *me*.

I looked at him with new uncertainty and said, "What will I do?"

"You'll be all right, because I can help you," said Bobby, all of a sudden brisk and cheerful. "You can be cured quite easily. Have you heard of hypnosis?"

I said that of course I'd heard of it, and even witnessed it. "There was a medical student at school who put people to sleep —just made them stare at a light bulb and told them they were sleepy."

Bobby made a call on my telephone, talking in German. He hung up and said, "We start tomorrow morning. I have a bed for you at my little hospital—a private ward, no less. Get up early if you can and do what you usually do in the morning—smoke if you like, I have no objections—but be there at nine o'clock. I'll write down the directions for the taxi-driver." He did so. Then, at the door, he added, "Heh-ven will try to talk you out of it, you know. Don't let him."

I said, "Oh no, Bobby, he wouldn't do that. This is my own affair, and he'd never interfere."

"Just don't let him, that's all. Don't forget a suitcase with your night things. You'll probably bring some opium pills, but if you do I'll find them, so save yourself the trouble."

Before I became an addict, I used to think that a confirmed smoker would be frantically afraid of the idea of breaking off. Actually, it isn't like that—or wasn't with me. At a certain stage, a smoker is cheerfully ready to accept almost any suggestion, including the one of breaking off. Stop smoking? Why, of course, he will say—what a good idea! Let's start tomorrow. After a couple of pipes, I was very pleased about it, and rang up Heh-ven to tell him. He, too, was pleased, but couldn't see why I was in such a hurry.

"Oh, wonderful!" he said. "But why tomorrow? If you wait, we can do it together. It's always easier with somebody else. Wait, and I'll ask Bobby to fix me up, too."

"I'd like to, Heh-ven, but he's got everything arranged for me at the hospital, and I can hardly change things around now. And, as he said, I haven't got much time—only a couple of weeks before I have to go to Chungking. It'll be easier when your turn comes."

The high sweetness in his voice when he replied was significant, I knew, of anger. "Of course, since you are so happy to take the advice of a man you hardly know . . ."

It was a struggle, but I hadn't given in by the time I hung up. Full of opium or not, I knew all too well what would happen if I consented to wait for Heh-ven for anything at all—a tea party or a cure. He'd put it off and put it off until it was forgotten. I shrugged, and had another pipe, and next morning I almost overslept, but didn't. The old man who took care of the house carried my bag out to the taxi, talking to himself, and stood there as I climbed in, a worried look on his face. He didn't trust anything about the project. "I come see you soon," he promised.

I had never heard of Bobby's hospital. We drove a long way through the shops and hovels that ringed the foreign town, so that I half expected we would enter the Japanese lines, but before we got that far we found it—a building about as big as most middle-class Shanghai houses and only a little shabbier. Over the entrance hung a dirty white flag and a red cross on it. Bobby was at the door, his teeth gleaming in a relieved smile, his spectacles flashing in the morning sun. Clearly, he hadn't been quite sure I would turn up, and he asked how Heh-ven had taken the news.

"He wants you to fix him up, too—someday," I told him.

"Whenever he's ready. Come in here. The nurse will look after your suitcase."

234

I followed him to a flimsily walled office filled with, among other things, filing cases, a heavy old desk, and one overstuffed chair, in which he told me to sit. He gave me a pill, and a tin cup of water to help it down. I stared around curiously. There were cardboard boxes piled against the walls, and an instrument cabinet. A patch of sunlight lay on the floor matting. The room was very hot. Sweat rolled down Bobby's face. Though smokers have little sense of smell, I could distinguish a reek of disinfectant. I asked what kind of cases the hospital cared for, and Bobby said it took in everything. He spoke absently, pacing up and down, waiting for the pill to work on me.

I said, "I don't see why you need to use a pill. The medical student just used a light bulb."

"Oh, I could do that, too, but it takes too long," Bobby retorted. "In the future, I want to cure whole roomfuls of addicts all at once, hypnotizing them in groups, and how far do you think I'd get if I tried to put each one under by making him stare at a light? No, barbiturates are quicker. Aren't you sleepy yet?"

"No. Why roomfuls of addicts?"

He explained. There were far too many for one man to cope with unless he employed such methods. In fact, he said, my case was being used to that end. If it worked—and it was going to work, it was bound to work, he assured me—he wanted me to exert all the influence I might have to persuade the authorities involved to hire him as a kind of National Grand Curer-in-Chief of opium addiction. He talked warmly and hopefully of these plans, until, as through a glass brightly, I saw a schoolroom full of white-clad Chinese, row on row, all exactly alike, with their faces lifted toward Bobby on a very high dais. He was saying . . . was . . .

"Will you permit me, while you are under, to make a little psychoanalysis also?" He really was saying it, and to me, not to the white-clad Chinese.

I stirred, and forced my tongue to answer. "Yes, if you'll promise to tell me all about it afterward. Do you promise?"

"Yes, yes." He was pacing again, and said it impatiently, over his shoulder. "You are now getting sleepy. You will sleep. In a few minutes . . ."

It was less than a few minutes, however, before I felt fully awake again, and sat up, saying in triumph, "Your pill didn't work."

Bobby, still pacing, was now rubbing his hands, saying over and over, as if to himself, "Very interesting, ve-ry interesting."

Suddenly the room had become dark again. I said, "It didn't work," and now I felt disappointed. All those preparations had been wasted. Bobby came to a halt in front of me.

"Do you know what time it is?" he asked. Once long ago, I dimly recollected, Heh-ven had asked the same question. But Bobby answered himself. "It's five o'clock in the afternoon, and you went under before ten this morning."

"But what's been going on?" I rubbed my forehead.

"You've been talking almost the whole time. I stopped for lunch."

I was staggered, but Bobby gave me no time to discuss the strangeness of the situation. He looked at me intently and said, "Do you feel any desire to smoke?"

I shook my head. It was true that the picture of the tray and the lighted lamp was no longer there in the middle of my mind. His question, in fact, surprised me. Why *should* I want to smoke?

"You have no wish, no thought of wanting it?" he insisted, and again I shook my head.

Bobby said, "Good. You will go to bed now, and eat something if you like. For tomorrow I've given orders that you're not to have visitors. That will be best for a little, but I'll be coming in later tonight to check up."

I started to stand, but paused as a sneeze overtook me. "I've caught cold," I declared. "Oh, Bobby—the analysis. What did you find out?"

"You are very interesting," he said enthusiastically. "Here is Nurse Wong to take care of you." He walked out.

Nurse Wong led me down the passage as fussily as a tug conveying a liner to its berth. She showed me into a first-floor room with an army cot in it, with whitewashed walls and a French window looking out on a wildly overgrown garden. The bed linen was worn and stained with rust. Nurse Wong had already unpacked my things and hung them on a couple of nails stuck in the wall. Of course, I thought drowsily after I got into bed, Chinese don't hang up their clothes but fold them away in boxes. . . . Later, a supper tray lay on my chest. I had no desire to eat the rice covered with brown goo, and after a while it was taken away. Bobby must have come in that night, but I don't remember him. There was no reason why I should have been so sleepy, I told myself when I woke up in the small hours. I wasn't any longer. I was uncomfortable, though I couldn't say just where the discomfort was. Throat? Arms? Legs? Stomach? It wandered about. The only place it seemed to settle for good was in the conscience. I felt very guilty about everything in the world, but it was not agony. It was supportable. Still, I was glad when the sun rose. Jan had once expressed the feeling of opium very well, I reminded myself; he had a bad leg, and after he'd smoked a pipe or two he'd said, "The pain is still there, but it no longer hurts." Well, I said to myself, that's what's happening. The pain has always been there, and now it hurts again. That is all. It is supportable. It is supportable.

One thing helped a lot. Never through the week that was worst did I have the thought that I would feel a lot better if only I could get to a pipe. That was where the hypnotism came in, I realized. Knowing it, however, didn't spoil the effect. It worked. I wasn't locked in my room, and there was no guard at the front door. If I'd wanted to, I could have dressed and walked out and gone home, or to Heh-ven's, but I didn't want to. Of all my urges, that one was missing. I counted the days after which Bobby said I would feel better. I fidgeted and yawned and sneezed, and my eyes wept torrents, and my watch simply refused to run, but I never tried to get out of the hospital.

For a while, whenever Bobby came and I tried to talk, my voice quivered and I wept. "Just nerves. I can't manage words,"

I sobbed, but he said I was getting on fine. He added that he realized I really wanted to stop smoking, because I hadn't brought in any pills. He said he knew that because he'd searched my things while I was hypnotized. The night after he said that, I had cramps. Cramps are a well-known withdrawal symptom. They might make themselves felt anywhere in the addict's body, but most people get them in the arms—they feel as if all the bones have broken. I had mine in the legs, all the way up to the hips, and at four in the morning I figured out that this was because I'd had to wear braces on my legs as a baby. I had never been able to remember the braces, but now, I said to myself, my legs were remembering. Then, as if I'd pleased the gods with this decision, I actually fell asleep for a full hour. It was probably the worst night of all.

Bobby let a few friends in to see me after that. I could go out into the overgrown garden with them and walk a little, taking shaky steps to the creek where ducks swam, and then we would drink tea under a tree. They helped the time pass, which was good, because without distraction it dragged terribly. "The mortal boredom of the smoker who is cured!" wrote Cocteau. Most vivid of all, though, was the way I felt about the bed. Night after night, I had to lie on it without sleeping, until I detested it with a bitter, personal spite. I hated the very smell of the mattress. I don't suppose it was really bad, being kapok and nothing else, but for the first time in some years my numbed nose was working, and any scent would have had an unpleasant effect on newly sensitive nerves. To me the mattress stank, and it was lumpy, besides. I knew every lump. I resolved to settle that bed's hash as soon as I was my own master. One morning, I asked Bobby what it would cost to replace it.

"Oh, I don't know. Twenty dollars, I suppose. Why?" he said.

"I want to buy this one when I'm through with it, and burn it in the garden. I hate it."

"If you still want to by then, you may," he said solemnly. "Hehven telephoned me today." He paused, looking at me with a cautious expression. "It is not the first time he has tried to reach you," he added, "but I didn't tell you before. Now I think I can trust you to see him. He's coming this afternoon. In fact, he's here now."

"Good." I must have sounded indifferent, because that was the way I felt. I'd almost forgotten Heh-ven. When he walked in, though, I remembered how well I knew him, and how many hours we'd spent smoking together. His eyes looked cloudy, I observed, and his teeth were dirty.

He said, "I'm taking you out."

Bobby said swiftly, "Only for a drive, remember," and looked hard at him.

Heh-ven laughed, and held up his hand reassuringly. "Certainly I'll bring her back. I do not want your patient, Doctor."

"You are not going to smoke," said Bobby, "and you are not taking her anywhere where she can smoke. Is that clear?"

"Perfectly clear," said Heh-ven. We walked out the front door —which I hadn't gone out of for a week—and into his car, and drove away. He was faithful to his promise. We went to a tea-room and sat there and looked at each other, and he said, "You look all right. How are you?"

"I'm all right," I said, "but Cocteau was telling the truth—you know, about the boredom. Still, I'm glad I did it." I was warming up, though Heh-ven still sounded and looked like a stranger.

"I tried, while you were out there," he admitted, "and I couldn't. It didn't last more than about thirty-six hours. I missed the lamp most of all. I find the lamp very nice."

"Well, that's easy," I answered. "Just light it and lie there." We both giggled. It was the first time I'd been able to make a joke about opium. Then he took me back to the hospital. His eyes when he said goodbye were wet, because he needed his tray. I felt smug.

The afternoon I was formally discharged, three days before I was to go to Chungking, Bobby said, "Well, goodbye. You're free. You're all right now. You can go anywhere you like. I don't want any pay, but remember—if you get the chance to convince some higher-up, tell him my method is effective. You'll do that, won't you? I would like to have that job."

I promised, and thanked him, and we shook hands. My bag was packed, and a car waited outside, but I hesitated. "There's one more thing," I said. "The analysis, remember? I've asked you more than once, but you haven't told me what you found out the day you did it."

All Bobby said was "Oh, yes, that. Very interesting."

What's more, I forgot all about burning the mattress.

FOR HUMANITY'S SAKE

Of all the people who, one time or another, have occupied the
spare room in my Shanghai house, I liked Miss Chu best. She
was a Communist and a Chinese patriot, to be either one of which
is conducive to a solemn state of mind, and in a way, I must
confess, Chu Ying was quite solemn. Yet she was a most likable
girl. A good-humored honesty beamed through her glasses and
she had sudden, unexpected outbursts of mirth. And nothing in
the world seemed to shock her.

One day, on the other hand, she shocked me quite a lot by
placidly confessing that she had a husband and a child. Ying

had been living with me as a paying guest for six months, and it had never occurred to her, evidently, to mention these two facts. I had never dreamed of them, for Ying seemed so completely the footloose student and her time was largely given up to mysterious patriotic interviews with other student-like people who came to see her, bearing briefcases. The meetings always took place in her room, which was bare as a Spartan's, even the bed mattress having been removed in favor of a roll of harsh Chinese blankets spread on the box spring.

That day, though, Miss Chu's visitor had not been a Communist student; it had been Mr. Pei. Because Mr. Pei carried no briefcase and seemed to have no particular political chip on his shoulder, I had long since guessed that he was Ying's boy friend, although she always referred to him severely as P. C. Pei. After he left she came into my room and preened herself in the mirror, an astonishing action, as she had never before shown the slightest interest in her appearance. Her hair stood out at the back of her head like a pigeon's tail.

"Why, Ying," I said, "you've had a permanent."

"Yes," she admitted, patting at the wiry mass. "I do not know why I wasted so much of the morning on it. I have three articles to prepare before next week." She sat down on the bed, pulled up her small, slippered feet, and sat on them. "P. C. Pei," she said in the same tone of voice, "has just asked me to marry him. Did you not hear us quarrelling just now?"

"No," I said, "I didn't hear anything. But why did you quarrel? I thought you liked him."

Over her spectacles her eyebrows lifted. "I do like P. C. Pei, but he asked me to *marry* him. I consider that in so doing he has insulted me." She hesitated, searching my face for signs of understanding. "Marriage," she added, "is degrading to a woman, and I am surprised that P. C. Pei should propose it. I had not thought he could be so atavistic."

I protested. Mr. Pei, I said, was a good-looking, strong, young man and had every right to turn atavistic now and then. "Anyway," I said, "I'm sure he didn't intend to insult you."

"He knows my feelings," said Ying, freezing up. We were

242

silent for a while. "But then," she explained more kindly, "you do not know, as he does, that I have once been married. I don't believe I have mentioned it to you."

"What?"

"Yes. It was at the university, quite a long time ago, and the man I married was a very selfish person. It was altogether a mistake." Ying glanced at her watch and decided she had time to go on with the story. "I should have arranged it more intelligently. But at that time we all felt that under the old capitalist system young people neglected important matters to a criminal extent in favor of their small personal love affairs. Therefore, just to save time and trouble, when this man wanted me so much I went to him, although he did not share my views. He had a job with a firm of foreign importers and this job was all he really cared about. He never gave a thought, if you can believe me, to the government of his country or to helping humanity. *Extremely* limited."

Ying mused a moment. "In a way it was excusable. I did it in the hope of being free to pursue my work. Also, I did not marry him outright. But it was very wrong of me to allow matters to slip into the situation which developed. In short," said Miss Chu, "we had a child."

"Oh," I said. "And where is the child now?"

"In Peiping," said Miss Chu carelessly, "with my sisters. They have no outside interests. . . . After this I permitted that we should be considered married, according, that is, to Chinese ideas. We shared a house. Only the missionaries who owned the school were shocked. To them, it appeared that I had been living irregularly, and even our joint household did not seem to satisfy them. Missionaries are also limited—in another way, of course." She lay back on the bed, her hands clasped under her neck, her eyes looking dreamily at the ceiling. "After that," she said, "the troubles began. We quarrelled very much. None of our ideas were alike. He could not understand my work and thought I should stay at home with the child. Oh, I resented that child terribly, although, of course, after it was born I liked it. But I am not the maternal type—he is much better off with my sisters. You now understand, I hope, my attitude toward marriage and my surprise at P. C. Pei's tactless suggestion." She paused. "What would you say if I were to tell you that I am thinking of divorcing my husband?"

Her voice had a new note in it, and when I glanced at her sharply, her eyes did not meet mine.

"It has nothing to do with P. C. Pei," she said. "Nothing can alter my resolution in regard to him. But do you not think I should have obtained this divorce long ago? I have not even seen my husband in three years."

"Oh, undoubtedly you should get a divorce."

She sighed. "It will be difficult. Perhaps my husband will not consent. He has still some feelings for me." She stood up and smoothed her permanent. "Anyway," she said, "whether I do or do not divorce is not really of much importance. I should not waste time speculating. It cannot matter to humanity."

Vastly cheered by the thought, she returned to her room, and presently I heard her typewriter clicking.

One morning at breakfast I noticed that Miss Chu was unusually pinched and wan. She had occasional bouts of indigestion, but she always said indifferently that she had eaten too much dry rice as a child. It was nothing. This time, however, she admitted that she was in pain. "Today I shall see a doctor," she said, and went out and was gone all day.

She had always been so casual about her health that I didn't worry about her, and that night, when she hadn't come back before curfew, I supposed she was staying with a friend. But when another day and night went by I began to worry, though not about her illness. I had never asked any questions, but I was fairly certain that Miss Chu was doing something or other patriotic and forbidden within the Shanghai limits. It was a tricky time in the French Concession, or "Frenchtown"—a large portion of non-Chinese Shanghai—and the International Settlement, which between them made up the treaty port of foreign Shanghai, though admittedly it was not as bad as it was for the Chinese peasants living outside our little plot of sacrosanct land. There the peasants were at the mercy of the two opponents, Chinese and Japanese, fighting this undeclared war. Both fought over peasant land, with first one and then the other winning for a while— though by this time the Japanese were in fairly firm control of the area. At least one saw their sentries all around us, just outside the gates and at the other end of the bridges in the Chinese city. They made us nervous. We were well aware that if we wanted to maintain neutral status we must *be* neutral. Suppose the Japanese had caught Miss Chu at the activities I suspected her of being engaged in? They could make life very uncomfortable for us if they wanted to.

The next night I was just trying to find P. C. Pei in the three pages of Peis in the telephone book when a Mr. Wang was announced. In the living room, sitting on the extreme edge of a chair and clutching his soft hat, was a small stranger. His brown eyes were as anxious and appealing as a dog's; his foreign clothes were neat; he looked very weak and childish and unattractive, and his lips trembled hysterically.

"How do you do?" he said. "I am sorry to trouble you so late at night. But can you tell me where is my wife? Perhaps I should explain that I am the husband of Chu Ying."

Between us we managed to get badly worried. Rather to my surprise, he said that P. C. Pei was his very good friend. "Tomorrow I shall ask him to help me find my wife," he announced. "And in the meantime, of course, you can have no objection that I occupy her room?"

I did object, but not successfully. An hour later I lay in bed wondering where Ying was, and worrying about what she would do if she should come home and find her husband in possession, and, finally, about the likelihood that Mr. Wang wasn't her husband at all. At that thought I sat up in bed and turned on the light. He might perfectly well be a Japanese spy. Perhaps Ying was even now being third-degreed by a Japanese officer while this little brown-eyed impostor went through her papers and found incriminating evidence.

Then I remembered my parting glimpse of him, going to the bathroom. He was wearing Ying's bathrobe and his head, with its stylish pompadour, was covered by a sort of skating cap with a pompon on top, patterned in concentric circles of green and black. Surely no spy would wear a skating cap in bed. I turned off the light and went to sleep.

In the morning, Mr. Pei and Mr. Wang found Ying in a Chinese hospital, paying fifty cents' fee a day and being treated for stomach ulcers. It developed that in her language "going to see the doctor" and "going to the hospital" were one and the same. For a week both young men visited her daily, and by night I shared my house with the stranger. It was all very peculiar, but I didn't know what to do. Even when Ying came home, very thin and weak, and moved into the room with Mr. Wang, I saw no way to put a stop to it. We never even had a chance to talk about it; wherever she went, Brown Eyes pattered after her. She spoke to me as from a distance, gravely and with all possible courtesy. "I regret so much that I shall be weak for a time and must have someone to look after me. May my husband stay until I am well?"

It was her own business, I said to myself. I knew he was sleeping on the floor, for the mattress had been brought upstairs again. Mr. Pei hadn't come to call since Ying's return from the hospital. I was very much puzzled.

The first day Ying could walk without assistance she came into my room, closed the door, and sank down on the bed. "Ai-yah, I cannot bear this much longer! Do we disturb you at night?" she asked.

"No. Why?"

She looked over her shoulder at the closed door. "I can never get away from him," she said fretfully. "At night we quarrel. Oh, I am tired!"

She lay back on the pillows with closed eyes. "At first he seemed so reasonable," she said, opening her eyes suddenly, "but now he is making threats. If I insist on the divorce, he says he will go to the police and charge me with desertion. Sometimes he wants to jump out of the window. What is the matter with him? How can he hang on to me if I do not want him? Is it love? What is it?"

I did not attempt to say.

246

"There is no arguing with him," she said. "He is like a child, and he is so violent about P. C. Pei!"

I asked, "Is Mr. Pei violent too?"

Miss Chu's face became even more wretched. "I do not know what P. C. Pei is thinking. He told me, when my husband first arrived, to go slowly. He said, 'Be nice to him.' And I am being very nice, but I cannot bear it much longer. He is always with me, always arguing. I have not done any work for days. He asks me to make promises. Already I have promised not to divorce him for a year, and I have promised not to see P. C. Pei for a whole year too."

"But why? Do you mean you might reconsider?"

"Oh no! I will never take my husband back."

"But then why did you make that promise?"

She pushed out her jaw. "P. C. Pei told me to be nice to him. So I made the promise, and if I had not, my husband might go to the police or kill himself. Only he must go back to Peiping soon or I shall go mad." She spoke wildly. "Going back in the boat, he will jump off. Somebody ought to go with him to see that he will not jump off."

"Mr. Pei," I suggested.

She looked sullen. "Perhaps P. C. Pei will not wish to trouble himself," she said coldly.

There came a fumbling tap on the door, and in the hall Mr. Wang wailed like a child. "Ying!" he called. "Ying!"

"I do not understand P. C. Pei's attitude," Miss Chu went on, ignoring the noise. "He does not come to see me anymore."

"He's jealous, that's all."

She shook her head. "Today when I phoned and asked him to come to see me he said he was busy. No, P. C. Pei has made up his mind to get away from all of it."

Suddenly she turned a more hopeful face to me. "Will you speak to P. C. Pei?" she asked.

"Me?"

"Yes. *You* can do it. Ask him how he thinks. Find out why he is so strange. Perhaps he will talk to you. Tell him how I feel. You *must*," said Miss Chu in quiet desperation. "Tell him I quite

247

realize I can have no claim upon him. But I want him to know that no matter what he does I will *not* go back to my husband. If I cannot have both," she said, with mounting agitation, "I will have nobody. *I cannot let him go like that.*"

"Ying!" wailed Mr. Wang. She started out, but at the door she stopped to say, "But perhaps P. C. Pei thinks I have gone back to my husband already."

"Of course. He's jealous, Ying."

"Well, but he told me to be nice to him. . . . Yes, I'm *coming.*"

I did my best with P. C. Pei to remember what she had told me. I gave him a rapid but vivid sketch of Ying's state of mind, while I wondered and worried about Mr. Pei and his attitude. If he was really tired of waiting for her, I said, it would be better to tell me now.

Mr. Pei stood up and began to walk around. "Perhaps you do not know," he said, "that I have always respected Miss Chu, even before this man Wang ever saw her. I thought her a remarkable girl; it was only my sense of unworthiness which kept me from—in short, I was astonished when I heard of her marriage. I had known Wang at school. For *him* to aspire—but no doubt, I thought, they have fallen in love, and for such sentiments there is no explanation. I tried to forget. Years later I again encountered Miss Chu, alone and free, in Shanghai. My respect has, if anything, increased. I respect her to such a degree—"

"She loves you, too," I said.

P. C. Pei relaxed pleasurably, waiting for more. I gave it to him. "In fact, although I am not authorized to say this, Mr. Pei, I think it safe to suppose that your recent—uh—disagreement as to marriage will never recur. Miss Chu now realizes that she cannot force nature to share her political ideal. She will be willing, even glad, to marry you; that is, if you have not changed your mind."

Mr. Pei said emphatically that he had not changed his mind.

"But there is Mr. Wang," I reminded him. "He threatens to go to the police."

Mr. Pei snorted. "He has no legal claims. I have been looking into the law, the latest one. There is no necessity even for a divorce. Legally, according to this latest law, she is free. Please tell her so."

I promised.

"As for the child, I shall be glad to give it a home; I shall treat it as my own. Please tell her that."

"Yes, Mr. Pei."

"Frankly, I was a little jealous," he continued. "I have been unable to sleep all this week. Please tell her."

I bowed. "It is all very satisfactory," I said. "There remains only one matter. If her husband should kill himself?"

P. C. Pei came to a halt in his triumphant walk about the room and looked appropriately grave. "It would cast a shadow over our lives for a time, of course," he admitted. "Still, perhaps he was fated to die young. Who knows?"

We looked at each other in complete sympathy. "Please tell her that," he said gently.

"In that case," said Miss Chu, looking years younger, "my husband—I mean this man—can leave for Peiping tomorrow. There is a boat. I looked it up in the paper."

"Splendid. And is he going alone?"

Miss Chu regarded me gravely. "Oh, yes. After all, we cannot take care of all humanity. Even if he decides to end it all, it will naturally cast a shadow over our lives for a time, but—"

"I think you are so right," I said.

Still she hesitated. "It's a pity, nevertheless," she said. "It is a pity he should be so weak. If only he could manage to think more about humanity and less about himself. I cannot help thinking that if he had good advice, if somebody would only show him these matters in the right light . . . I don't suppose," said Miss Chu, "that *you* would talk to him?"

SOUTHERN TOUR

Our steamer moved briskly downstream to the mouth of the river. When we were free of the gap-toothed ruins of Yangtsepoo and Chapei and had left behind the little, beetlelike Japanese boats running about the edges of Shanghai, the sky was blissfully clear. After three years I had forgotten how blue the open sea can be; the Whangpoo colors even one's memories of water. When I said this, the British captain grumbled that the water along the China Coast is never really properly blue, but I was satisfied.

It was a small boat. None of the officers would promise when we might get to Hong Kong. Ordinarily the trip took three days —two in the big ships—but at the Shanghai office, when I bought my ticket, they had been not only discreet but downright silent on this subject. Once we got outside the Whangpoo into the bay, everything was explained; the ship would try to pick up cargo here and there—Chinese cargo—and because of the Japanese gunboats it would be a game of hide-and-seek. There could be no schedules in such a game. Gently we moved between islands, between sunrise and sunset. Sometimes from the wireless cabin on high there came word of radio orders: we were to stop here, we were not to stop there; people were waiting for us at such and such an obscure village and we must not disappoint them. The news of the day came through now and then and after a fashion, but it was so chopped and misspelled in the Chinese radio operator's handwriting that it could not seem real. Every day carried the outside world further into oblivion. In the saloon we still listened politely when the captain read the news to us, and we sighed at the Soviet-German pact, and were interested when we heard of another foreigner in Shanghai clapped into jail for offending the Japanese Emperor in the diminished person of a sentry. But it was not real; we followed the world's doings as if in a novel. Each of us made an effort only for the sake of the others. What was real was the throbbing of the ship's engines and the luncheon menu.

Even when, by order of the inscrutable authorities, our engines were stopped and anchor dropped, we passengers paid little attention. The scenery was well painted, to be sure. We spent a long time near a town on a golden beach with a white customs house perched like a palace on an overhanging green hill. We were half a night near a city of piled houses, on an island with a coastline like Greece. Always we steered our way delicately among the rearing junks and the little fishing boats which drift forever among the islands.

One morning I woke to find that we had gone round in a circle during the night. Some radiogram had not come through in time, and the captain, when he received it at last, had cursed and turned back a hundred and sixty miles to the town on the golden beach we had visited before. To return, he had slipped up a sort of back alley, behind a large, fat island, so that a Japanese gunboat reputed to be on our port side would not see the maneuver and grow too inquisitive.

The mention of the gunboat was slightly interesting to me, but I didn't go up on deck on the chance of seeing it. Neither did the others. I don't know how they felt about it, but I simply didn't care to see or to think about a Japanese gunboat.

We anchored once again off the golden beach. It was bright and breezy, an enchanting day. Clustered about us were fishing boats disgorging coolies—men and women—who hurried to the lower deck to sell food to the crew. They were all carrying what looked like bunches of queer red bananas. Later, seeing the things spread out to dry on the deck, I recognized them for red octopuses. Our own food continued to be filling but unimaginative—mutton curry and cold cuts. It didn't matter.

I began to prefer being at anchor to progressing. The sea was calm and the waves, with their slow lift and fall, were as soothing as a cradle. The fisher people had all cleared off now except for one boat, and the air was very silent. As the sun strengthened, everything—the yellow sand, the green hills rising from the blue water, the white houses, and quiet boats—took on a childish clarity of primary colors. It was very, very still, so still that the quiet almost droned.

The quiet *was* droning. It grew louder and louder; it developed a heartbeat, and then a double beat, and then, just as we all rushed for the rail—crew, kitchen boys, passengers, and soldiers—the planes flew over from the east. There were three of them, small and supple, above the islands.

Nobody said a word at first. Then the engineer's mate, quite unnecessarily and probably without realizing it, cried, "There they are!" By this time they had swooped down over us so near that we could see the pilots' figures. Then the planes lifted and soared off, pointing their sharp noses away as though they had never dreamed of our existence. Our heads, like those of a ten-

252

nis-tournament crowd, turned as one head, following them. They crossed and re-crossed the sky, making loops and twists and turns.

Just behind a point of the big island lay a junk. I had noticed it before, mainly because I could see nothing of it but the tip of its mast and a little of the ragged sail, blackened with pig's blood to make it last longer. I remembered it as we all walked to the other rail to watch the planes, because the one fishing boat still left on our flank was now completely empty. Its crew had climbed aboard our ship and was crouching beneath the deck rail—a skinny bearded man in a loincloth, a plump middle-aged woman with her hair in a braid down her back, a little boy about eight years old, and a naked baby who could just stand up. They all, except the baby, squatted on their heels, hiding unnecessarily, for the planes' pilots could not possibly have sighted them where they were. The bearded man grinned wryly, flashing his teeth. The woman's eyes were dull and flat, and the little boy was impassive. Only the man seemed awake, almost merry; then I saw that his hands, holding the baby around the waist, were gripping so tightly that the knuckles were pale.

Everybody connected with the ship—officers, sailors, and soldiers—ignored this huddled group. A few moments before, the crew had been shooing the coolies off the sacred deck; now they were not bothering about such trifles. Their eyes and souls and hearts were following the swooping silver insects, which were skimming gaily over the point of the island. I heard first two and then three slight noises—pop pop. Somebody shooting off a cap pistol, I thought. Then came a noise like a very quick motor, louder than the hum of the planes, a merry burble of noise, monotonously regular—machine guns. Each plane dipped behind the island's skyline and then came up again, one, two, three. They wheeled like swallows and dipped again at the same place. The machine-gunning stopped from time to time as if for breath, and then went on. The junk's mast and blackened sail moved a little, and jerked uncertainly, and seemed to sag. It was hard to see just what happened. Nobody said a word.

This went on, over and over, for quite a time. Then all three planes suddenly rose, soared, righted themselves with a swaggering shake of the tail, and in neat formation winged away toward Japan.

Around the point of our island, where no mast or sail now showed, there came another sort of noise, a cry that was loud and then soft and then loud again, like the crowing of a rooster.

We were all watching the fisher's family as they put off. The bearded man waved and grinned again, mischievous and triumphant. The woman held the oar; the little boy was absorbed in working the boat hook and getting away cleanly. The baby was tied to something, and it leaned over the water and wiggled its hands as they all moved off.

I was left alone with the second mate. I had something to say, very urgently. "Those planes," I said. "They did it to show off to us. If we hadn't been here they wouldn't have—"

"Nonsense. I've seen 'em at Pakhoi. They came alongshore in a launch, all along the beach where the junks were pulled up; they machine-gunned the whole row and the people, too, as they ran away up the beach. Pure murder," he said offhandedly. "*We* didn't make any difference."

The sea had turned from blue to vivid green, and it was more choppy than before, so that the sun glittered on splinters of water. Everything was peaceful and almost the same again, except for the noise from behind the point of the island. For a long time I said nothing, but at last, "That noise," I said. "Listen. Is that a rooster?"

"No," said the second mate.

DR. BALDWIN

It didn't seem at all peculiar at the time, but later I began to see how very odd it was.

At five-thirty on an October afternoon I broke a front tooth. It wasn't a real front tooth; it was a porcelain crown, and so I was not in pain, but I didn't like it. Nobody would care to go around with a small gold swivel showing in the gap where a nice white tooth ought to be. Even in China, where they are not so particular about teeth, I was uncomfortable, and I refused to wait until next day to see about it, because after the insane fashion of Shanghai residents, I of course had a dinner date. My roommate Mary and I always had dinner dates during the crisis

255

at Shanghai. There was something comforting about talking the matter over in large groups.

We telephoned dentists all around town, and none of them were in their offices and none of them were home. We called American and Swedish and Chinese and English dentists; there were none. Some of them were at hospitals—it had never occurred to me before that wounded soldiers might get the toothache—but others must have been at cocktail parties, for we telephoned until six-fifteen, to no avail.

It was my intention when I began to tell this story to conceal one important point, but I see now that it must be told. This point relates to the manner in which I had broken my tooth, and I am ashamed of it, but unless I explain fully there will be some question in the minds of my readers as to why Russell Pong should have been willing to help me out of my predicament. These are the facts:

We had a gibbon, Mary and I. He was called Mr. Mills and he was very small, which may be why people insisted upon calling him a monkey, thus annoying me a good deal. Monkeys are easy to come by, but silver gibbons are not. Besides, Mr. Mills had no tail, he didn't scratch, he didn't break things except in revenge, or imitate, or do anything monkeylike—except bite.

He was a complete success except that he sometimes bit people. Now, I had a theory that the only way to carry over an idea in animal-training is to make the animal see you as one of his own sort, as it were. In other words, one should make the punishment fit the crime, and that is how I broke my tooth. It was because of Mr. Russell Pong, a Chinese friend of ours who had called to pay his respects. Mr. Mills bit him without the slightest provocation, and so I bit Mr. Mills, forgetting in my enthusiasm about this porcelain crown. Therefore it was broken, and now we are back again where we started.

Russell Pong sat there politely listening to our frantic effort to get a dentist. At last he said, "I have one dentist in Jinkee Road. I am almost sure that he is at home. He is always at home."

I said, "Is he good?"

"He is splendid," said Russell. "He does all my family."

I looked at his teeth and was about to refuse as tactfully as possible, but Mary said, "Well, he wouldn't do anything important anyway, not at this time of night. All you want is to cement that old jacket crown back on for the evening until you can get to somebody good tomorrow. Why don't you go and try it?"

This was quite true, so I asked Russell to make the appointment. The dentist, it seemed, had no telephone; he was that kind of dentist. There was nobody else, simply nobody, and I almost gave up, but in the end we telephoned a girl who lives in Jinkee Road and asked her to send over her houseboy to make the appointment, and we waited fifteen minutes, and finally I had the appointment.

Dusk had almost fallen when Russell and I started out.

"But of course I must come with you," he had said. "You have hurt yourself in my defense!"

I got out my car and drove hastily, ignoring the sounds of battle, which had increased in strength after sunset. I remember that I was trying to explain my theory of ape-training to Russell, who is a scholarly type and considered my methods cruel.

"The thing you don't understand in ape mentality . . ." I was saying.

Whereupon we forgot all about gibbons. We were plunged into the middle of a jewel-filled atmosphere. Hissing, spitting tracer bullets and shells fell around us; the deep-blue air was like water in which swam glowing fish, always in parabolic curves. There was a general impression of sparkles, glitters, and crash. I stamped on the brake, so that the car skidded and then stood still in the middle of the street, its door swinging open, as we ran for cover. I remember a smell of sulphur, and how Jinkee Road presented a terrifyingly unfamiliar aspect of closed doors and shuttered windows, before a gate of iron grating opened just a little and somebody called in Chinese, out of the dark behind it, "Hurry up!"

We scrambled through the crack and the gate swung closed behind us, and we all stared at each other in the flashing, fragmentary light. The man who had opened the gate was some sort of coolie, and further back, where they could watch without being in too much danger, were other men and women and children, dressed like poor servants and such. The shadows of the gate bars moved and slipped past their features. We were in a deep, dark, long, narrow courtyard, surrounded by steep zigzag staircases and fire escapes with doors huddled beneath. Two or three bombs burst while we looked around at all this.

As our panting stopped, we began to laugh. It is always the first thing one does after an escape. The coolie people laughed, too, and Russell chattered with them. Outside it was quieter, save for the pingggg of one rifle bullet which was evidently travelling straight along Szechuen Road at right angles to Jinkee, singing as it went. Then the bombardment began again. Russell turned to me.

"They say we can get through to the dentist, through this building. It is all one house in this block," he explained. "Let us try."

A little girl in trousers led us up a rickety fire escape. We came to a second-story door and entered a long hall cluttered with rubbish and sleeping forms. After traversing this we went downstairs again almost to the level of another courtyard, and then through a door with a lot of broken glass and into a gas-lit corridor of shabby green plush, and then at last to the dentist's own door. "F. BALDWIN" was in half-obliterated letters on the frosted glass. We rang a bell and waited a long time. The noise of the bombardment was now muffled.

"They ought to get their range soon," I whispered. "Isn't anybody at home here?"

Somebody pushed aside the cloth and peered at us, and then the door was opened, halted by a chain, closed again while the chain was taken off, and then at last flung wide. A Chinese boy in a dirty white pinafore took us through a pitch-dark room, very large, into a tiny three-cornered dentist's office. Nothing there was white save his pinafore and the shirtfront of the man who greeted us.

Russell evidently did not recognize this man, who was a tall, wrinkled Eurasian in shirtsleeves. "We wish to see Dr. Baldwin," he proffered timidly. A second white-pinafored boy hovered in the doorway. The only light came from a reading lamp on a buffet.

"*I* am Dr. Baldwin," said the man, smiling with his teeth. "What can I do for you?"

Russell laughed too loud. "Of course; it is your brother whom I know."

"Yes," said the Eurasian. There was a silence. I was very sorry to have come.

"How *is* your brother?" asked Russell at last.

"He is dead," said the Eurasian in an even voice. "Died eight months ago."

"Oh." Russell was very much embarrassed and shocked. "Was —wasn't it very sudden? Was it heart disease?"

"Yes," said the Eurasian. "And what can I do for you?"

I cut in here. "I think I'd better wait. If Mr. Pong's dentist isn't—isn't—"

"I also am a dentist," said Dr. Baldwin inexorably.

"Aren't these your brother's sons?" asked Russell. The Chinese boys shuffled their feet. The tall man gave that smile again.

"Yes. We are carrying on the practice. Is it your front tooth, Madam?"

There was nothing for it; I sat down in the worn leather chair and allowed myself to be lifted higher. Dr. Baldwin peered into my mouth gingerly, and when I gave him the two pieces of broken porcelain he shook his head. "It wouldn't stay," he said. "You need a new one."

"I know, but if you'll just put it on for tonight, I—" Here I hesitated, and then lied nobly, "I could come back tomorrow and let you start work on the new one, do you see? But I've got to have this tonight. I'll be very careful and not bite on it."

Still doubtful, Dr. Baldwin the Second gave directions to the boys. While cement was being mixed, Russell made conversation, standing well back of the chair. "She broke it biting a monkey—I mean an ape," he said. "A gibbon it was, really."

"So?" said Dr. Baldwin, without interest. "Wider, please." He turned to the dusty cabinet and searched for another tool. Outside, the noise seemed to have ceased altogether.

"Where has your brother been buried?" asked Russell. And when he had been told that, he asked, "Under which name, foreign or Chinese?"

Dr. Baldwin hesitated and measured porcelain. "Chinese," he said after a second, and added, "Of course."

"Of course," said Russell hastily.

One of the boys had plastered my crown into place, and now there was nothing to do but wait, gaping, while it hardened. I saw that all the blinds were down and that the walls were covered with family photographs in ornate frames, photographs of very mixed-looking groups. But everything was so faded and dirty that I forgot how important my tooth was and wanted only to get out. I was permitted to do so at last.

We came out through a different door into Jinkee Road. Everything was quiet, and windows had been opened and doors unlocked. My car still waited in the middle of the street, untouched, its door swung open. Across Soochow Creek we heard bombs exploding.

"They've got the range," I said. Everything was fine. Whatever was happening over there was no business of ours. We drove away, turning as soon as possible toward the other side of town. When I had dropped Russell off, and driven home, there was just time to change for dinner.

That is probably all I will ever know about Dr. Baldwin, except for his bill, which came in at the end of the month. It was for five dollars, and was made out to "Mrs. Russell Pong."

ROUND TRIP TO NANKING

Nobody said not to go. The young man at the airline office, a friend of mine, did sound a little surprised when I called him on the phone and said not to bother about getting our plane tickets to Nanking after all, that we were going by train instead. This was Wednesday, I explained, and we'd just go on up by train the next morning and get back to Shanghai Sunday night. The school where I taught English to Chinese youths was to start its fall term on Monday, so I would be back in plenty of time. The young man said "Oh?" in a cold, funny little voice, but I thought that was because he is English and had probably gone to a lot of bother over the tickets, and perhaps was peeved. I was sorry, but in a hurry, so I said goodbye and hung up.

Even now it doesn't seem such a damn-fool thing to have done. All summer, waiting for war, Mary and I hadn't gone anywhere, and Mary was new to China and did very much want to get out of Shanghai just for a little. We lived in a small house, very quietly, and it had been dull for us both. We felt we must go somewhere after giving up our long holiday; we had to go, we agreed, to Pootoo or to Tien Mu Shan or to Nanking. All these are just short trips.

It was I who decided on Nanking. There were young men, dinner parties, and dancing in Nanking, I pointed out. We wired two of the young men that we were coming, and we left Shanghai on the eight-o'clock express Thursday morning. That, it happened, was the very last train to get through, but we had no way of knowing. Nobody said not to go.

We had a little car and an undersized coolie-chauffeur. He took us to North Station early (someone called to warn us, I found out later, but we had left the house) and I told him to meet the evening train Sunday. Then we left him and went into the station. I said, looking round, "Oh, good! It's much better than last week. Not so many refugees. The exodus must be slackening."

For about a month frightened Chinese had been pouring into Shanghai from outside, and out of Shanghai from inside, glutting the trains, sitting all night on their bundles, smiling or eating or just looking dazed, but never crying or wailing. We had got used to it, and now only said, "Poor things. Why do they? They don't know where they're going, or why." The latest Incident which called forth these refugees—and now the warships—had been the shooting of two Japanese at the Hungjao airdrome. But there had been so many Incidents.

The train was crowded; we had expected that. We found one foreigner in the first-class carriage, and we knew him. He was an Englishman, a government man. There was a Chinese we knew,

262

too—a Mr. Wing. The Englishman told the car porter to look after us, which I resented just a little, as the porter would have anyway. (I traveled to Nanking a lot—I mean I used to.) We got seats in a half-compartment, sort of a drawing room, which ordinarily you can't get in the daytime.

We each had a hatbox with some day clothes in it and one cotton evening dress apiece, and Mary also had Sweetie Pie in a basket. Sweetie Pie was a baby duck I had bought for ten cents on the Bund and brought home to Mary. My Chinese teacher told us it was incubated and couldn't possibly be expected to live, but it had withstood stomach trouble and pneumonia and everything. The duck's name was Li originally, but Mary grew so crazy about him—it used to make me uneasy to hear her talk to him—that he became Sweetie Pie. He was full of personality, and had got to be quite famous, in a small way, in Shanghai. He was awfully tame, and followed her everywhere and cried like a child if she wouldn't pick him up, and he would climb up her legs to her lap on a towel. On cool nights we even let him sleep with one or the other of us. He was still downy, and was incredibly tiny. We had decided to bring him along because our maid didn't treat him very well when we weren't there. The cook had brought us a round woven basket with a lid, just right for him, but he yelled his head off when the top was down. He wasn't old enough to quack; he peeped, like a chickabiddy.

We settled down in our compartment, bought a bottle of drinking water, and let the duck out and laughed at him and waited for the train to go. It didn't start for an hour and a half. We strolled about and talked with the Englishman and Mr. Wing. The Englishman said, "What a nuisance! We shall be so late!" He said he was taking some lobster to the British Embassy staff in Nanking because they were running short of such things. He hoped it wouldn't spoil, now that the train was so late.

Then the train did start. Very soon it stopped, and waited an hour or so more. Troop trains came by, and we looked at the soldiers in their tin hats, and the machine guns, and I said,

"But why toward Shanghai? The war's in North China." Mary said, "Oh, it's those soldiers we saw at Mutu near Soochow last April. Remember?" We felt fine, but people around us began to look worried, and Mr. Wing said he would get off at Soochow and go back to his wife. Something was wrong, he said. But he didn't know whether we could go back if we got out, and the Englishman said it would be better, now we were started, to go all the way and be stuck, if necessary, in a big town like Nanking. Himself, he said placidly, he had a plane reservation back to Shanghai for next day. "You girls shouldn't have come. I thought so when I saw you, but didn't like to say anything," he said.

I was worried. I thought of my school on Monday. We looked at each other apprehensively, but Sweetie Pie wanted a drink, and we got busy on him.

It took sixteen hours to get to Nanking, which is usually a five-hour journey. We picked up nineteen coaches before we were through, and the engine broke down a few miles outside the city wall, but we got in at last, after midnight. My young man was waiting at the station; Mary's wasn't. Mine was a British naval officer, and he looked smart in white shorts, and was tired of waiting. He said, after a disdainful glance at Sweetie Pie, "See here, that's the last train between Shanghai and Nanking. The line's cut now, at Soochow. There are no planes. You can't go down by river. It's mined below Chinkiang."

Mary, who always believed what she was told, was alarmed, and I laughed at her and said, "He's just teasing us. Don't believe him." Navy looked at me oddly, but said nothing more. We had tea and fruit at the hotel. Everything in Nanking closed at midnight, and so I wasn't surprised that the lights were all out, and we laughed heartily at a sign in the room: "Visitors are warned that air raids are expected at any time; please keep lights off and shutters closed." I said, "Lord, these diplomats get scared, don't they?" We talked about the tiresome trip—we felt very ill-used—and gave Sweetie Pie a swim in the bathtub, and

Navy invited us to lunch next day on his gunboat and left. Mary tried to call her friend, but couldn't get him. It seemed he had gone to Shanghai.

Next morning we began to find out it was all true—planes full, river mined and closed, and trains promising to take people only as far as Soochow, which is more than an hour from Shanghai by ordinary train. Sitting at lunch on the gunboat and listening to the radio, we found out why. Sniping at Japanese sentries in Shanghai had grown suddenly serious, the Chinese had sunk junks across the river off their Bund to keep the Japanese out, and . . .

It seemed so unreal. Still, I couldn't eat lunch, and said we must see about trains, and I wrote a wire to a Chinese friend in Shanghai and asked him what he thought. I never found out. Navy was vague and slow about sending his boy with the telegram and with our tickets to get reservations on the next Shanghai train. I said, "There is an eight-o'clock train tomorrow morning. We must try to get on that," and he said, "Oh no, ducky. Take the afternoon express." We tugged him off the boat between us and went back to our hotel, and he didn't want to do anything until we had heard about the tickets. He acted as though the train service was all right, the planes were all right, the boats were all right. I can't describe it; he just *lagged.* Then we found they wouldn't promise a train at all for next day. He went about arranging a dinner party with some Nanking people, and I wandered down to the lobby in a distracted and aimless sort of way.

Nanking hotels were all a bit casual, and this one was very much so. You could never find a clerk at the desk, and it took a half-hour to find the manager. I saw servants hanging around avoiding my eye, and heard a frantic German voice, which belonged to a big, fat man, talking of hiring a bus to go overland to Hangchow, a ten-hour trip, and then to Shanghai. It was uncomfortable. I didn't want to go back to the room and look at Mary's worry and at Navy's strange sulkiness. Then, near the door, I saw a young man in a cap, talking to the big German, and

265

I heard him say, "Train tonight." I didn't know him, but we were all foreigners together, so I rushed up and said, "Is there a train? Do you know?"

The young man, who also had a German accent, said, "There is one tonight. I don't know what time."

I said, "Oh, wonderful! They told me there weren't any more. I must get back to Shanghai."

The fat man said, "There can't be a train today. Are you sure?"

The young man said, "Yes, because they have stamped my ticket. But of course there is only third and fourth class."

"Oh, that's all right," I said confidently.

He looked at me and added, "It gets only to Soochow. From there we must change and go around the city and on the Hangchow line. It will be five hours more after Soochow."

I said, "I must get my ticket chopped," and ran upstairs.

Navy said, "Today? Don't be a bloody fool. Why today?"

Mary and I, without answering, called the hotel porter and told him about the train, and sent him to the station to have our tickets stamped. He thought the train must be leaving at midnight, at which Navy cheered up a little. He could have his dinner party anyway.

I couldn't understand him. The British, I said to myself, are calm, but why need they be definitely unhelpful? It isn't really so important. We were wrangling half-heartedly when I was called to the phone. "Is this the lady," said a German voice, "who wants to go to Shanghai? . . . I am sorry I do not know your name, but perhaps you would like to hear that a train is leaving in an hour. I am here at the station and I have seen. If you can hurry, I will save two seats. But there is no second class, you know, only third and fourth. All right? . . . All right."

We couldn't find the porter with our tickets. We packed anyhow. Suddenly—it was now six o'clock—Nanking had turned dark and stormy. We had the manager, but no taxi, and no rickshaws. There were clouds in the black sky, and the manager shivered and said, "There *must* be a war!" He stared about foolishly, his good-natured manager's face puzzled. "My boys have all run off to get their things and bring them here," he said. "I'm awfully sorry."

At last we got rickshaws. Navy had gone back into the hotel; we didn't wait. We started off down the wide dusty street that leads away from the Wall. We heard the feet of the rickshaw men pattering in the dust, and saw black clouds over the fields, and wondered about catching the train, and if the train would get through, or if we would. I had forgotten Navy, but suddenly he was there, sitting upright in a rickshaw and looking straight ahead. We all swung along to the station.

We could not find the man with our tickets and had to buy more. There was just about enough money left over for food and things like that. Then we ran into the Army. Right through the station hundreds of men marched, with all their kit on bamboo poles. They were strong, but some of them had too much to carry, and they kept coming between us and our train until I would have screamed except that everything was so quiet. They were all young and awkward and cheerful, and they marched well, horribly well, and we could not get through. At last the hotel porter stopped them—by having on a more gorgeous uniform, I think. Navy was not there; we ran and ran, and climbed down off the platform and ran across tracks, and passed a lot of crowded cars. I couldn't find the German. But we climbed up into a first-class carriage, which must have been put on just then, for there was still one seat. Just one. The porter got it for us; we both crowded into it and sighed. Then Navy came up and gave me all the money he had in his pockets, and said it was because he didn't want us to have such an uncomfortable trip. He was acting a little better by now, but unmistakably English. Hundreds of refugees and soldiers were marching all round us, and the trains were crazily arranged at the wrong places, and anybody, anybody but an Englishman, could have seen it was War. But Navy went on talking in his round-tongued, loud-voiced, faintly amused, masculine way. He said he had just heard that the train was not leaving until morning, so we might as well get off and have our dinner. It was no good telling him we had to keep our seat against the hundreds of people now trying to get into the train, hammering on the doors. He just stood outside the window and smoked his pipe and looked down his nose. We had been sitting there an hour and it was really hot and stuffy, because we were just outside the train kitchen. We couldn't let Sweetie Pie out in that crowd, and he kept saying "Peep!" Navy finally went away to get some supper for us.

Then the German came along, and his face lit up when he found us. With him was a tall East Indian in gray flannels, smoking a pipe. He had a lovely face, very gentle and humorous and sweet. When I told them my name, and Mary's, the German introduced himself as Wally and the Indian as Gandhi. We all talked, and bought some hot beer and handed the bottles around.

Navy came back after a while. He had a packet of sandwiches and eggs and things, from his friend's house, and a Thermos of lemon squash. Navy said, "I'm going to dinner now, and in one or two hours I'll be back to see you." Very safe and clean and cool and nasty, he walked away. It was hot and getting foul in the car, and outside it looked cooler, but still it felt good having a chance—just a chance. We didn't see Navy again, because pretty soon the train started. We were on our way to Shanghai.

Hatboxes are better to sit on than any kind of luggage. We took turns with the chair and one of the boxes while Wally sat on the other. At his side, Gandhi sat on his own black bag, at the feet of a Chinese couple with two little boys. There was also a new man, Mr. Lee, a big, plump Chinese with a beaky nose, who spoke English mixed with very pure Nanking dialect. At every stop, we got out to walk and rest on benches or on the ground. After eight hours, when we thought we could not bear being so cramped and miserable, we stepped over the line into another existence, where we didn't feel anything.

Gandhi, his face sorrowful and greenish, slept on the floor propped again my hatbox. Wally's face was pillowed on his arms. The couple with two children slept. Behind me other people slept; only Mary and I could not. At five the sun came up; it made everything look different and hopeful. Even Soochow might be all right.

We bought coffee and toast, and fed Sweetie Pie. The little duck had got dirty and wanted to swim. Still, whenever we would let him sit in our laps he would sing softly and liquidly, and peep now and then.

We got to Soochow at nine o'clock. Each of us grabbed something—I got Gandhi's bag, almost empty—and Wally and Mr. Lee carried our heavy hatboxes. We climbed down and up more platforms and trains, round and round old sidings and tracks. At last we came to a train very far from the station, which was full of screaming, battling people. We couldn't get in that train. People were hanging onto the outside, and onto all the windows, like leeches after you have gone swimming in a creek.

Wally sat us down in a field, on our boxes, and went with Lee to complain. We stayed there under the soft morning sun in the middle of the ugly-smelling field, and looked at Sweetie Pie and agreed that it was he who made everyone else kind to us. People jammed upright in the train peered out dusty windows at us.

Wally ran back to us, saying, "Hurry! Hurry!" We rushed wildly, back over those sidings and tracks, round empty freight cars, in front of slow, chugging locomotives. We fell into a car on the Shanghai train just as it was opened for use; we each got a seat this time. We let Sweetie Pie out for a little, holding him carefully. We ate some sandwiches and all the eggs, and drank the lemon squash.

What we were doing was making a detour around the fighting. Lee jumped out and tried to buy papers everywhere, but there were no Chinese papers ready so early. The country after Soochow was emerald and jade and gold, with pools of clean, blue water, and windmills turning here and there, and lush bushes and trees. It was cool and showery. We were all hungry, but there was nothing to eat on this train, not even tea. At Kashing, three hours after we started, we bought grapes that were wonderful, and lotus pods with seeds that were good to eat, and a kind of sweet. Wally and Gandhi brought out a tin of sardines and one of peaches. We filled the Thermos with tea there. It was noon and then afternoon, and we had been shunted to a siding, and left there for a long time. Suddenly, after two hours of eating and then dozing, a signalman shouted at us to get out of this train; another one was going, not this. There was a scramble, for we were not anywhere near a platform. Several people just jumped down and ran back to the station with their things. Before we could get out, the signalman shouted that this train would go on after all, and sure enough it did.

All afternoon we went slowly through flat, rich country, stopping every few yards. We saw airplanes, more and more, over the fields. Toward evening, a Japanese plane came along directly over us, but that day the Japanese were not bombing trains—not yet.

About six in the evening we began to sing. Gandhi could play a sort of tune on the flat wood bottom of a matchbox. He was wonderful. He wouldn't eat our ham sandwiches, but said if he were starving he would eat ham, though he is a Mohammedan. He smiled softly and asked me if I had ever been to Liverpool. "There is a mosque there, wonderful. I have never seen it, but I have heard." Mr. Lee asked for tunes, and Wally played on a comb and I sang, and Mary used our two fans for drumsticks on the table between the seats. Sweetie Pie came into the chorus, "Peep, peep! Peep, peep!" or, as Cocteau would spell it, "Huit, huit!" We saw Lunghwa pagoda, and Mary said to me, "This was too easy. It has been almost twenty-four hours, but not bad really."

We were going to get off, we told each other, at South Station, and not ride downtown to North. Then we came into South Station, and we were mobbed. There had been freight cars and boxcars and flatcars full of Chinese riding out in the country toward the end of the day, crowded indescribably, with people standing on the roofs. We should have expected this mob, but we were tired, and then they were on us before the train was stopped. We didn't know, of course, that they had been under fire and bombs all day. We only knew the train was arriving, not going, and there was no sense to all this. The mob was forcing us back into the train. People climbed in the windows, even. They didn't look bad, just dazed. Wally climbed through a window on the side away from the mob, pulling my hatbox and telling me to come. I screamed, "No!" and with Mary behind me, I threw myself into the crowd at the door. I am heavier than most Chinese and they let me fall through, and I thought Mary was right behind me. When I got to the platform and turned and saw her still on the train, I felt suddenly sick. Mary is very small and thin.

Then something happened. Mary was being tossed around as if she were in surf, and she looked down and saw that Sweetie Pie's round basket was being squashed flat. His head had reared up like a snake's and his eyes were starting out of his head. She yelled loudly—I found out afterward it was "God damn you, let my duck alone!"—and began hitting out and scratching, and before I knew it she was out of the crowd, too, with Sweetie Pie in her hands.

It took a long while to find Gandhi and Wally and Mr. Lee, but we did. Then we began to walk. It was about this time, just as night fell, that we realized we were hearing bombs.

The street in the Chinese city, where all was fair in war, was full of people drifting like leaves, peering uneasily into a cloudy sky. We walked fast down the middle of the street. It wasn't true: it was too much like a woodcut in a nightmare. Wally had got a rickshaw, just one, to carry the luggage. He was exclaiming in indignation at the prices the coolies wanted, and he would not listen to me when I told him Mary couldn't walk. But Mary did walk, we all did, over cobblestones, almost running. He was feeling awful anyway; he is a movie-maker, and had missed a lot of chances to make money by not having his camera. "Two gold dollars a foot," he said, and shook his head. So we walked, and heard bombs very near. I had never heard them before. It was endless, not exciting at all, not frightening, not real.

No other foreigners were around. The volunteer police were out very thickly, telling us where we couldn't go. We described a semicircle, I think; I think we must have walked four miles before we came to the only gate into the French Concession which was left open. (I don't know why, even now.) When we came to the big iron gates at last, there were foreigners, Frenchmen in uniform with a big camouflaged truck, staring at us, amazed. A big man called, "Vhere are you from?" I yelled, "Nanking," and we passed through the gates. He said, "On *foo-oo-oot?*" and roared with laughter. We swung into this new street, and then behind us, behind the gates, there were airplanes dropping bombs.

We turned to look. The sky was almost dark now, and we saw five planes, and then flashes of electric blue which Wally said were anti-aircraft guns. I didn't care anymore if we were bombed or not. I was angry with everyone except the innocent Chinese, peering up into the sky; I was furious. Mary suddenly was scared, though, and begged us to run, and the men came along reluctantly. It was then I insisted on a rickshaw for Mary, and said I would pay.

From then on it was really dreamlike. A truckload of dead bodies went by, quite fast. The rickshaws kept stopping because their lanterns went out. There were flames in the sky. I saw a pair of Chinese lovers sauntering along under that horrible canopy, hand in hand, heads bent.

At last we found a taxi, and then we were home, and Wally and Gandhi said they would stay to dinner. The bombs went on, and we ate dinner and talked very hard to the cook, who was glad to see us. We had coffee and brandy, and cigarettes, and Sweetie Pie had a long swim in the bathtub. Twelve hundred Chinese had been killed in Shanghai that day—by Chinese bombs.

PEACE COMES TO SHANGHAI

The war went roaring northwest and we thought complacently
that, anyway, we had had ours. Things quieted down, though
they continued to simmer. A few people hurried home, there to
eke out their lives, dull thereafter, with amateur movies of
Nantao burning by night, and lecture tours, and interviews with
the home-town newspaper; but most of us were left in Shanghai.
Times were hard, of course, but even hard times in Shanghai are
pretty soft when you compare them with the old days in Berlin
or Lyons or Columbus, Ohio. So most of us gave up the extra

house coolie, the young men stopped playing polo for a while, and we all went on working at the customary mild pace.

There had been lots of stories about interviews between Japanese officials and our own during the weeks past. There was the tale of the Japanese admiral who requested the French admiral to remove his gunboat from its place in the river, so as to be out of danger of gunfire and bombs. The French admiral is supposed to have agreed with the utmost alacrity. "On one condition," he added. And what was that? "That you supply me," said the Gaul, "with a boat large enough to tow all of Frenchtown downstream with us."

Again, there was the meeting of all the Western admirals to discuss what should be done now that the combatants were getting so careless about the American cruiser Augusta and other foreign craft. The British admiral said, "We'd better be diplomatic, eh? Even if one of their silly little airplanes does happen to fly over us now and again, we'd better—er—ignore it diplomatically, what?"

The American admiral said, "Well, the next time they fly over the Augusta I shall wait upon their Admiralty and deliver a very strong protest."

The French admiral leaped to his feet, bristling. "If one of them comes anywhere near my ships," he stormed, "I shall shoot off all my guns in every direction!"

After the earlier excitement, life would have seemed almost dull if it had not been for the fantastic rumors which flew about town. At first we just amused ourselves with the stories, but as certain acts classed by the papers as "terrorism" became more and more frequent, the Municipal Council police of the Settlement and the French police, upon whom most of the direct responsibility for keeping order always lay, grew rather hot under the collar, and we were impressed. Hand grenades were thrown now and then at Japanese-owned factories. Headless bodies were found in the streets. Heads were found without their bodies. These relics were always supposed to be Japanese, or Chinese in the pay of Japanese. The Japanese theory was that under the protection of the foreign nationals dastardly Chinese who called themselves patriots were taking this cowardly method of heckling the enemy.

Every time any Japanese suffered from one of these incidents, the Japanese authorities looked grave and made cryptic threats. We had all become more or less placid; we had forgotten the possibility of our land being taken over outright, but now we were reminded of the danger. It was not the worst that could happen, we realized, to be deprived of the liberty to motor to Minghong or to Hangchow of a Sunday. It was not the most distressing thing in the world to be sideswiped in our cars by some reckless Japanese driver who would immediately gallop to safety over the bridge to Hongkew. They might demand more. They might yet take more.

None of us could swear to how much our home governments would stand by us, either. People went about feverishly adding up the capital invested by their own nations in China. Would this sum justify any resistance against more aggressive Japanese action? And why didn't we have more troops, for God's sake? At the daily press conference, where bored foreign correspondents had gathered of an afternoon to listen to a glib Japanese spokesman tell them whatever propaganda was good for them to hear, the atmosphere grew brisker. Theretofore everybody had accepted the conference as a rather tiresome joke, and on Christmas Day in '37 the correspondents presented to the spokesman a carefully wrapped length of bologna. Now military-looking gentlemen attended the meetings and consented to answer questions, and their answers grew less and less equivocal. Japan, they said, smiling flashily, would do in Shanghai what seemed to her most consistent with her policy of expansion. Japan expected other nations to recognize that the whole situation here in Shanghai had changed since the old days when France had acquired her sovereignty from the now outmoded Chinese.

Then there was the slapping epidemic. Japanese sentries seemed suddenly to have developed a mania for slapping. An English lady crossed Garden Bridge on what was, according to unannounced Japanese rules, the wrong side; the sentry shook her arm, hustled her across to her proper place, and slapped her face. She reported it to the British Consulate. They made representations. Next day she prudently went down to another bridge to do her crossing and all unwittingly walked through a gap reserved, for no particular reason, for rickshaw coolies. She was again slapped, and again she reported the incident to the British Consulate. They made representations.

An American vice-consul in Nanking was slapped for trying to enter his office. He just stood there and thought things; he could do nothing else. An elderly British nature-lover in Shanghai walked too near the lines; he was arrested and bayonetted a good many times, not deeply, of course, mostly in the small of the back, before he was released. The soldiers who arrested him took turns slapping him. Tourists in Peiping who were being no more offensive than tourists naturally are to the natives got slapped all the time. These slappings usually happened to the nationals of non-Fascist countries, though sometimes the Japanese made mistakes and didn't recognize Germans or Italians when they saw them.

In the light of the uncertain conditions, the foreign consulates and embassies could do nothing but sit tight and counsel patience. As the first anniversary of the war's beginning drew near, they expected many dangerous demonstrations of Chinese patriotism. In vain might all the papers scold the Chinese community and point out that they were enjoying our protection and owed us peace; most Chinese had long since come to the quiet conclusion that Shanghai is China, after all, and that the foreigners, by refusing to fly to China's aid, had sacrificed this claim to consideration. A very practical people, the Chinese.

Therefore the police and the civic authorities took extraordinary precautions as the August anniversary approached. They put up their wartime barbed-wire barriers again on most of the roads running between Frenchtown and the Settlement. Frenchtown was policed by the French, and the International Settlement was managed by a mixed "municipal council," on which a number of countries, including Britain, the United States, Germany—even Japan—were represented. Everybody passing through the lines was liable to search and Chinese were patted all over to make sure they carried no firearms or grenades. Suspicious-looking foreigners were patted all over, too, for though it had been announced that Generalissimo Chiang and the Communists were kissing and making it up out in Hankow, you never know with these Reds, said the police. Even some Japanese were searched, though they objected shrilly. Their leaders protested, too, but the police had their orders.

The war's birthday dawned. By noon, several cars full of Chinese had been grabbed for throwing pamphlets to the populace. A few dozen hand grenades were dumped in empty fields by men who lost their nerve at sight of the search parties. A lot of armed terrorists were caught, too, brandishing rifles. By two o'clock in the afternoon, foreign and Chinese Shanghai was rocking with decorous laughter and Japanese faces were red, for in every case these captured terrorists turned out to be Japanese, or Chinese in Japanese pay. The ensuing five weeks saw a relaxed Shanghai and a very quiet Japanese community, and nobody heard any careless talk of Nippon taking over. It was pleasant and the night clubs did a boom trade.

Then Europe turned over in her sleep.

At first the full significance of the Czechoslovakian dispute did not occur to most of us. We said hilariously that after all little old Shanghai was just about the best place to be if that was the way things were going to be managed in Europe. After a week somebody remarked in print that a European war would remove our protection, and we suddenly sobered and commenced to think about it. It didn't look so good.

Panic began slowly, then swept the town. As the American dollar and sterling began to fall, the Chinese dollar went up, but for once nobody paid any attention to the exchange. Everywhere we were asking each other, "What do *you* think the Japanese will do?" A few hardy souls said, "They won't do anything. Why should they?," but they lied in their teeth and they knew it. Grim realists figured it out this way: "The first thing they'll want, of course, is full control of Frenchtown, because, of course, Japan will line up with Germany, so that means Japan against France. The Japs have already got the International Settlement where they want it. We'll all be interned."

Once again, and for the tenth time, the unfortunate Chinese refugees clinging to their nooks and crannies in nice, safe Frenchtown packed their little bundles and shouldered their children and marched in long, ragged lines back to the International Settlement. At least there were two British regiments there—the Seaforth Highlanders and the Durhams—and there were always the American Marines. These wouldn't let them down, they said.

The French authorities, without fuss or bother, went all around their outside lines and added to the barbed-wire barrier and strengthened their guards. There hadn't been such efficient preparation even in the worst days of the hostilities. Nothing could have reminded us more vividly that other dangers besides Japanese occupation lay in wait for us. Outside the city were the Chinese guerrillas, some of them working directly from Hankow, others acting like the simple bandits they had been before. The Chinese had no particular reason to be loyal to foreigners, we remembered.

During the hostilities we called "the Shanghai war," when Japanese and Chinese had battled for control of the country all around us until the Japanese gained the upper hand and occupied Chinese Shanghai, we had taken comfort from the presence of the British troops and to a lesser degree from the American Marines, whom we had always had with us. We tried to feel that way now, but it didn't look so good, it really didn't. More rumors added to our discomfort. Every day somebody would announce that latest report from Reuter's or Domei or somewhere that war had already broken out in Central Europe.

Many of the old-timers in Shanghai had fought in the World War. They were still on reserve. They got their old equipment ready and began to wait for telegrams. Among the French, a good many officers were actually recalled; they took ship and went away. Gunboats, which had come back since the war went away to the northwest, began to disappear by night; one by one they vanished, until we stopped counting the vacancies.

The German community held a secret meeting at their schoolhouse and made plans. At the first sign of trouble they were to remove their women and children across Soochow Creek, where they would be dependent upon Japanese protection. It would be quite safe there for Germans and Italians.

I think we were more badly scared than we had ever been under fire in 1937. Yet nobody stopped working. With one eye on our everyday competitors and the other on the news from Europe, we worked feverishly, squabbling over contracts, packing trunks, counting money, telephoning the newspaper offices for the latest bulletins, and clamoring for more business in offices which might before another week be deserted forever.

The conversation must have been very much what it was in other parts of the world: "It can't happen again," "There's no way out," "Better get it over now while it's easy," "A war to end war," "That's what they said last time."

But some of our topics of conversation were probably unique. We laid bets as to where we would be interned—in our own homes, or in concentration camps in Japan? Shanghai was peculiarly international, with a long-standing internationality; there existed there a generation of people born in Shanghai, though they held European and American passports. German boys brought up in Frenchtown, who were French in speech and habits of thought, found that they must report to Berlin for orders. Eurasians had to hold themselves in readiness to fight for England, a country they hated with the hatred born of a lifetime of snubs. Italians were faced with an extra dilemma; many of the most important members of the Shanghai-Italian community were Jews who had suddenly been deprived of their Italian citizenship. People of all nations had been sending children to mixed schools. What were they to do? Then there were the many Austrian-Iraqians who had travelled so long on Chinese passports. What was going to happen to them?

Underneath it all the Chinese refugees waited dumbly, only wondering in which direction to run this time.

We all stopped moving about at last. We were quiet, waiting for the deadline. It was all too uncertain, and anyway it was too late for anybody to attempt to get away by boat. There was only one comfort: the English troops and the Marines were still here.

Then at ten o'clock one morning the Seaforths marched down to Yangtzepoo, got on a ship, and sailed away to Hong Kong. It happened before most of us knew anything about it. A few people saw them marching, but nobody could believe they had gone until it was announced in the papers. The Seaforths, said the authorities briefly, had been ordered to Hong Kong "for manoeuvres."

But what about *us*? The English were too patriotic to ask the question aloud. At first they gave themselves up to despair, and no rumor was too silly to be repeated; then they reminded each other that they still had the Durhams and the Marines. There had always been the Marines. Why, of course, the Marines! Good chaps, too, and they'd held their own every time during the hostilities. Maybe it had been arranged secretly that America was to take over from England. That might be it. Why, yes.

We went on doing our office work. We went out at night to the movies or to the night clubs, too nervous to sit at home and think. It was noted, but not mentioned, that one didn't see Japanese around anymore. Wherever we went during those few days and whatever we did, our eyes were turned toward Soochow Creek and beyond. What were they planning over there, anyway?

After that, you remember, things happened very swiftly in Europe. Chamberlain's first trip by airplane broke the spell and the relief was so exquisite that nearly an hour had gone by before the diehards began to grumble, "Let us down, he did," "Great loss of face for England," "We should have seen it through."

The Shanghai Club bar, which had been quiet though never quite empty, now hummed with discussion and rang with cries for whiskey and yet more whiskey. A sigh of relief that shook the city rose gustily to the autumn sky. The Shanghai dollar went down to its normal place. War veterans began to ask themselves if they were after all a little bit disappointed. People renewed contracts which had been awaiting renewal for a week.

In Hankow there was mourning, for the Chinese had decided that Japan, with the other Fascists too busy in Europe to help her Chinese campaign, might have stopped advancing. Everybody there felt strong sympathy with Czechoslovakia, in whose fate they saw a similarity to their own. The rich Shanghai Chinese soberly congratulated their foreign acquaintances, then went home to curse quietly in the bosom of the family. All over Shanghai wives and mothers put away their trunks and suitcases, wiped their eyes, powdered their noses, and went out to play bridge. Over in Hongkew, an American sailor slapped a Japanese.

PILGRIM'S PROGRESS

Step by step, life in Shanghai became more constricted. First we couldn't go outside the town limits, and then some of my friends were shot at while riding, and we had to give up hacking even inside the Settlement. The shops ran short of things, Chinese acquaintances quietly disappeared, and there came a time when the staff of my college, with the exception of me, moved to Hong Kong because, it was explained, students from the interior could no longer get to Shanghai. This was just about when the European war started. But Europe was a long way off, and in any case the war didn't so much break on the world as slither onstage. I didn't really notice it until I tried to get an entry permit for Hong Kong—for I was going to Chungking, and had to cross the colony on the way—and found a bit more difficulty travelling than I had encountered in the past. I got the permit, of course: I had a good reason to go to Chungking, I explained, because it was arranged that I should interview Madame Chiang there, where the government had withdrawn from the advancing Japanese. But it meant filling in more forms.

In the meantime I had met and fallen in love with Charles, an officer in the British army. Though he wanted to go to Europe where the action was, the authorities said that someone had to stay in Hong Kong, so that was that.

I was in Chungking when the news arrived that the phony war had ceased to be phony. Even then, from where I was it didn't seem crucial that the Germans should be crashing their way through Holland, Belgium, and France with such surprising ease, especially when they paused, or were halted, at the Channel before they could invade Britain. But the British and American authorities in charge of the Far East, who took things harder than I did, began shipping their women and children to countries considered safer than Hong Kong and the Chinese treaty ports— countries such as Australia, Malaya, the Philippines, and the Dutch East Indies. I returned to Hong Kong where Charles was and resumed working at the college.

In October 1941 our baby Carola was born. Six weeks later the Japanese attacked Pearl Harbor, Hong Kong, Malaya, and so forth. Hong Kong held out until Christmas Day, but before the surrender Charles had been seriously wounded, and like everything else the hospital was taken over at the surrender. Military and naval prisoners were put into their own camp, and the Caucasian civilians—enemy nationals, they were called—were rounded up and put into another, but I wasn't. I wriggled out of imprisonment by claiming to be Eurasian, for the Japanese made a point of leaving all "Asians" alone. Though this action left Carola and me without means of support, we were no worse off than all the others outside, the Chinese and Eurasians and Portuguese-Chinese from Macao, along with a sprinkling of neutral whites, and I thought this existence would be vastly preferable to life in prison camp. The decision might easily have led to catastrophe, but our luck held and for the following two years we managed to survive.

Two exchanges of civilian prisoners were arranged between Japan and the United States during that time, one early in 1942 and the other late in 1943. I refused to accept passage on the first exchange because the women outside were being permitted to send food to their men in camp, and Charles, like the others, needed the extra nourishment. When the second chance came, however, in 1942, he got word smuggled out to me that this time Carola and I must go if we could. He implied that something serious was about to happen in Hong Kong for which he wanted us out of the way. Though I didn't understand the veiled warning I accepted it. Carola and I, on the list as an American-born Chinese woman with her child, sailed off with a shipload of other exchanged people two days before Charles with a number of associates was caught and put on trial, charged with taking part in espionage in camp. Fortunately I knew nothing about this for several months, until the American papers printed the story that he had been found guilty and beheaded. Fortunately again, I didn't believe it when I read it. I suppose people never do believe unwelcome news until it is absolutely proven, and this turned out to be untrue, as a matter of fact. But it was another two years before one could be sure.

On returning from a long absence, I am always surprised and even resentful to find friends and landmarks changed. I never seem to remember that I, too, must have changed, but lately I've been thinking a little about that side of it, and I've come to the conclusion that inveterate wanderers like me must be pretty hard for their families to take. A nephew brought it home to me the other day. After having remained silent on the subject for more than twenty years, he told me how he'd reacted back in 1943 to the news that his Aunt Mickey was coming home from China. "I didn't like it at all," he admitted. "I wished that you'd stayed away."

"But you didn't even know me!" I protested.

"Of course I didn't," he said. "I was about two weeks old when you left that time, but you don't understand—you yourself had nothing to do with this. It was just that all the time you were over there I could boast about my aunt in China. None of the other kids I knew in Winnetka had a relative so exciting, and it gave me a certain standing. In fact—though it's an awful thing to say, and I apologize—things got even better after the war started, when you were supposed to have been killed by the Japanese. I was riding high until we got the word that you hadn't been killed after all and were on the way home with a baby daughter, named Carola. It seemed sort of flat."

I suppose it always does seem flat when a traveller returns. Even Marco Polo, back in Venice after years in the Far East, met with a disappointing reception from the townspeople. They respected him for bringing home a fortune, I'm sure, but they refused to listen to what he had to tell. All the glitter and pageantry of the court of Kublai Khan—the temples and the silk and the spiced foods, the Forbidden City, the lakes like jewels, the caves of idols, the tombs, and the incense, and the junks with painted eyes, arched bridges, wind bells—the Venetians said he'd made it up.

Their disappointing reaction is on record, but what is not written is a description of how Marco Polo's *relatives* felt about the situation. I'm willing to hazard a guess, however. I'll bet anything that they found their celebrated kinsman an awful nuisance to have around. For one thing, there was the way he expected the young people to listen whenever he felt like telling an anecdote. And the extravagant habits he'd cultivated. Though slaves were a luxury, Marco Polo expected to be served as if he were a Chinese emperor. If it hadn't been for his wealth and the children's prospects . . .

Ulysses is another case in point. No doubt Penelope was glad to have him back to rescue her from that difficult situation, but, once the excitement of homecoming was over, she may well have found it difficult to adjust to him—a man who had grown all too used to the rough life of the seafarer. By day, he would complain that Ithaca was dull, and would mope around the estate. By night, he would sleep badly, often starting up out of a nightmare to shout hoarsely about alarms and excursions. Anxious times for Penelope.

There is no doubt that people away from home collect unfortunate habits and forget to slough them off after returning, but—characteristically—I didn't think of this when I stepped off the Gripsholm late in 1943, an exchanged prisoner of war from Hong Kong. It's hard to remember what I *was* thinking. At best, I was pretty groggy after the hours of questioning I'd been put through by armed-forces Intelligence men who were suspicious of me because I hadn't lived in prison camp with the other Americans caught in Hong Kong. I realized that they had every reason to be suspicious, and I wasn't indignant about it, but I was awfully tired, especially of telling them the truth over and over—how I'd seen a loophole right after the surrender and had grabbed it by telling the Japanese officials in charge of internment that I was Eurasian. They were mostly young, green, and bewildered, and they believed me and let me stay out of camp because they figured any Eurasian should have the benefit of his Asian blood. So I'd taken my chances with the other non-internees—the Chinese and neutrals who went on living at large in the town as best they could. I'd tried to tell the Intelligence men why I did it, but I couldn't have been very clear—they kept asking the same questions all over again, and I kept replying that the comparative freedom I had got out of the lie was important. It wasn't only that the very idea of being herded behind barbed wire was revolting. Outside, I was able to carry food and medicine to the military camp where Carola's father was incarcerated. We all did, every week, a draggletailed group of women whose men were locked up—Chinese women, and Swiss and French and Danish and Eurasian and Russian, and me. The thing grew, too. There were two military camps, and in time we were visiting not just our own particular camp but the other one as well, whether or not we had somebody inside.

Even a Mrs. Weston sometimes showed up with her daughters, though she lived over on Pakfulam, a long way off, and every-

286

body knew her husband wasn't even in Hong Kong but had been caught, as it happened, in Manila. What saved Mrs. Weston from being interned as the Englishwoman she was born was the fact that her husband was Irish, and Ireland wasn't at war with Japan. Perhaps I should have cited her case to my questioners. But I wasn't thinking about her, of all people, that day on the dock in Jersey City. I probably wasn't thinking anything except that it was awfully cold in New York and that Carola seemed heavier than usual. At two, a child has the right to be heavier than a newborn infant, but she was a very small two-year-old. She was almost hairless. She cried a lot. She'd cried steadily all the time I was being questioned, until the Intelligence men got tired of the noise and gave me permission to take her off the ship and hand her to my sister Helen, who, according to a note I'd received, was waiting for me on the dock. Then I must come back for more questioning, they said, and, to make sure I did, a woman in uniform came along with me.

As I stepped down from the gangplank, a whole lot of lights flared up in our faces. Carola screamed, of course, and started hitting out at the world, most of the blows landing on me. Beyond the ring of lights, I could see the dark figures of men trying to get closer, past the policemen who were keeping them at a distance. The men shouted, "Names? What are your names?" They were reporters and photographers who had been there for hours to catch us repatriated people and get our stories as we disembarked. They were cold and damp in the Jersey City fog, but still excited—far more excited than I was. I just stood there blinking and holding down Carola's fists, until a woman broke through the wall and came over past the policemen and said, "Mickey!"

I stared at her utterly strange, emotion-suffused face, and then, just before she put her arms around us, she turned into my sister Helen. I almost laughed because I hadn't known her at once, but there was no time to tell her about it. The uniformed woman was waiting grimly, so I pushed Carola at Helen and said, "Here, take her home with you, will you? She's awfully tired. I'll be along as soon as I can. Oh, and if she makes a fuss, sing to her. She knows 'Six Honest Serving-men,' remember? By the way, where do you live? Where shall I go?"

A man who had come up behind Helen said, "That's all right. I'm waiting for you until you're off for good. I'll take you to Helen's."

Several hours later, I joined the man—a friend of Helen's husband—again on the dock. Almost everybody else was gone by that time, and even to my eyes the city looked strangely dim in the night as we came out through the gate. The man said, "You must have had quite a session up there. How many panels did you go through?"

"Panels?" I repeated blankly.

"Groups of people. You had different groups interviewing you, didn't you?"

"Oh, groups. Yes, there were a lot. There were—let's see—eight different groups, I think."

"Eight panels!" He whistled, and stopped short. "Listen," he said. "It's late, and Helen's probably worrying her head off wondering what's happened. Let's telephone and say we're on our way." He found a drugstore, got Helen on the phone, and handed it over to me.

I said, "Helen? I forgot to tell you—Carola doesn't speak English."

Her voice sounded tense. "We—have—already—found—that—out," she said, clearly controlling herself with great effort. "Hurry up."

I said I would try to. Outside, the man had hailed a taxi. "Your brother-in-law asked me to stand by. That's where I come in," he explained as we got into it. "But I've got a lot of work piling up at the office, and if you don't mind I'll just take your things up to the door and leave you. O.K.?"

I was alone, therefore, when I rang the bell at last—Ulysses back from his wanderings, Marco Polo with a head full of visions. The door opened; Mother stood there. I knew her at once. She said, "Well, *Mickey*," just as Penelope might have spoken— more crossly than anything else. I half expected her to continue, as she so often had in the past, "This is a fine time . . ." Instead, she hurried me through the little hall, saying, "We've been having a real struggle with that child of yours. Helen! Here she is, and high time, too."

Helen and her husband, who stood gloomily contemplating a large sofa along one wall, gave me only a short glance and turned back to the sofa. It was at an angle, having apparently been shoved out at one end. A bowl of water that stood on the carpet had slopped over, and near it lay a gnawed piece of bread. Under a chair was a small shoe that I recognized as Carola's. Helen said, "Oh, hello, Mickey. The baby's under the sofa. She's been there a long time. She won't come out."

I extracted Carola, wiped her dirty, wet face, and sat down on the sofa. The others found seats, too. We all looked at each other. I said, "How's everybody, and where are they?"

They told me. It took a long time, naturally—it always does—and there was more than usual to say, what with the way they kept interrupting each other and contributing more information. We hadn't been able to exchange letters for two years. Little by little, the clan was charted: Rose and Dauphine and Mannel in Winnetka, with their children; Dot in Burlington, with hers. Charless and Hattie had a daughter just Carola's age, or did I know that? Mitchell's nephew was dead from an accident at his Army camp. It went on until Carola fell asleep on my lap and I nodded over her, nearly asleep myself. Ulysses was home again.

It wasn't to be simple in the following days, for the others or for me. Momentarily, however, the pressure relaxed. I moved into an apartment and found a nursery school for Carola, the principal of which advised me to have her thoroughly examined by a doctor. She said, "Let me recommend our man. He's a perfect darling—just a young man, but he knows his job. I'll give you the name. Benjamin Spock."

Dr. Spock did examine Carola, though it must have been difficult, since she spoke only Cantonese. She had sternly resisted all blandishments and refused to learn English. And, as was to be expected, she wept several times during the interview.

"An apprehensive child," the Doctor said when he had finished. "Doesn't she ever seem happy?"

I said, "Yes, she's happy enough when we go to Chinese restaurants, where the waiters gather around to watch her eat with chopsticks. They talk to her, and she talks to them. Oh, she's fine in Chinese restaurants, but we can't spend all our time there, and—well, you can see for yourself. And she doesn't sleep well, either. She's apt to wake up any time in the night and howl."

He mentioned something about children's reflecting the moods of their parents.

"But I'm all right," I said. "I'm perfectly all right. I'm just waiting for the war to finish, that's all. Her father's in prison camp."

Dr. Spock nodded, and repeated that the child seemed apprehensive. "I don't see anything wrong otherwise—nothing we can put a finger on. The lack of hair is probably due to malnutrition, and the growth should speed up now. Keep an eye on her teeth. For the rest, if I were you I'd spoil her, let her have what she wants, within reason. At night, don't let her go on crying in the dark. You might move her bed into your room —anything to give her reassurance. Get a night light."

I got a night light and did the other things, and, sure enough, Carola improved. Her hair grew out, she learned to eat American food, and soon she was speaking English, having dropped the Cantonese completely. At nursery school, she made friends and enemies. By the time we went out to Winnetka for a visit, she could have been any child in town. The family had no problems at all with Carola. It was I who gave trouble. I didn't mean to—I was never aware I was doing it until it was too late— but there it was: I bothered them. There was the time, for instance, when I went out shopping for a blouse with my sister Rose at a place she often patronized. Among the models the salesgirl showed us was one that particularly pleased us.

The girl said to me, "Would you like to try it on?"

I assented, and began forthwith to unbutton my own garments

right there in the middle of the floor. Rose said my name in a horrified tone and stopped me. "Go into the dressing room," she said.

I muttered an apology and trotted off, blushing, toward the curtained alcove. Behind me I could hear her saying apologetically to the salesgirl, ". . . no inhibitions left. Absolutely none."

There was an explanation I could have made. Living six or eight in a room and sleeping all over the floor—customs not conducive to modesty—had been my way of life for two years, and you don't drop all such habits in a hurry. But what would have been the use of explaining? You can't learn things like that at second hand. Rose would have listened courteously and accepted what I said, but she'd have had mental reservations just the same.

Additional awkwardnesses arose. I swore a lot—quite unconscious of what I was doing until it was too late—and ladies don't swear in Winnetka. When rebuked, I reverted to childishness and swore even more. Who did they think I was, anyway? And though nobody liked to mention it to me, my table manners were quite deplorable, for I would start eating as soon as food was on my plate, regardless of whether other people had been served or not—a hangover from mealtimes in Hong Kong, when if you didn't gobble you didn't get enough. However, all these misdemeanors were relatively insignificant in my family's eyes compared with one outstanding, glaring trait I had developed. I had become dishonest. Not only did I deal in the black market in New York, I *talked* about it. I seemed proud of it.

I still think it was natural enough, that period when I was half a criminal. If you look at it from my point of view— Well, it was this way. In Hong Kong, there were good reasons for black-marketing. If you tried to live on the rations the Japanese granted, you starved. The rice ration alone, for example, would have been insufficient even if it had been honored, and most of the time it wasn't. Peculations, graft, and plain mismanagement emptied the storehouses, so that cardholders were either told to come back later, day after day, or given a miserable dollop of floor sweepings. Within the first few weeks, most of us gave up trying to use our ration cards for rice; instead, we sought it on the black market. The same thing happened with cooking-fat, sugar, and all the rest of it. Like everyone else at large in the town, I had sold things, bartered, begged, and black-marketed without the slightest sense of shame. Of course without shame; what was shameful about it? The overriding consideration, it hardly needs saying, was to feed Carola and myself, but if I'd ever been challenged and asked to justify myself I would have added that it was a good thing in any case to buy and sell on the black market because the Japanese had ordered us not to do it. Under enemy rule, it doesn't take a person long to become chronically anti-government. What does take long—longer, at any rate—is to shake off such almost instinctive feelings when the person gets out from under. I'd come home from Hong Kong wearing a chip on my shoulder, and it wasn't to be jiggled off all that quickly. I couldn't have explained any of this to the family—I didn't understand it myself. As I look back, however, it's clear enough, and so is my realization of an additional reason I black-marketed: doing these things in occupied territory is fun.

To anyone who hasn't experienced it, it would be hard to describe the boredom of life under enemy occupation. You might not expect a person who is harried and apprehensive to have the time to be bored, but in fact he has all the time in the world, because constant fear and worry are not demanding of attention. They move in, select their places, and adhere firmly to the sides of the heart, but when the host has got used to the slight discomfort they are just added parts of the furniture. Time remains as it always has been, but the host is in a grayer world and his day-to-day life is less punctuated. In fact, it is endless. In Hong Kong, the only alleviation of this ennui, aside from the occasional alarm of a drunken soldier in the street or a spot-check search of the house, was the black market. It could be deliciously exciting to buy or sell commodities you had no right to deal in. I learned to love the intrigue of it—the whispered colloquies on street corners, the dropped word on the ferry as an acquaintance passed by seemingly unacknowledged, the furtive deliveries in the dark, and the little parcels at the bottom of a shopping basket smuggled past a guard. Of course it terrified me—that was the whole point. I grew to love being terrified and all that went with it, including shaking knees and breath that refused to fill the lungs. I loved it all. No other addiction could have been as satisfying.

Admittedly, that was in Hong Kong, whereas in New York it was different. Looked at with clear eyes, the black market in New York was just trading—a question of buying stuff under the counter. There was no spice in it, no real danger. It wasn't even a pallid imitation of the real thing. But I wasn't looking at it, or at anything else in New York, with clear eyes. I had the black-market habit. I had a grudge, too, against law and order, and I still had my reasons for that. Time still stretched ahead with no break in sight, since nobody could possibly guess when the prison-camp doors would open, and Charles might well be dead anyway. And even though Carola and I were safe at home, surrounded by friends, I was lonely, because the friends and family seemed shadowy, not quite real—nothing like as real as people I'd lived among in danger. The only bit of solid life that remained was the black market. There, at least, even though I was acquiring butter and nylons instead of peanut oil and powdered milk, I could feel that I had my feet on the ground. Once again, I could experience the old familiar thrill of outwitting authority. That I had changed governments since leaving Hong Kong meant nothing. Logic didn't enter into it. How could I explain this to my relatives? They would never understand me, just as I would never understand them—never again. The situation was a stalemate.

Or so it seemed at the time. I am not sure even now what broke it up and brought me back to normal. Probably it was just ordinary attrition, the erosion of the once-familiar, that sandpapered me into recognizable shape at last, but I can be pretty certain when the change began making itself felt. It was on the day I wondered what had happened to Mrs. Weston.

Until the summer of 1943, a couple of months before I found I was being sent back to America, I knew her story well enough

—how she and her two little girls had stayed on in their old flat, the way people in Hong Kong did, until they were evicted by a Japanese officer who wanted the place. Then how they found less desirable premises where, presumably, they wouldn't be disturbed again. She'd told me all this when we met at the prison-camp gate to hand in our offerings. Sometimes we happened to meet otherwise—at the new shopping center (rows and rows of barrows along the sidewalks downtown) that sprang up after the Japanese closed all the shops—but we weren't really chummy, in spite of having so much in common. For one thing, she lived so far away, and both she and I were too busy scrounging to spare effort for mere sociability. However, when I thought of her—*if* I thought of her—it was as a nice woman and a courageous one, and I owed her gratitude for at least one favor she had done. When we did happen to encounter each other—the Weston girls taller and thinner every time I saw them—we would swap useful bits of information about available supplies and current rumors. That time, she told me I'd better stay at home next day because a friendly guard had told the girls that a Japanese prince was going to pay a visit on the island. We all knew what that would mean—a curfew. I don't know why the Japanese used the word as they did, since it had nothing to do with nighttime regulations. It meant that all persons out-of-doors, as soon as they got the signal from policemen or guards, had to stop, kneel down, and freeze there until they were given the order to relax and continue on their way. A curfew was called every time an important visitor—a general or admiral from overseas, usually—was in town and moving around on a tour of inspection. They were tense, uncomfortable periods, and could go on for hours.

All this, however, is by the way and not what I thought about in New York when I suddenly remembered Mrs. Weston. What I thought about was the last time I had seen her, in the summer of 1943, when I met her as usual among the barrows downtown. She was alone, for once, but otherwise looked the same as always, shabby and determined. I asked about the girls, and she said they were busy at home, getting ready. Before I could ask,

"Getting ready for what, for God's sake?" Mrs. Weston stepped closer, looked furtively over her shoulder to make sure she wouldn't be overheard, and said in a low voice, "We're leaving, you know—we start out tonight."

I knew enough not to exclaim, though I was startled. It had been months since anyone I knew had slipped out of Hong Kong. At the beginning, during all the confusion, it hadn't been too hard. You hired a junk and sailed off during the night, and the crew landed you somewhere on the mainland where the Japanese weren't in strict control and you could make your way overland to Free China. In those early days, some people even left Kowloon, over on the mainland, by bicycle, crossing the border. It was that simple. Then there was the time-honored system of disguising yourself as a Chinese peasant and hiking past the guards, though it wasn't advisable to try this unless you talked fluent Cantonese or Swatow dialect. On further thought, I decided that all these systems might still work, though the controls along the border were tighter. Mrs. Weston was probably bribing somebody with a promissory note.

"I'm telling you so you won't say anything about it when you don't see us around anymore," she said in a half whisper. "If you didn't know any better, you might ask somebody quite innocently where we are and start an inquiry—not that they have any reason to keep us here, for heaven's sake, but you know how it is with them." She paused. "I'd better not tell you anything more—how we're going to get out and so on."

"Well," I said, "all the best."

"I've been thinking of doing it for some time," Mrs. Weston continued, an apologetic note in her voice—people on the eve of escaping always felt apologetic, for some reason. "At first, I thought we'd just see it out. It might be an adventure. That was when everybody believed it would be over in a few months, remember? It looked like an amusing game for the girls, if we lived like gypsies, and I admit that I quite enjoyed it myself." She pushed back a strand of gray hair and looked over her shoulder again, purely out of habit. "But for days and days now it hasn't been at all amusing. Goodness knows when it *will* be over, and the girls have been growing up so fast—" She paused as if she had just realized whom she was talking to. Then she went on, "Now, in your case it's quite a different thing. You've got something to stay for, your husband here as a military prisoner and all. But for us, what's the point? Still, I might never have come to the decision if it hadn't been for a small thing—the smallest thing, really. Let me tell you. Just a few days ago, we were walking near our house, the three of us, through a little market that's grown up there, where we often look for supplies. We walked and stopped here and there and compared prices—you know how one does—and then we went on toward home, and just around a bend in the road my Joan —that's the younger one—pulled out an orange from under her jacket and showed it to us. *Proudly.*"

Mrs. Weston paused and searched my eyes for signs of horror. I don't know if she found any, but I think not, because she became urgent. "She'd filched it from one of the barrows, you know. She'd *stolen* it. Well, the incident set me back on my heels, I can tell you. I thought it over and asked myself, 'How is she to know the difference?' You see, from the beginning of all this, we've lived on what we could find in abandoned houses— everybody else has, too; I expect you have—and we took whatever we could find that was left by the first looters. Pieces of furniture for fuel. Piping. Sheets. Tins of food where they'd been overlooked. Everything, really. Now, strictly speaking, those things did belong to other people. It doesn't matter—if one's speaking strictly—that the owners had been taken away. We appropriated things, and a child like Joan couldn't be expected to know the difference between picking up such, well, flotsam and jetsam and stealing an orange from a barrow. Not in these surroundings, and in this life." She rubbed her forehead as if to smooth out the wrinkles of worry. "At any rate, there it is. Suddenly I saw it all quite clearly. I have no right— I had no right—to take such a risk. I blame myself."

"You didn't have much choice," I pointed out.

"Perhaps not at the very beginning, when everything was so

desperate, but I could have tried to get away before now. So we're really going at last, before it's quite too late."

We didn't shake hands, because people might have noticed, but we nodded before she strode away.

It was months later, as I've said, that I thought about Mrs. Weston again—just about the time I gave up black-marketing, because it wasn't fun anymore. The truth is, I suppose, that I'd stopped being bored, and the people I'd left behind were getting shadowy. In New York, on the other hand, they'd become quite distinct and real. By the end of the war, when Charles got out of camp and the relocating began, I was actually feeling respectable.

THE SCREAM

I was awakened that morning by a shriek so loud I thought it was in the room. Then I heard it again, and knew it was just outside, below the bedroom window. It sounded like a syllable or a word, foreign but quite plain—"E-e-e-eh! E-e-e-eh!"—and yet I knew, half asleep as I still was, that it wasn't a human being screaming. It wasn't a parrot, either. What other creature, though, could talk?

"E-e-e-eh!"

This time, I sat up, wide awake and trembling. I knew I must get out of bed immediately and do something, but I was afraid.

I didn't move. I didn't want to see what was going on outside the drawn curtains. My husband hadn't stirred, and I wondered if anyone else in the house was listening. Now the screams seemed to come from different directions, as if whatever desperate thing made them was running back and forth, trying to get away.

"E-e-e-eh!"

The sound grew weaker and came from farther off—down the hill, perhaps, where a path runs between blackberry bushes. At last, I made myself get up and go to the window, push the curtain aside, and look out. There was nothing there that could scream. The peaceful English countryside seemed, in fact, particularly tranquil. It was dawn, the grass was powdered with a light frost, and the air was brighter than it would be later. The noise had stopped. Everything was familiar; nothing was terrible. I saw the old rosebush at the top of the path leading into the woods. I couldn't see any animal or bird. It was too early even for the cheerful grating of the rooks that nest in the trees on the hill. Still, I knew I hadn't dreamed that noise. I had never had a dream that real. It was worse than a human voice, I kept insisting stupidly to myself, because it was so *nearly* human.

The sunrise was as lovely as any I have known, and the day was sure to be fine and delicate. It might have been a screech owl, I thought—but I didn't really believe that. There are owls in our woods, but they make a noise one recognizes—crooning, ghostly little hoots. I felt better, though my knees were still shaking and I was wet between the shoulder blades, as if I had had a nightmare. I looked again, carefully, at the woods and the rosebush, and at the brambles, their branches just softening and blurred with early buds. There was no wind. Everything was still. I dropped the curtain at last and went back to bed.

"Whatever was that this morning?" asked the children's nurse at the breakfast table.

"Oh, Nanny, did you hear it?" I asked.

"Hear it! Of course I heard it," she said. "It was almost in my room. To tell you the truth, I got up and went to look at the baby."

This shocked me. "You never thought it was her, Nanny! You couldn't have, even for a minute. It wasn't human."

"I know," said Nanny, "but it was nearly."

Carola took a spoonful of porridge and said calmly, "Well, I didn't hear it. I only dreamed I heard it."

"That's good," I said. I looked down to the other end of the table, where my husband was reading a book. "Charles, you didn't wake at all, early this morning, did you? I almost called you to ask what it was."

"What *what* was?" said Charles. "Was there a noise?"

I told him about it.

"A rabbit being taken by a stoat," he said.

"Oh, no, it couldn't have been a rabbit," I said. "They only squeak. This was terrible. It was loud and terrible, like something with a shark after it, or—"

"Yes, that's it. Rabbits scream when stoats are after them. They act as if they're paralyzed, but they scream. It's the only time they do."

"But that's perfectly horrible!" I put down my spoon.

"Yes," he said noncommittally. He glanced warningly toward Carola and went back to his book. Thus reminded of Carola, I was silent, and waited remorsefully for her comments, but apparently she hadn't listened.

I managed to keep the whole thing out of my mind most of the day, but that night, when I was getting into bed, the sight of the drawn curtains brought it back to me. I said, "I hope I won't hear a rabbit again tomorrow morning."

" 'Nature red in tooth and claw,' darling," said Charles. He turned off the light.

I couldn't go to sleep right away. I felt depressed and frightened, and I was angry with myself for this. It seemed unreasonably squeamish to be so upset by one rabbit. I told myself that it wasn't as if I were unused to the sudden death of animals. I was used to the country, too. "I love our house," I said to myself. "I love our woods and countryside. I feel happy whenever I come back to them from London. Everything around us is so wide and quiet and clean and cool."

I went through all this like a lesson, and in defense of our home I made a list in my mind of the bad things I have seen elsewhere—all the crimes and accidents and cruelties. I've seen people starving, I thought. I've seen rows of torn bodies being sorted out on the ground after a bombing. I've seen an African village during an epidemic and in a famine.

My thoughts were not peaceful ones, but now that the light was off, there was nothing to keep me reminded of stoats at dawn—not even moonlight picking out the openings in the curtains—so at last I went to sleep.

The next day was Sunday, and again the weather was lovely. Part of the satisfaction I find in our house is the way I can sit and be conscious of the children, somewhere nearby, growing and playing and learning, within call but not cooped up. It's a good place for both of them, in their different stages. The baby takes her milk and then she sleeps in her cot or in her pram, under a pine tree near the kitchen garden. As a matter of fact, now and then I don't quite like her sleeping outside, though I know it is necessary. I sometimes feel worried, all of a sudden, for fear a branch, or even a cone, may fall on her. When I stop to reflect, I know this is nonsensical. Branches are pretty certain not to fall in any weather in which she would be sleeping outdoors, and she is covered with a net that would deflect most lighter falling things, but there it is, and I think about it. It's not a strong anxiety. I know perfectly well that I have inherited fears of this sort from the war and that lots of other people entertain these irrational worries.

As for Carola, no such neurotic misgivings interfere with my feelings about her. She is outside all day, all the time. There is no motor road nearby to tempt her to danger. She can ride her small-sized bicycle on our drive as far as she is likely to want to go. She can climb any number of trees to her heart's content. It's good to sit in one's house with a child playing outside quite safely, quite happily. There aren't many better sensations in life.

Once during the afternoon of that Sunday, I heard Carola calling "Patrick! Patrick!" and looked out of the window to see her running across the lumpy, weed-grown tennis court with her big water-spaniel puppy after her. Patrick, his ears flopping, was making heavy weather of it, running like a cart horse on his enormous paws. Francis, the cat, stalking at the edge of some bushes, saw them and crouched motionless until they had got past. They ran out of sight behind the rhododendrons, and Francis stood up and went on with his hunting.

Carola came indoors at teatime. "Wash your hands," I said mechanically, and then, looking at her, I added, "And your face as well. It's all smudged."

"I was crying," she said cheerfully.

"Oh? Why?"

"I was so cross with Patrick," she said. "He had a dead mouse in his mouth that Francis must have killed, and I was afraid he'd get germs, so I tried to take it away from him, but he wouldn't let me."

"Those germs wouldn't hurt Patrick, honey," I said.

"Wouldn't they? Well, and then I scratched my leg on a stick, so I cried, but it's stopped hurting now."

"You go and wash your hands," I said.

While we ate, Patrick stood outside the dining-room window, with his paws on the sill, and whined to come in. He looked like George Eliot. Carola ran out as soon as she had finished, and, later, I went up to my sitting room. I heard her calling Patrick, and I said from the open window, "Not so loud, Carola. You'll wake the baby. She's over there by the hedge."

She disappeared in search of the dog, and a hush fell over the house and lawn, broken only by the rooks' cawing as they came to the trees. The baby was brought in and given her bottle. I mended some socks. Faintly, I heard music from Nanny's radio. A cow called to her calf, the rooks grew quiet, and the day slowly faded out.

If I had turned on the light in my sitting room five minutes earlier, Carola might never have told me. I think she would have tiptoed past my door, gone straight to her own room, and tried to bury all thought of what had happened. As it was, my room must have looked inviting and safely closed in, because it was almost dark and yet she could see that I was there. She stood just at the threshold, looking at me, and she spoke in a strange, dull voice. "Hello, Mummy," she said, sounding just as if she had been on a long journey and had got back very tired.

I looked at her as well as I could in the dark. "Why, hello," I said. "Is anything the matter?"

She said, "Nothing's the matter," and waited awhile. Then, suddenly, words came in a flood, passionately, indignantly, accusingly. "There was a little rabbit, a tiny baby rabbit, only this big. This *big*, Mummy!" She came closer to show me, with her thumb and finger, how small the rabbit was, and she began to cry. "And Francis got him," she sobbed. "The rabbit let me pick him up and pet him, and he jumped away and ran into a bank, and Francis got him. Oh, Mummy, he was only this big! He had a little white tail!"

I realized that I had stood up. Carola came close and leaned her forehead against me. She cried quietly; she was too tired to make much noise. "Did Francis—" I began, but I stopped. I knew all about it anyway; I have seen the cat with rabbits. "Darling," I said, "I'm so sorry. Did he get it right in front of you? I'm so sorry."

"It ran away. It ran into a place with ferns and moss and a log, but Francis—I know he got it. I know he did."

"Did you try to chase Francis away?"

"Oh, yes, I tried and tried, but he wouldn't run." She was still leaning against me, but she was not crying so hard.

"I'm awfully sorry," I said, rubbing her head, "but cats are made that way, you know. All animals kill other animals."

"I hate cats," she said. "I hate Francis. I don't want to see him." She rubbed her face against me and wailed a little. "I prayed, too," she said. "I prayed four prayers, but God didn't help."

"Did you?"

"Out there under the trees. I was crying all the time I prayed, but Francis wouldn't go away. He was there a long time. I couldn't do anything for the rabbit anyway. I couldn't stop Francis. Oh, Mummy, I couldn't do anything!"

There it was. Not even our house was safe. She *had* been on a long journey, after all. I stood smoothing her hair, feeling small and weak in our small house surrounded by dark space, by stoats and shrieking rabbits and pine trees and all the endless outside—the earth with hunters prowling on it, the sky from which things fall.